Magnus Magnusson is an Icelander who has spent nearly all his life in Scotland. Educated at the Edinburgh Academy, he won an Open Scholarship to Jesus College, Oxford (1948–53), from where he graduated in English and Old Icelandic literature.

He became a journalist in Scotland before moving to current affairs television on programmes like *Tonight*. His main interest, however, was in making historical documentaries. He was the founder-presenter of *Chronicle* (1966–80), a monthly series on world archaeology and history, and he presented two other major series, on the archaeology of the Bible lands and on the Viking Age.

As a writer and historian, Magnus has published more than a score of books, dealing with archaeology, Iceland, Irish history and Lindisfarne, as well as translating Icelandic sagas and modern novels and editing the 1995 edition of the *Chambers Biographical Dictionary*. In 1989 he was awarded the Medlicott Medal of the Historical Association.

Magnus is now chairman of Scottish Natural Heritage, the government's environmental agency in Scotland. He has been awarded honorary doctorates by five universities, and the honorary Fellowship of his old college. But his proudest honour is the honorary knighthood (KBE) he was awarded in 1989 for services to the heritage of Scotland.

Also by Magnus Magnusson

I've Started, So I'll Finish

The Story of *Mastermind*

MAGNUS MAGNUSSON

WARNER BOOKS

A *Warner* Book

First published in Great Britain in 1997
by Little, Brown and Company
This edition published in 1998 by Warner Books

Copyright © 1997 by Magnus Magnusson

ISBN: 0 7515 2585 5

Typeset in Bembo by M Rules
Printed and bound in Great Britain
by Clays Ltd, St Ives plc

Warner Books
A Division of
Little, Brown and Company (UK)
Brettenham House
Lancaster Place
London WC2E 7EN

'Comment is free but facts are sacred.'
Apt are the words of C. P. Scott.
Let us not ponder the why and wherefore,
Better to bank on the who-did-what.
Cheers for the things that they remembered.
Tears for the things that they forgot.

'Who was the aunt of Uncle Vanya?'
'Who cottoned on to Arkwright's frame?'
Milking the mind is purest torture,
More like a war than a harmless game.
Somewhere at home a shout of triumph:
'I know! – Wasn't it what's-a-name?'

Think of the books and the midnight oil,
Think of the numberless cups of tea;
All roads lead to the seat of anguish,
The bitten lip and the nervous knee –
All for the sake of a smile from Magnus,
All for the joy of the third degree.

These are the few who air their knowledge,
Bright as the dew on morning grass,
Candidates all for a job at Delphi,
Eager to enter the riddle class.
Still there remains the unasked question:
How do you fathom people? – Pass.

ROGER WODDIS, 'Remembrance of Things Past'
Published in the *Radio Times*, 30 August–5 September 1980,
at the start of that year's season of *Mastermind*

Contents

Acknowledgements

In the preparation of this book I have been helped by a host of people who have been connected directly or indirectly with *Mastermind*, and to whom are due endless thanks – not least Alan Samson of Little, Brown, a *Mastermind* contender in 1985, who took this book under his wing and did much to nurture it to completion.

Past and present colleagues from the programme have helped immensely with their memories and memorabilia, especially Martin L. Bell, Toni Charlton, Andrea Conway, Penelope Cowell Doe, Mary Craig, John Gilpin, Peter Massey and David Mitchell. Julie Corcoran, our production assistant, Boswell Taylor (our specialised questions organiser for twenty years) and Sheila Wright were tireless in responding to appeals for material and information. My main debt of gratitude, however, is owed to Dee Wallis, our senior researcher and latterly assistant producer: no query, however marginal, went unanswered or unsolved by her.

The Mastermind Club has also been a tremendous help, individually and collectively. Committee members, both past and present, like Peter Chitty, Tony Dart, Phillida Grantham, Lance Haward, Paul Henderson, Sue Jenkins, Gerald MacKenzie, Mike O'Sullivan, Patricia Owen and Craig Scott, and former editors of the Club magazine, *PASS*, like Martin Leadbetter and Sheila Ramsden, all provided me with copious archive material and reminiscences. More than a hundred contestants entrusted me with loans of precious copies of cuttings, audio cassettes, photographs and videos; all of the *Mastermind* champions co-operated to the hilt, too, allowing themselves to be interviewed or sending me long written accounts of their memories.

There are also three Club members who have been indefatigable in their help at every stage, from researching to writing to proofreading, far beyond any call of duty: Margery Elliott, former Club Secretary and former Editor of *PASS*; Christine Moorcroft, the current Editor of *PASS*; and Ray Ward, who delights in his unofficial Club title of Chief Nitpicker. For myself, if he's going to pick any nits I would much rather he did it before publication than after! It is with much pleasure and affection that I record my thanks for their outstanding contributions.

I am also grateful for permission to cite from poems and other television programmes which have given me particular pleasure: thanks to Martin Newell, the *Independent*'s regular 'pop' poet and author of *Poetic Licence*, for allowing me to quote from 'Disastermind'; to David Renwick, Ronnie Barker and Ronnie Corbett, for their classic *Two Ronnies* sketch; to Stephen Fry, for his spoof *Mastermind* skit; and to Charles Plouviez and the late Roger Woddis for their poetic contributions. My thanks also to Bamber Gascoigne for his generous Preface.

The illustrations are all on kind loan from the BBC, apart from a few in the plate section: on page 6, thanks to Nick Baker, Mac and Solo Syndication Ltd; on page 12, thanks to Syndication International and Margery Elliott; and on pages 14 and 15, thanks to Gena Davies and Christine Moorcroft.

Preface

I remember very clearly the day we heard in the office that the BBC was launching a high-level quiz to rival *University Challenge*. High time too, we thought. We had had the field to ourselves for ten glorious years. When we went on the air in 1962 the only other quiz games on television were *Take Your Pick*, *Double Your Money* and *Criss Cross Quiz*, none of which was calculated to test the nation's brains.

It had seemed odd that BBC1 and BBC2 had no serious quiz on television while commercial Granada was putting on a game with often extremely difficult questions at a peak time (in those days the half-hour before *Coronation Street* each Wednesday). We drew an audience of some 10 million, they said, though a massive surge in viewers towards the end of the game must have helped our average.

Now at last the Beeb was coming up with its reply, and a brilliant one, too. It seemed from the start an ideal fit with *University Challenge*. We were a team game, while *Mastermind* was to have individual contestants; we were purely general knowledge, they found an opening for impenetrably arcane information; we tried to be friendly, they set out to be terrifying. And the Black Chair was, from the start, the perfect symbol. Our double-stack of students was a bit of a laugh, a bit of a puzzle. Nobody was very surprised when the top team in *The Young Ones* were able to pour their water down on the students below.

And then the final stroke of genius, the inquisitor himself, great son of great, Magnus. Nobody else could have provided so well the necessary gravitas, the essential blend of stern and yet just. He has had in his Black Chair an astonishing parade of eccentric, quirky, brilliant people. And *Mastermind* has wisely kept tabs on them. As members of the Mastermind Club (of which I am proud to have honorary membership too, without having undergone the terror), they are a living record of the programme's twenty-five years.

Magnus and I were quiz-masters for exactly the same length of time. But I only provided the starter for ten. He started and he finished. It is excellent that he is rounding it off by telling the whole *Mastermind* story under the title of his famous catchphrase.

Bamber Gascoigne
March 1997

Foreword

The 'Dear John' letter came late in October 1996. It was from John Whiston, the Head of Youth & Entertainment Features in the BBC – the department to which, for some convoluted planning reason, *Mastermind* belonged:

> *Dear Magnus,*
>   *I'm sorry to be the messenger of unwelcome news, but after the last round of commissioning meetings it has been decided not to re-commission* Mastermind *beyond this next run. The sentiment which lies behind this decision is genuine: a wish to 'quit while ahead', while the programme is as fresh and confident as it's ever been, rather than watch the programme die a slow death shunted into marginal slots and ending up a shadow of its self in some daytime backwater.* Mastermind *has done the state great service and deserves much better than that. So the decision has been made to call a halt after the 25th series . . .*

It was an elegantly phrased letter, and the BBC was determined to give the programme a 'memorable and fitting' send-off, 'to allow the series to go down in history in a proper way'. The press reaction was equally gratifying: the *Independent* made it the lead story on its front page ('I started, so now I'll finish'); the *Daily Mirror* devoted its centre-page spread to it; the *Telegraph* gave it a tongue-in-cheek obituary ('by

Christopher Howse, Obituaries Editor', ending '*Mastermind* never married'); the *Sun* conducted a telephone poll which indicated that 84 per cent of its readers thought *Mastermind* should stay; and *The Times* gave it the major lead on its Home News page, and bestowed on it the signal honour of a magisterial leader ('Masterful Mastermind: The programme's passing will be much mourned').

Certainly, the programme had never been in better shape. Although *Mastermind* could once boast viewing figures of 20 million (in 1979), this was a complete fluke: ITV was on strike at the time. Throughout the 1980s the viewing figures averaged some 10 million. In the 1990s the figures declined as the programme was transmitted later and later on Sunday evenings, and in 1996 it was moved to 7.30pm to take on *Coronation Street*. To everyone's surprise, it more than doubled its viewing figures during the series (from 2.3 million to 5.3 million) and, according to the feedback received by the production team, the audience (which was considerably younger than before) enjoyed it more than ever.

Nevertheless, I cannot pretend that the letter came as a surprise. In fact, I had been half-expecting it for twenty-three years! *Mastermind* was never designed for a long run. I was never contracted for more than a year at a time, and the production team seldom knew if there was to be another until it was time to appeal for applicants for the following year, halfway through the current series.

But what a wonderful twenty-five years it was. It certainly changed my life. Yet it all happened, like many good things, completely out of the blue.

I was a print journalist who had drifted into television. After an Oxford degree in English and post-graduate work on Old Norse literature, I had joined the *Scottish Daily Express* as a cub reporter in 1953, and then the *Scotsman* as assistant editor in 1961. In the late 1950s I did one or two television programmes in Scotland soon after the first commercial station, Scottish Television, started up in Glasgow. As a result of that I began doing occasional documentaries for BBC Scotland (after being rejected on the basis of an audition in 1959). In 1964 I was 'discovered' by the old *Tonight* programme, and was given a year's leave of absence by the *Scotsman* to join the programme alongside Cliff Michelmore, Alan Whicker, Fyfe Robertson, Kenneth Allsop and the rest of that great band of television pioneers.

When *Tonight* came to an end in 1965 I was invited to stay on for its late-night successor, *Twenty-Four Hours*, but I had no wish to bring up my family in London, and so returned to Scotland and the *Scotsman*. The call of television proved irresistible, however, and I decided to go freelance: I produced some dramatised documentaries for BBC Scotland, and presented its major weekly current affairs programme. The big breakthrough came when I was invited to present a monthly programme on archaeology and history called *Chronicle* (1968–80). This was really my life's achievement on TV: serious, thoughtful work on projects all over the world. It culminated in two major series – *BC: The Archaeology of the Bible Lands* (1977) and *Vikings!* (1980). The start of *Mastermind*, in 1972, changed all that. Suddenly I was a 'celebrity', a television 'personality' – and all because I was playing a popular parlour game in public.

With the twenty-fifth series of *Mastermind* on the horizon, I had already begun researching a book on the programme to celebrate its silver jubilee when the 'Dear John' letter arrived. Now the book is a valedictory celebration.

What a fascinating task writing the history of *Mastermind* turned out to be. I studied and transcribed videos or audio cassettes of practically every programme since recordings were kept. I read every newspaper cutting I could lay my hands on. I interviewed all my past and present colleagues on the programme, and the other key people who had been associated with it over the years. I also published an appeal for help in *PASS*, the in-house magazine of the Mastermind Club; as a result I was able to build up lengthy dossiers on the experiences and reminiscences of nearly two hundred individual Masterminders, cross-checked against the transmitted programmes. Obviously I have not been able to use everyone, or everything, in this book, but they all in their own way helped to shape it and my thinking for it, and I thank them, one and all.

It may be the end of the *Mastermind* programme – but it is by no means the end of the *Mastermind* experience. The Mastermind Club lives on. So does the memory of a great programme of which I shall always be proud, and to which I shall always be grateful.

Magnus Magnusson
March 1997

1

The 'Onlie Begetter': Bill Wright

In June 1942, RAF Flight-Sergeant Bill Wright thought his last moment was at hand. His plane had been shot down over the Netherlands and he had been captured wearing civilian clothing given to him by the Dutch underground. The Germans were convinced he was a spy and kept him in solitary confinement for three weeks; the Gestapo refused to believe his story that he was a British airman whose Wellington bomber had come down in flames. They kept threatening to shoot him.

'Name?' his interrogators barked. Name, rank, number – name, rank, number: that was all he had to tell them, under the rules of the Geneva Convention for prisoners of war. It was not until another survivor from the stricken Wellington, the pilot, was captured, and confirmed his story, that the threat to Bill's life was lifted.

For decades afterwards, Bill would have nightmares about those wartime interrogations, always punctuated by the thudding litany of 'name, rank, number'. And twenty-nine years later, when he was a successful BBC television producer and needed an idea for a new quiz game, that's the formula which came to him in his nightmare: 'Name, occupation, specialised subject'.

Over the next twenty-five years the programme which grew from this idea was to develop into a chronicle of our times. Its story provides a wealth of anecdotes and yarns of triumph and disaster, of blunders and bizarre events, of camaraderie and shared endeavour. It is the people, both those in the Black Chair and in the production teams, who made *Mastermind* the best-loved and most respected television quiz programme on the air: a broadcasting legend.

The story can only start with a very special individual, the 'onlie begetter' of *Mastermind*, the man who devised it and deserves all the credit for making it the huge success it became: Bill Wright, the man whose nightmare became a dream. He was the real mastermind of *Mastermind*.

Bill Wright was the archetypal post-war BBC man: a man who rose steadily from page-boy to producer, always totally loyal and completely committed to the BBC. He was a gentle man, a reliable craftsman, scrupulous about every detail of his work and always ready to try something new. As executive producer of Outside Broadcast quizzes he found exactly the right outlet for his fertile wellspring of ideas; he moved with the direction of the BBC and helped to shape it, too, in his own dogged way. His major claim to fame is *Mastermind*; but he took part in, conceived or produced many other programmes worthy of remembrance. Early Masterminders from the 1970s recall his unfailing courtesy and kindliness towards them during their auditions. Former colleagues remember him with profound affection and respect and say, simply, 'He was wonderful.'

Bill was born in London on 19 December 1921. In 1936 he joined the BBC at the age of fourteen as a page-boy in Broadcasting House. He delivered messages and cleaned the Director-General's telephone, but a memorable duty every morning was to line up in the foyer of Broadcasting House with all the other page-boys, waiting for the Director-General's arrival in state. He had worked his way up to junior clerk and was studying for an engineering exam at night school when the Second World War broke out.

In 1941 he resigned from the BBC in order to volunteer for the RAF, and became a wireless operator/air gunner on Wellington bombers. It was on Midsummer's Day, 24 June 1942, on his fourteenth operation, a bombing raid to Krefeld, that his plane was shot down and he fell into the hands of the Gestapo. It was the start of nearly three years in various POW camps. During that time Bill did a great deal of studying, reading everything he could lay his hands on, including the whole of Shakespeare and the classics of English literature and a great deal of history (always one of his favourite subjects), as well as science and astronomy.

In captivity he dreamed of a future of freedom as a countryman. He sketched out detailed management plans for running a small-holding. Instead, when freedom came he returned to the BBC as a despatch clerk, then completed a course in the BBC's Engineering College in Evesham and landed a job as an assistant television cameraman, working in Outside Broadcasts.

Bill was an Outside Broadcast (OB) cameraman for nine years (a senior cameraman from 1947) – pioneering years which saw him take part in a number of early programme 'firsts': the first camera on a launch following the University Boat Race in 1949; the first cross-Channel programme from Calais (with Richard Dimbleby) in 1950; senior cameraman in Westminster Abbey at the pioneering live broadcast of the Coronation in 1953; stage manager for the Queen's first live Christmas broadcast from Sandringham in 1957.

In 1958 he was promoted to producer. His roll-call of credits as an OB producer included Dr Jacob Bronowski's first major BBC series, *Insight* (1960); a science series called *The Nature of Things* with Sir Lawrence Bragg (1962); *Mr Universe* (1963); a Light Entertainment series broadcast from a boat cruising on various rivers (*Song Boat*, 1964); and Sir Winston Churchill's state funeral in 1965.

The quiz king

In 1965 Bill's career took a decisive turn: he was asked to form an OB Quiz Unit. For the next fifteen years it became a veritable quiz factory, churning out an astonishing number of programmes.

Bill had recently appointed Mary Craig, a young Scots-born production secretary, as his production assistant; she was to become celebrated as the 'Dark Lady' who sat beside me during *Mastermind* programmes. Their first foray into the quiz business came when Bill took over *Television Top of the Form* (1965–75), which had been running for a couple of years as a direct transfer from the long-running radio programme *Top of the Form*. They made some changes to make it more televisual, using only sixth-formers rather than teams of graded ages. The permanent anchorman was Geoffrey Wheeler in the 'master' location, and there were various other presenters in the secondary locations, including John Dunn and a young David Dimbleby.

Two years later Bill developed an international spin-off from *Television Top of the Form* called *Transworld Top Team* (1967–73). The winners and runners-up of *Top of the Form* would take part in an international tournament against selected teams from abroad.

Meanwhile in 1966 – England's World Cup year, when football fever was at its height – Bill and Mary kicked off a new programme series called *Quizball* (1966–71). It was based on an idea brought to Bill by George Woolley, an electronics buff who had created an electronic board with lights like a football pitch. Bill transformed it into an inter-club game, with opposing sides of three club players and a celebrity guest. It was a game which was won by scoring goals through answering four, three, two or one questions, in descending order of difficulty. The referee was David Vine.

It so happens that I appeared on this programme myself in the 1968 series. I was 'supporting' the Scottish club Kilmarnock (although Kilmarnock would probably have disputed that). Late in the game I was awarded a penalty which allowed me a one-shot question which, if correctly answered, would give us victory. The question was an absolute sitter: 'Who was the American playwright who married Marilyn Monroe?' Ha! *Death of a Salesman*! *The Crucible*! Easy as falling off a log, it might have been tailored for me. Take it easy now, son, take your time, the game depends on it, there's a breathless hush in the close tonight – all these thoughts flashed through my mind. The only thought which did not flash through my mind was the name of the man who had written those familiar plays. Nothing. A blank. Imbecilic vacuity. The paralysis of mental processes was total, and seemed never-ending. Then, like a man slowly beginning to recover the power of muscular movement after a stroke, something started stirring in the sludge to which my brain had been reduced. Sluggishly, a name began to form. It was not the name of the dramatist, but something like it: my mother had just had a kidney operation and the name of the surgeon was Douglas something . . . Douglas . . . Douglas – could it be Miller?

As my team-mates sat back contentedly, assured of a place in the next round, and as David Vine started harrying me with his eyebrows, I began fumbling for the answer. 'Douglas,' I said hesitantly. 'Douglas . . .' (and here the association started firming up), 'Douglas . . . Arthur . . .'

At this point David Vine, who had already given me the benefit of extra time, blew the whistle: 'No,' he said, 'not Douglas Arthur. It's Arthur Miller.' With that, Kilmarnock were out of the game. And so was I. It left me with a very real empathy for all those who fail to organise their teeming brain-cells into a semblance of order when the chips are down – and a sense of awe at the people who can, under pressure, scour the recesses of their minds and dredge up half-forgotten facts when the need arises.

The Kilmarnock programme was the first time I had met Bill Wright and Mary Craig, and it has always been my private belief that Bill thought of me for *Mastermind* on the simple principle that I could not possibly make such a mess of asking the questions as I had made of trying to answer them.

Quizball was good fun, and attracted huge audience figures; but the BBC was looking for something more – it wanted an up-market 'brainy' quiz which could match the intellectual standard and appeal of *University Challenge* on ITV. So in 1969 Bill was asked to translate radio's *Brain of Britain* to television, as *Television Brain of Britain*. It ran for two years (1969–70); but it never quite worked – certainly not as well as Bill had hoped. He wanted an original television-generated concept, and kept on worrying the idea in his mind; Bill was terrier-like in his persistence. He was looking for a new format which would provide something 'a little more intellectually demanding than the average quiz'.

Mastermind

No programme idea is born out of thin air: inspiration is a matter of sparking between the steel and the flint of ideas from all quarters. For several months there had been sporadic discussion about the need for a new top-of-the-range television quiz programme. But it was not until a weekend early in January 1971 that all the disparate thoughts in Bill Wright's mind gelled, triggered by the nightmare. He came bounding downstairs one Saturday morning and said to his wife Sheila, 'I've got it!' There and then he sat down and sketched out the set and the shooting script for the kind of programme he had liter-ally dreamed up. It relied entirely on the concept of one contestant at a time being interrogated against the clock – the simple con-frontation of questioner and questioned.

On the following Monday he marched into his office in Kensington House with a beatific smile on his face, lighting one of his favourite little Henri Winterman cigars and waving it around his head, and saying to the world at large, 'What do you think of this idea?' He then proceeded to describe the idea for a new quiz programme, based on intensive head-to-head questioning. Those present in the office were Mary Craig and two of his directors, Peter Massey and Martin L. Bell. They spent the rest of the day brainstorming it, and by nightfall the basic plan had been worked up and typed, and the basic set and camera script had been outlined. It was such a simple and effective idea that it didn't really need very much in the way of embellishment. And with that, *Mastermind* was born.

On Christmas Eve 1979, Bill first became aware of the symptoms of the illness which was to cause his death within a year – motor neurone disease – although he had no inkling of what ailed him. He mentioned to his wife Sheila that he was having trouble lifting his left arm, and she prevailed on him to visit his doctor, who sent him to a consultant for tests.

The term 'motor neurone' was new to all of us on the production team. We really had no idea what was wrong with Bill. Nowadays, of course, everyone knows about it because of Stephen Hawking, the professor of mathematics at Cambridge and author of the best-selling *A Brief History of Time*, who has made the disease a household word. All we could see was a grimly progressive failure of Bill's muscular system. Little by little the muscle failure spread through his body, until his throat and chest muscles began to be affected. Towards the end he could not feed himself unaided and had to be helped into the scanner van when he was producing the programmes. For all of us it was heartbreaking to watch.

Only a week before he died he and Sheila travelled to Aberdeen University to record the last two heats of the 1980 series. He was desperately unwell at the time and Sheila said to him, 'Bill, do we have to go to Aberdeen tomorrow? Why must we go?' And Bill said, 'Of course we're going, I'm really looking forward to it.' But in the middle of the night before the recording he became very ill indeed and had to be taken back to London by train. It was the last time I saw him. He died, peacefully, at home in Highgate on 30 September. He was only fifty-eight years old.

Mastermind had meant more to Bill than any other programme he made. It was Bill's programme *par excellence*. He received no fewer than three BAFTA nominations for it: in 1975 (Best Specialised Series), 1976 (Best Light Entertainment Programme) and 1980 (Best Programme/Series Without Category). Sheila Wright continued her involvement with *Mastermind* after Bill's death by contributing general knowledge questions for many years. She was also elected a Life Honorary Member of the Mastermind Club and has remained a regular attender at Club functions.

It is to the fond memory of Bill Wright that this book is affectionately dedicated.

2

Origins

Mastermind was a remarkably innovative idea for its time. It had no technological gimmicks or electronic gizmos, no flashing lights or flashy prizes: just the concept of a severe interrogation under a spotlight with the slightly melodramatic overtones of the Inquisition. Bill Wright believed that there was nothing more interesting than the human face, and he was also sure that a quiz programme which featured people from all walks of life (not just students, as in *University Challenge*) would strike a chord in viewers. In later years he would tell audiences during his 'warm-up' sessions that the secret of *Mastermind* was twofold: the essential simplicity of the format, and the sense of viewer involvement. With hindsight, it is easy to see affinities with the techniques so brilliantly exploited by John Freeman in *Face to Face*: the probing questioning, the use of light and darkness, the camera tightening on the 'talking head'. But it had a lot more going for it: for one thing, it was TV-generated, unlike *Television Top of the Form* or *Television Brain of Britain*, which were derived from radio. For another, it was a genuinely indigenous programme idea, instead of being bought in from the USA.

Bill Wright's original concept concentrated exclusively on *specialised subjects*, and there was no thought of featuring general knowledge as well. Nor did the embryonic programme have a title. It was Mary Craig, the Quiz Unit's researcher, who came up with the inspired title of 'Mastermind', to emphasise the mastery of a chosen specialism – any subject on which the contestants felt expert, not necessarily an academic one. Very soon, however, in the course of further discussion, a *general knowledge* round was added to give the programme broader appeal, but the 'Mastermind' title stuck – it was much too good to discard.

The music: 'Approaching Menace'

An early priority was to find a theme tune. Bill Wright found the music he wanted on a 'mood' disc, one of those collections of recordings made and copyright-cleared specially for incidental use in films and in broadcasting. He had asked the BBC Gramophone Library for a selection of music which would engender a feeling of foreboding and expectation, and the very first title to which he listened was a piece of music called 'Approaching Menace' by Neil Richardson: a highly-charged, atmospheric theme, heralded by a drum-beat like the thud of a heart. As Jean Rook wrote in the *Daily Express* on 8 May 1983, 'It's like a cross between a State funeral and the Amityville Horror theme.'

Neil Richardson had composed 'Approaching Menace' the previous year. He was even then well-known as a composer, conductor and arranger. He had always been closely associated with the BBC, and had recently founded the BBC Northern Radio Orchestra (he was also its conductor for several years). Since then he has composed, arranged or conducted music for a host of singers and bands and programmes; recently he wrote some of the music and conducted the score for the film *Four Weddings and a Funeral*.

The pilots

By the end of January 1971, Bill had formally submitted his idea for a new quiz programme and put the appropriate BBC wheels in motion. Permission eventually came to make a couple of pilot programmes, to find a presenter and to see what it would look like on-screen; this was arranged for September of that year, at Westfield College, in Hampstead, as an Outside Broadcast event.

The director was Peter Massey, who was to come back to the programme as director in 1974–78 and producer in 1985–88 and

1990–91. The assistant stage manager was John Gilpin, who from 1982 onwards would become the programme's resident floor manager. The PA was Hilary Jones (now Warner), who had been with Outside Broadcasts since 1964, working with the 'royal' producer, Antony Craxton; she had been attached to the Quiz Unit as PA/researcher on loan from the Royal Unit because Mary Craig was so heavily engaged in other programmes.

Various possible presenters had been discussed. Bill Wright was looking for a professional presenter – and somebody who could make an intellectual contribution to the programme rather than just front it. The names of Bernard Levin and Robert Mackenzie (the BBC's main political pundit at the time) had been raised. In the event, two possible presenters were asked to audition for the part by doing a pilot programme each – myself and Alan Watson. Neither of us was an obvious choice, because we had no background in quizzes or Light Entertainment.

Alan Watson was a specialist in current affairs and politics and had been a founder-presenter of *The Money Programme* on BBC2 since 1964; he would soon be working on *Panorama* before moving to Brussels as Head of the European Commission's Radio and Television Division (1976–80). He stood three times as a Liberal candidate for Richmond (in 1983 he gave the Tory candidate, Jeremy Hanley, a close run with four recounts before losing by only seventy-three votes), and was Liberal Party President in 1985. He is now chairman of Burson-Marsteller/Europe (the international PR firm), as well as being Erasmus Visiting Professor in European Studies at the Catholic University of Louvain.

I, too, considered myself a current-affairs specialist. I had spent a year as a studio presenter on the old *Tonight* programme with Cliff Michelmore (1964–65) and was now fronting the monthly history and archaeology programme *Chronicle* on BBC2, which entailed filming all over the world. I think I regarded the possibility of presenting a quiz programme, however high-brow, simply as a casual ancillary to my main broadcasting work.

Alan Watson and I each did a trial programme with four different contestants who had responded to an advertisement in the *Daily Telegraph* that summer. One of them was a London schoolteacher, Doreen Simmons (now a media consultant in Japan), who was auditioned in a vast sound studio where she had to answer a series of taped questions. As a result of her answers she was accepted for the pilots, where she offered 'Mythology' as her specialised subject; she was later invited to appear in the first series, but her subject was narrowed down to 'Greek Mythology'. Another of the contestants was a Cockney greengrocer with a university degree, Robert Kift, who took 'French Literature'; he won his pilot contest and he, too, was earmarked for the first series. Bryan Cowgill, the Head of the Sports & Outside Broadcasts Group (and later Controller BBC1), was greatly taken with the fact that a London Eastender could 'take on the egg-heads and beat them at their own game'. Another of the pilot contestants was Ralph Whitlock, the celebrated broadcaster on country topics, who answered questions on 'Country Life'; he did not take part in the series itself.

Despite having had his briefcase stolen at the college that afternoon, Alan did very well in the preliminary run-throughs, but he failed to do himself justice during the recordings. He was not surprised to hear that an audience questionnaire taken after the programmes indicated a substantial preference in my favour. Looking back on it now, he tells me that he never felt totally happy about the prospect of becoming a quiz-master; it would not have sat comfortably with his career ambitions at the time. But he still allows himself the occasional wistful thought about how his life would have been affected *if* . . .

Mastermind was formally accepted over the winter of 1971–72, for production in the following autumn. On 7 March 1972, Bill Wright held a production meeting with his team to discuss the logistics of the operation, and how to fit it into the massive schedule of productions in which the Quiz Unit was already engaged. Boswell Taylor, who was setting the questions for *Transworld Top Team* at the time, was asked to organise all the questions, both specialist and general knowledge, for *Mastermind* as well; he had both the general range through his work for *World Book Encyclopedia* and the necessary familiarity with the academic world to find the right specialised question-setters. Because of the ferocious pressure of programme output, Mary Craig had to forgo taking on *Mastermind*, even though Bill wanted her to do it; instead, Cherry Cole, Phil Lewis's PA, was appointed as research assistant. Peter Massey was similarly overstretched, and Martin L. Bell took over as director.

The set and the bleeper

Martin Bell's first task was to have a set designed. Because it was to be an Outside Broadcast production, the challenge was to create a set which could be taken all over the country by OB units, so scenery which required carpenters and painters to repair it was out of the question; instead, the backdrops were to be the audience.

The chosen designer was thirty-year-old Philip Lindley from the BBC's Studio Design Unit. Philip was summoned to come and discuss ideas for the set, and caught the shuttle minibus from Television Centre to Kensington House. Straight after the discussion he took the minibus back to Television Centre and started sketching on the way. By the time he had arrived the concept had been defined; instead of going to his office he simply returned on the same bus and the plan was agreed with Martin. Philip's original idea involved the notion of 'walking the plank', and he wanted the Chair to be on an island surrounded by water with the walkway retractable so that the 'victim' was trapped – a sort of inquisition – to add visual drama to the programme. The water idea was simply not practicable for an OB programme, and so a shiny black-ribbed floor was the closest he got to achieving his aim.

The celebrated bleeper was made by the BBC's Special Effects Department. Martin Bell wanted something which sounded menacingly high-tech; Special Effects came up with the idea of altering the circuitry in the warble generator of the then newly-fashionable Trimfone, slowing the warble and raising its pitch. It worked first time.

The Black Chair

Finally, there was the Black Chair. Martin Bell and Philip Lindley were greatly exercised by this; they knew that it was likely to become a trademark of the programme. Really comfortable chairs are usually unsuitable for television because they cause the sitter to lounge. They were looking for something in black leather upholstery with arms and a high back which could still be seen in a close-up shot.

It took a long time to find a chair which was imposing, distinctive and would be suitable for contenders of all shapes and sizes, as well as being 'right' for the programme. Philip eventually found it in a catalogue of executive-style office products. However, it had a swivel base, which meant that the contenders would be able to move about too much; it also had castors, so the base was swapped for a fixed base from another chair. The original arms were of chrome; but they would have caused too many reflections from the stage lighting, so they were given a covering of black leather. So *Mastermind*'s Black Chair is actually an amalgamation of two chairs, custom-made for the programme.

The Black Chair was to become very much the trademark of the programme. As an emblem it became instantly recognisable. Strangers who meet me tend to say one of three things: either 'Pass!' or 'I've started, so I'll finish!' – or else, 'I'm glad you haven't brought the Black Chair with you!'

There is a widespread misconception that I am superstitious about sitting in the Chair. Not so; I have often sat in it, and very comfortable it is, too. On the other hand, I have previously declined to be *photographed* in the Chair for publicity purposes, because I never wanted to give the impression that I am any kind of Mastermind myself.

In fact, there are *two* Black Chairs now – because the original was 'kidnapped' on two occasions. In the 1978 series it was kidnapped by students as a rag-week prank before the recordings of Heats 3 and 4 at the Cranfield Institute of Technology, the air base in Bedfordshire. It all got slightly out of hand; the students demanded a ransom of £50 for their Cambodia Relief Fund, but the vice-chancellor insisted that no ransom should be paid on any account. We had to rehearse without it, which was a nuisance, and it wasn't returned until just before the recording. It was all a bit unnerving.

In my Introduction to the programme I tried to make light of the episode:

This is our first visit to a Technical University. Mind you, we had rather mixed feelings about that this morning, when we discovered that the famous Black Chair was missing. Horror of horrors! It turned out that it had been kidnapped by the students here in the hope of a ransom. But since its value is above rubies, and the BBC doesn't have that kind of lolly, it was eventually returned to us,

*unharmed, for nothing. Actually, we shouldn't have been surprised
at the kidnapping, because Cranfield students have a well-earned
reputation for merry pranks of this kind; the last time a police
convention was held here at Cranfield, the students nicked all the
blue lights off the police cars. That's poetic justice. Anyway, you're
only young once . . .*

The second kidnap happened the following year, before the
recording of two of the semi-finals at the New University of Ulster
in Coleraine, when Antonia (Toni) Charlton was in her first year as
director. After this we decided that enough was enough, and Toni
bought a second chair as a spare (although it wasn't an exact match).
The spare chair travelled to all locations with the original, but it was
never used in a programme. It was used for the opening titles and as
a prop in sketches by various comedians; it was also used in rehearsals
for a time, but even the small difference in height made it difficult
for the cameramen to determine their shots in advance, so the real
Chair was used for all the rehearsals as well.

Latterly, the Black Chair was always bolted to the floor of the set,
as the result of an accident in the 1993 series. In one of the semi-
finals, recorded in St Paul's Concert Hall at Huddersfield University,
Malcolm Edwards, a retired bank official from Leeds, crashed into
the chair as he went to it for his first round and knocked it over. I
said, 'You're the first silly bugger in the history of the programme
who's managed to do that!' As it turned out, he was also to be the
last.

Game and set – now for the match.

3

1972 and All That

'Are you a Mastermind? What exactly is a Mastermind? This week's new quiz on BBC1 is a nationwide search for just that. Challengers on the programme include a dentist whose speciality is Tudor history, a pig-farmer who will defend his claim to know all there is to know about pigs, and a greengrocer who feels he knows as much about French literature.' That was how the *Radio Times* of 7 September 1972 heralded the new series. It was the culmination of a summer of frantic work by the tiny production team to get everything ready.

There were to be fifteen programmes in the series – eleven heats, three semi-finals and a Final with three finalists; that meant finding forty-four contenders, as I always called them. The BBC announced the new series and advertisements were placed in quality journals such as the *Listener*, the *New Statesman* and the *Daily Telegraph*. These elicited responses from people like Nancy Wilkinson, a part-time lecturer at the Cambridgeshire College of Arts and Technology; Robert Crampsey, a Glasgow schoolmaster and TV football commentator; Ivan Limmer, a 34-year-old National Council for Civil Liberties field officer from Burnley; and the Rev. David Drake-Brockman, an Anglican curate in the parish of Lymington in Hampshire.

Other potential participants were approached because of previous appearances on BBC quizzes and were invited to audition. This system produced contenders like Joan Taylor, a lecturer in modern history at Newcastle University, who had been runner-up to Irene Thomas on *Brain of Britain* in 1961 and had won the first series of Bill Wright's *Television Brain of Britain* in 1969; the Rev. Dr Michael Dewar, a Church of Ireland clergyman who had been runner-up to Joan Taylor; and Bill Rennie, municipal correspondent on the *Scotsman*, who had taken part both in *Brain of Britain* and *Television Brain of Britain*.

However, Bill Wright wanted to avoid a preponderance of so-called 'professional' quiz contestants – people who made a habit or hobby of quizzes; so he turned down the inestimable Irene Thomas, the charismatic doyenne of *Round Britain Quiz*, and Ian Gillies, the omniscient question-setter (Robert Robinson's 'Mycroft') of *Brain of Britain*. But perhaps the most spectacular refusal concerned Tim Rice who, with Andrew Lloyd Webber, had recently earned celebrity status with *Joseph and the Amazing Technicolor Dreamcoat* and *Jesus Christ Superstar*. He applied for *Mastermind*, offering as his specialised subjects 'Pop Music' and 'The Solar System', but he didn't even merit an audition, on the grounds that *Mastermind* in those early days was far too highbrow for such down-market subjects as pop music. Tim Rice still recalls this episode, with a chuckle, as one of the few failures of his enormously successful show-business career.

There is no record of precisely how many people applied for the 1972 series. But for much of the summer, Bill Wright and his research assistant, Cherry Cole, toured the BBC regions holding auditions for aspirant Masterminders (perhaps 'interviews' would be a better term). Selected applicants would be given a 45-minute audition, consisting mainly of an oral test of twenty reasonably difficult general knowledge questions (but not against the clock). After the test, the choice of subject would be discussed. As John Hall was to write in the *Radio Times* on 17 August 1977:

> *An interview with Bill Wright weeds out the cranks and the fibbers, the frail of spirit and the quarrelsome. Then follows a taste of the real thing – the same twenty general knowledge questions for each candidate, framed to throw into high relief the most common failings of your quiz attempter – rambling, slowness, failure to see the point of the questions or sheer blue funk.*

No amount of rejections or weeding-out would put some would-be Masterminders off, however. Graham Bell, from Sheffield, an employment researcher with a training agency, made no fewer than thirteen applications, starting as a mature student at Sheffield in 1978; he had almost a dozen auditions, nearly all of them in York, and the near-annual audition by the producer at the time became something of a jolly jaunt. He eventually won a place in the 1994 series – he took 'The Life and Reign of Edward IV' and scored 23.

The all-time record for the number of applications, however, is held by Gordon Troughton, a retired telephone engineer from Rugby in Warwickshire, who came second to the eventual champion, George Davidson, in another heat in the 1994 series. It was his seventeenth application for the programme, and his third audition (1981, 1993 and 1994). Over the years the subjects he had offered included 'The American Civil War', 'The Miss Marple Novels of Agatha Christie', 'Wellington in the Peninsular War', 'The Pern Novels of Anne McCaffrey', 'The European Cup 1955–91', 'England v. Australia Test Cricket', 'Stage Musicals' and 'The Novels of Isaac Asimov'. In the event he took 'Classical Ballet Since 1870', and scored 27.

There was someone else who nearly got on to *Mastermind* without even trying. It happened back in 1980 when auditions were being conducted by Mary Craig in Southampton. For once, Dinah Long, our PA at the time, had forgotten to bring from London all the paperwork for the auditions – the names of the applicants, their application forms, the times, and so on. Consternation! There were one or two applicants waiting already, so Mary arranged for the application forms to be rushed to Southampton by despatch rider while she tried to busk her way through the morning appointments.

She interviewed the first few people 'blind', taking copious notes against such time as the application forms turned up. As one interview ended, the hotel porter ushered in 'your next gentleman'. Mary had no application forms in front of her, of course, and asked for his name and address and so on; they chatted about his career and television in general, and then Mary said she would try him out on some general knowledge questions. 'Sure,' he replied, 'fire away.' He was very good, answering some of the most difficult questions with great presence of mind and aplomb, and Mary realised she was dealing with a very strong candidate for the programme. It was only when she started asking him about his specialised subjects that he said he thought there might be some mistake. It turned out that he was a CID man in the local police who had come to the hotel to be interviewed by a Police Promotions Board, and had thought he was being given a rather eccentric initiative test.

I have done my darnedest to discover the identity of this phantom Masterminder, but the combined detective efforts of the Hampshire Constabulary failed to identify him for me. I rather like the idea that the police were helping *me* with *my* enquiries. Whoever he was, it seems that he was never tempted to apply for *Mastermind* for real. Pity.

Selecting the contestants was never an exact science. What they scored didn't matter all that much. Just as his successors were to be, Bill was more concerned about *how* the candidates answered – how they set about trying to work out what the answer should be. He used to say that there should be sufficient information *within* a question to indicate the direction in which to seek the answer; his classic example of a good general knowledge question was: 'In which English city would you find the Dyson-Perrins Museum?' The clues are a) since it's a city it is likely to have a cathedral, and b) Lea & Perrins are the makers of Worcester sauce – *ergo*, the answer is Worcester.

Above all, Bill was trying to find the blend which would make good television – not just the standard knowledge-brokers but also people with unusual jobs or interesting backgrounds or imaginative subjects. He looked for two or three 'bankers' in each programme, people who could be relied on to have done their homework; but in each programme he wanted at least one person who was a bit more risky – interesting for various reasons, more extrovert perhaps, but more unpredictable. Hence, in the first series, the Glasgow dental surgeon who specialised in Tudor history (Julius Green); the Skegness pig-farmer taking 'Pigs' (T. F. Smith); and the Cockney greengrocer taking 'French Literature' (Robert Kift). None of them won, but they added freshness and piquancy to the programmes.

Bill was also desperately keen to get as many women to take part as possible. Right from the start, the problem for *Mastermind* was that the ratio of women applying, compared to men, was only one to four. As it turned out, for the first series in 1972 he recruited thirty-five men and nine women.

The first programmes

The first two programmes were recorded in the Mountford Hall of the Guild of Undergraduates of the University of Liverpool, on 6 September 1972. The occasion was deeply overshadowed by the news from the Munich Olympics the previous day – the massacre of the Israeli athletes by a band of 'Black September' Arab terrorists. Looking back on it, my recollection of the early 1970s is curiously indeterminate: the decade had not acquired any defining characteristics, as the 1960s had done; perhaps Europe would be that determining factor, because it was in January 1972 that Prime Minister Ted Heath signed the Treaty of Accession in Brussels which brought Britain into the EEC. Of course, as a national of Iceland I found that many of the things connected with my homeland provided some of the landmarks and milestones for 1972 – the Spassky–Fischer World Chess Championship which was held in Reykjavik that summer, and the start of yet another Cod War between Britain and Iceland. But for the rest, the general impression is one of mayhem and murder and disasters at home and abroad: of that 'Bloody Sunday' in Londonderry's Bogside which heralded twenty-five years of turmoil and torment in Northern Ireland; of the escalation of the Vietnam War with the bombing of North Vietnam; of aircraft being hijacked and blown up by Palestinian terrorists; of the massacre of tourists at Tel Aviv airport.

That was the sombre world backcloth to our modest attempt to make a little bit of domestic television history. On Monday 11 September, at 10.45pm on BBC1, a week after the recording, the new late-night programme went on air:

> With this programme we begin our search to find the 'Mastermind of the United Kingdom'. Our aim is to discover the person who can best use this incredibly complex and sophisticated piece of computer machinery which we call the brain. Our competitors not only have to specialise in their own field but need to be someone who also works things out intelligently and fast, the person who knows the formula of applying his or her mind to open up a new world of knowledge.
>
> We have four selected competitors with us here in the Guild of Undergraduates at the University of Liverpool. One of these will emerge a Mastermind. He will be required to meet other area winners

*until eventually the Mastermind of the United Kingdom reigns
supreme.*

　　So may I have the first contender, please?

Thus spake 'The Interrogator', as I was somewhat pretentiously
labelled throughout the first series.

'Your name, please?'
'Alan Whitehead.'
'Occupation?'
'Print-maker.'
'And your specialist subject?'
'"The Visual Arts".'
'Mr Whitehead, you have two minutes on "The Visual Arts",
　　starting – now. Picasso's Guernica was a protest about the
　　bombing by Spanish [sic] planes of a village. What was the year
　　when the event took place which inspired the painting?'
'Nineteen thirty-seven.'
'Correct! Name the artist who was responsible for the windows in the
　　new Cathedral at Coventry.'
'John Piper.'
'Correct!'

Alan Whitehead was followed by Charles Coleman, a marketing
executive, offering 'British Politics Since 1900'; then by Ivan
Limmer, from Burnley, a National Council for Civil Liberties field
officer, offering 'Classical Greek Theatre'; and finally by Basil
Sabine, a civil servant, taking 'Nineteenth- and Twentieth-century
Financial History'.

The winner was Ivan Limmer, who scored 9 on his specialist
subject and 10 on general knowledge for a total of 19 and a place in
the second semi-final. When the programme was transmitted I was
on location in Salisbury, filming a *Chronicle* programme with my
producer, David Collison. We watched it together in the hotel
lounge, and David remembers my saying, 'Well, that was okay, I suppose – I guess we'll have to wait and see.'

And so the familiar pattern of *Mastermind* was set, twenty-five
years ago. It was the template, almost the stereotype, of what was
to come. I cannot tell now what the programme looked like; alas,

neither the *Mastermind* office nor the BBC archive has kept videos of any of the programmes (apart from the Finals) from the first five years of *Mastermind* (1972–76). All I have had to work on is a dog-eared copy of the very first working script, some occasional billings in the *Radio Times*, and the memories of some of the early Masterminders.

Paradoxically, it was this lack of archive material which has made researching the material for this book such an enormous pleasure – the fun of tracking people down, the thrill of finding the right person after hours of journalistic detective work. Some were easy to find, because they had joined the Mastermind Club as soon as it was founded in 1978; others just turned up out of the blue. Take Ivan Limmer, the winner of the first heat. I found him through another Masterminder, Andrew Grealey (1992 series), a member of the Mastermind Club, who wrote to tell me that he had harboured an ambition to appear on *Mastermind* ever since one of his colleagues in Blackburn Social Services, Ivan Limmer, had taken part in the very first programme in 1972 – did I remember him? I was on the telephone in a flash; happily it turned out that they were still in touch, and Andrew was able to give me Ivan's address and phone number.

Ivan had been a probation officer in Inner London before he became the first field officer to be appointed by the National Council for Civil Liberties (now Liberty). In the early summer of 1972 he had seen the advertisement in the *New Statesman* inviting applications for a new kind of television quiz show. He sent off for an application form: the only question on the form he can remember was: 'Why do you think you would be good on a TV quiz?' Ivan replied, 'Because I know a lot of useless facts and I enjoy showing off.' He reckons that clinched it. He was interviewed in Manchester. He had not given any thought to the matter of specialised subjects, and had to come up with an idea. He reckoned that he needed something about which not a great deal was published (which would limit the number and range of questions which can be set), but which he knew at least something about. He remembered that at school he had done a sixth-form project on 'Greek Theatre Production in Athens', and that he still had his notebook on it. So his specialised subject was decided: 'Classical Greek Theatre'.

A score of 19 would be considered modest nowadays, but it was sufficient to earn a place in the semi-finals. Ivan, who had by then left the NCCL and joined Blackburn Social Services, had to offer a different specialised subject, and this time chose 'The English Legal System'. He scored 31 this time, but even this score was not enough to beat Joan Taylor, who went on to the Final.

Looking back on it now, Ivan is amazed at how essentially naïve he and his fellow Masterminders were. They had no idea about tactics. They did not realise how vital it was to get a move on: to answer without hesitation, to give a quick wrong answer rather than to think and then pass. Since it was the first programme, they had no way of knowing that the format was so radically different from that of other quizzes. I was delighted when Ivan, now fifty-eight years old, applied to have another go and took part in the first heat of the Silver Jubilee series in 1997, which was recorded in the august setting of Blenheim Palace in Oxfordshire. He didn't make it to the semi-finals, but he enjoyed it all immensely.

The first challenge

We were all feeling our way in those early days, questioned and questioners alike. In the second heat (also recorded at the University of Liverpool) I had my first taste of facing a challenge from the Black Chair – and a correct one at that. It came from a clergyman from Northern Ireland, the Rev. Dr Michael Dewar, who was offering 'England Before 1066'. In his general knowledge round he was asked: 'Who wrote "Onward, Christian Soldiers"?' He replied: 'Sabine Baring-Gould', only to be told that it was Sir Arthur Sullivan. The Reverend Doctor replied magisterially, 'Sullivan composed the *music*; it was Baring-Gould who wrote the *hymn*.' I conceded the point without demur; it was the first of many salutary lessons in the importance of absolute accuracy in the precise wording of questions.

By 1972 Dr Dewar was already a seasoned quizzer. He had been a finalist on *Brain of Britain* in 1965, and again in 1970. After *Mastermind* he went on to star in *Round Britain Quiz* from 1974–84 as a member of the Northern Ireland team. His elder son, history teacher David Dewar, also reached the final of *Brain of Britain* in 1986, and took part in the 1992 *Mastermind* series, where he, like his father before him, reached the semi-finals.

Birth of a catchphrase

The 1972 series brought us other lessons, in addition to precision in the wording of questions. It also brought a change in the rules – and gave birth to a familiar catchphrase.

In the earliest programmes each question-and-answer session would end abruptly, the moment the bleeper sounded, whether or not the contender was ready to answer. The most striking instance came in Heat 4 of the first series, when Bill Rennie, a journalist on the *Scotsman*, was answering questions on 'The First World War'. Bill was no stranger to quizzes; he had already taken part in *Brain of Britain* and *Television Brain of Britain*.

When I had almost finished reading out Question 15 the bleeper sounded and the round came to an instant end. The question was: 'Where did a British fleet under Admiral Sturdee destroy—' (*bleep bleep*). I stopped speaking at once (the rest of the question was 'Vice-Admiral Maximilian von Spee's fleet'). Bill knew that the answer was 'the Falkland Islands', because the Battle of the Falkland Islands was the only decisive victory ever won by a force under Sturdee; but since the bleeper had gone he was not allowed to answer. That extra point would have been enough to produce a tie on points with the eventual winner, James MacGregor, headmaster of Morebattle Primary School near Kelso, who took 'Words' as his specialised subject and went on to the semi-finals.

As a result of this and other similar occurrences we changed the rules to allow a question to be completed and answered *after* the bleeper had sounded; and to emphasise this change I would say, 'I've started, so I'll finish'. It was only when viewers started writing to the programme saying 'I wish Magnusson would stop saying that damned silly sentence' that I realised that a catchphrase had been born.

In her 1990 book on her *Mastermind* experience, . . . *And No Passes*, Mary-Elizabeth Raw (1989 champion) noted an occasion when it was used by the Speaker of the House of Commons, on 7 February 1990:

> *Some MPs were saying that they were not being allowed enough questions during Question Time. Mr Weatherill replied that he was being urged by the Procedure Committee to speed up Question Time, and went on to talk about the efficiency of one of his*

predecessors, Dr Horace King. At this point he was interrupted by
Andrew Faulds, urging him not to quote Dr King. 'I've started, so
I'll finish' came the swift reply, amid laughter from all sides.

The catchphrase has also achieved a modest immortality as an entry
in the *Bloomsbury Dictionary of Popular Phrases* (1990), edited by Nigel
Rees:

I've started so I'll finish! Stock Phrase > Catch Phrase. *In BBC*
TV's Mastermind *quiz the chairman, Magnus Magnusson, would*
say this if one of his questions was interrupted when the time ran out.
It became a figure of speech – sometimes also given a double meaning.

The media, in those early days, tended to be ambivalent in their
response to the new series. After three programmes Clive James – in
the *Observer* on 1 October 1972 – set the tone which many other
commentators were to follow:

Mastermind *has now settled in and is ripe for judgement. This is*
the kind of élite-seeking stuff that would send Mao into a positive
frenzy of contemptuous inscrutability. Magnus Magnusson – who,
unless my dazed ears deceived me, is actually called the
Interrogator – comes on accompanied by doom-laden music, like the
Grand Inquisitor in Act III of Don Carlos. *At a signal from*
Magnusson's omnipotent forefinger, the patsy is released on to the
catwalk and stumbles forward to where the Chair awaits, like the
beginning of the long fall in San Quentin. A fierce overhead key-
light picks him out like a rabbit in a fog-lamp.
  I won't go into what happens next, except to say that the toll in
ruined lives must already be a national disaster. Men who have spent
thirty years enjoying an unchallenged reputation as the village
wiseacre are revealed, after only two minutes in the hot squat, to be
riddled with ignorance even in their formidably recondite specialities.
The programme is compulsive viewing: a really gripping, totally
useless quiz.

My own favourite newspaper cutting, however, was an enchant-
ing misprint in the *Belfast Telegraph*. The reviewer was reasonably
complimentary, but the compositor supplied the real comment

when the title of the programme came out not as *Mastermind* but as 'Masterwind'. That said it all.

Knowing the score

The biggest problems we faced in the early days were not so much intellectual as technological. Television was still relatively young, and a great deal of improvising was still going on. Our scoring system, for instance, might well have been devised by Heath Robinson himself; it was diabolically complicated and precarious. The original *Mastermind* scoring device (called Gensign) was one of those leaf-type flip-over mechanical devices similar to the system used on airport display boards. It was alarmingly prone to jamming and often needed a thump to reset it; what's more, it couldn't go backwards once the score had been keyed in.

Gensign was wildly temperamental. Sometimes it would work sweetly enough: I would ask a question, the answer would come back and, lo and behold, the correct score would appear on the screen. That was on the good days. But on bad days (and it seemed to have a malevolent mind of its own) there were no half-measures and we all suffered. I would steal a glance at the screen and see the numbers flapping furiously and the wrong one appearing. The recording had to stop while it was sorted out. Then we would start again, but we would have to re-record the last question and answer in order to keep the finished product looking seamless. That was nuisance enough if the answer had been right; if it had been *wrong*, I had the task of saying to the contender, 'Do you mind giving me the same wrong answer as you gave before?' The audience, at least, quite enjoyed it (although I certainly didn't). The contenders themselves always took it in good part, and I marvelled at their outward composure and their capacity to take set-backs in their stride under stress. But it was undoubtedly hard for them. The stopping and starting and repeating (sometimes several times in a single programme) inevitably interrupted their flow. Who knows how many contests would have ended differently if the scoring device had been more efficient?

The other element of the scoring system was the 'caption scanner'. This was a small camera fixed inside a wooden container and permanently focused on to a lit caption-area framework about twelve inches away. At the end of a round, when I would say 'Now let's look at the scoreboard', it produced a shot of a magnetic scoreboard. This caption carried the contenders' names with a blank space for the scores which would be filled in by a scene-hand as the programme progressed, using magnetic numbers. As I announced the score for the fourth contender, and the audience applauded the walk back from the Chair, the scene-hand had to complete the scoreboard and drop it into the slot which brought it into view of the camera inside the caption scanner. The positioning of the scoreboard in the frame was critical: the slightest jolt would knock the graphics askew, or a magnetic number would drop off. The director used to have nightmares, wondering whether that particular operation would be completed without incident.

The end credits – the list of those responsible for making the programme – could provide the final nightmare. Each credit had its own caption card, and two cameras were required in order to cut from one to the other. It also required two scene-hands, each changing his captions one after another as the director cut from camera to camera to match the beat of the closing music; it was a fiendishly complicated operation, and there were very few recordings which did not involve retakes of the closing titles. The audience sometimes must have wondered if they were going to see their beds that night at all.

Life became a lot easier when the captions began to be generated on an electronic typewriter called Ryley, around 1982. But the real revolution came in 1992 with 'Archimedes'. Archimedes was our salvation. It is actually a make of computer, but I always used the name indiscriminately for a system which made programme recordings run much more smoothly and made my own task infinitely easier (only twenty years after the programme began). It also enabled us to do away with the recording break in the middle of the programme when we used to have to regroup for the second half. And for that we had an engineering computer genius called Peter Byram to thank.

Peter was the Special Facilities Manager in the BBC at the time. The most spectacular of the special facilities he had developed was the miniature camera inside a cricket-stump which offers dramatic pictures of batsmen being bowled out. For *Mastermind* he devised the software for a new scoring system, using the Archimedes computer.

This programmed the computer to do all the work which the Ryley had been doing; but whereas Ryley was a dedicated caption generator, Archimedes could store first-round scores (and passes) and reset for the second round in an instant. It meant that we could move straight into the second round without the recording break at halfway while the scores were being totted up. Its operator, Bob Richardson, could also show me, in one of the two little monitors built into my desk, the name and running score of the occupant of the Chair – and the name of the next contender to be called.

The first Final

The first Final was recorded in the Polytechnic of North-East London in Walthamstow, and transmitted on Boxing Day 1972. Despite the fact that only nine women had taken part in the series, the Final (which had only three finalists) was an all-woman affair. In their wake they left a trail of beaten male hopefuls who had challenged them in the three semi-finals. Many of them were experienced quizzers already, like Dr Michael Dewar and Ivan Limmer; there was also Robert Crampsey, Glasgow schoolteacher and TV football commentator, one of the best-known voices in Scottish sport, who had been the first Scot to win Franklin Engelmann's *What Do You Know?* (the forerunner of *Brain of Britain*) in 1965; and the Rev. David Drake-Brockman, an Anglican curate from Lymington in Hampshire, who became one of the first married Anglican clergymen to be received into the Roman Catholic Church as a layman in 1985 (he was ordained as a married priest in 1991 and now serves in the diocese of Leeds).

The three women finalists were all rather remarkable in their own way. Two, as college lecturers, were professional knowledge-brokers; the third was not, but had an equally impressive background.

Mrs Nancy Wilkinson was a part-time lecturer in French and German literature at the Cambridgeshire College of Arts and Technology. She had won her heat with 'French Literature', followed by 'The History of European Antiques' in the semi-finals. She was now offering a new subject, 'The History of Music 1550–1900'.

Mrs Joan Taylor, a former Roedean teacher, was a lecturer in modern history at Newcastle University, married to an electrical engineer who managed a small company. A seasoned quiz competitor, she had been runner-up in the *Brain of Britain* radio programme and winner of *Television Brain of Britain*. She had reached the Final with 'Modern History', followed by 'The History of Music'; she was now offering 'International Relations Between the Wars 1919–39'.

Mrs Beryl Leatham Thomas was labelled 'a butcher's wife from Oswestry in Shropshire'. Her potential career as an academic had been disrupted by the war and early widowhood, whereupon she had bought a smallholding to rear poultry and had ended up as a wholesaler and retailer of every kind of fresh country produce; with her partner, a cattle-dealer and butcher, whom she later married, she had built up a small chain of market-stalls, shops and a restaurant. 'Butcher's wife' may have been a snappy journalistic label; but in fact she was a member of Mensa, ran a writers' group, wrote newspaper and magazine articles on literary matters and had appeared on *Television Brain of Britain*. She had reached the *Mastermind* Final with 'Twentieth-century English Literature', and 'Murders and Assassinations'; she was now reverting to 'Twentieth-century English Literature'.

Because there were only three Finalists, the normal two minutes of the earlier rounds in the series were considerably extended: two and a half minutes on specialised subjects, and three minutes on general knowledge.

At the halfway stage, Nancy Wilkinson and Joan Taylor were almost neck and neck (20 to 19), with Beryl Leatham Thomas trailing on 9. The outcome, in a cliff-hanger of a finish, was a win for Nancy over Joan (37 to 35); Beryl came third on 24.

Twenty-five years after that historic first Final, two embarrassing aspects of it stand out in my mind with appalling clarity. The first was a crass blunder which I made during Beryl's general knowledge round. Her second question was: 'Which character in *Richard II* described England as "This precious stone set in a silver sea"?' After a slight pause, the answer came back – 'Lancaster'. 'No,' I said with sublime authority, 'it was John of Gaunt.' I still cringe when I think of it – because the Duke of Lancaster *was* John of Gaunt, of course, and I had given a blatantly wrong adjudication. Yet the error was not picked up at the time, either by the producer or the researcher. Beryl herself merely blinked and looked surprised, and clearly spent the next few questions going over it in her mind.

However, in the taxi on the way back to the hotel, Nancy Wilkinson mentioned it to me. I was flabbergasted and mortified. It probably made no difference to the final result – Beryl was already trailing badly – but I was deeply concerned that it might have put her off her stride and robbed her of the chance of pulling off a sensational victory. Whatever disappointment she must have felt at the time, she hid it bravely; when a member of the production team apologised to her after the programme, she merely said, 'It's only a game, isn't it?', thereby setting an enviable standard of sportsmanship and grace in defeat.

The second stark recollection is the fact that we ran out of questions at one stage! The rounds were longer than usual, as I said, and we did not time questions in advance as rigorously then as we did latterly. On her specialised subject, 'The History of Music 1550–1900', Nancy was so quick on the draw that I had no questions left with fifteen seconds still to go. We had to stop the recording and compose some new ones in a hurry from *Pears Cyclopaedia* and any other sources to hand. Meanwhile Nancy sat on in the Chair and exchanged banter with the audience – and eventually turned to me and asked, very sweetly, if I would like *her* to ask *me* some questions!

The first Mastermind champion: Nancy Wilkinson

In the annals of TV quizzes, Nancy Wilkinson has earned herself a place in the pantheon of winners: the first Mastermind. She went on to win the first *Supermind* contest in 1975 (despite having suffered a mild stroke three weeks beforehand), and also took part in the 1982 Champion of Champions tourney (see Chapter 9).

Nancy Wilkinson (*née* Bird – she was a cousin of the cartoonist Kenneth Bird, 'Fougasse') had been one of the most brilliant girls of her year when she went up to Girton College, Cambridge, with no fewer than five scholarships in 1938. She took two degrees – a BA in Modern Languages (French and German) and a Mus.B. Recruited into the ATS (Auxiliary Territorial Service) she was put into the Intelligence Corps and worked on the Enigma project at Bletchley. After the war she married a classics lecturer, John

Nancy Wilkinson

Wilkinson, and moved into a delightful 700-year-old rectory in the Cambridgeshire village of Kingston. She held a number of part-time lecturing posts in French, German and English Literature, with a bit of Latin, biology, music and commerce thrown in, at the Cambridgeshire College of Arts and Technology (now the Anglia Polytechnic University).

Ever since childhood Nancy had taken pleasure in acquiring knowledge for its own sake. She told a Girton College annual meeting one year that as a child she had often wondered why her elders and betters spent so much time and energy arguing over matters of *fact*; to her way of thinking, the only things worth arguing about were *ideas* – if it were a matter of *fact* she thought one should look up the answer in a reference book at once and settle the matter. She went on to say that she thought a house should have a dictionary in every room, and an encyclopedia on every floor! She looked on *Mastermind* as a spur to read up on subjects which she had always wanted to have an excuse to study.

In *The Times* on 27 December 1972, Penny Symon gave her win fulsome coverage:

Mrs Nancy Wilkinson's ideal home would have a Bible, the
complete works of Shakespeare and a set of encyclopedias. Her
success in last night's final of BBC Television's quiz programme
Mastermind, *a cross between* Brain of Britain *and* University
Challenge, *comes partly from having piles of reference books, not in*
every room but certainly in the kitchen . . . She beat two other
finalists, both women, because of her retentive memory, curiosity and
wide interests:

'I am interested in almost everything. Ornithology, flora, domestic
architecture, local history, painting, composing, and I could get
interested in sport if necessary.'

Nancy's win made her a household name – for a time. In 1973
there was a by-election to the Church of England General Synod,
and three pairs of supporters independently offered to propose and
second her if she were a candidate. The fact that she was elected, she
feels, must have had something to do with the fact that people knew
her name through *Mastermind*. She was a member of the General
Synod for seventeen years, until 1980. Indirectly, membership of the
General Synod got her on to various committees which chimed in
with her interest in the conservation and maintenance of churches.

I cannot imagine a more fitting winner for the first *Mastermind*
championship than Nancy Wilkinson, the polymath who set the
pattern for the future.

The Mastermind *trophy*

David Attenborough, then the BBC's Director of Programmes, presented Nancy with her trophy. The only prize for winning
Mastermind was a rose bowl designed and engraved by Denis Mann,
of Caithness Glass. A northerner born and bred, Denis lives in Wick,
where Caithness Glass was founded (by Viscount Thurso) in 1960.
The basic design always involved depictions of the nine Greek
Muses, the nine patrons of the arts and sciences; they were divine
singers whose chorales and hymns delighted Zeus and the other
gods, but they also presided over thought in all its forms: eloquence,
persuasion, knowledge, history, mathematics, astronomy. They made
a highly appropriate theme, because they were the daughters of

Zeus and Mnemosyne, the personification of memory, which was just about the most useful of all the many attributes required to win the *Mastermind* title. Mnemosyne herself ought to have been the patron goddess of all aspirant Masterminders.

Each year the design became more and more the inspiration of its artist. At first Denis researched for ideas in the British Museum collection of Greek pottery, and used live models. Later he would sketch a rough design and draw it directly on to the plain glass with fibre-tipped pens of different colours so that he could see the effect through the bowl and judge any distortions. Then he sand-blasted the design on to the bowl, to give a fixed base on to which he could sculpt. This sculptural technique (the most skilled part of the design), using a copper-wheel engraving lathe, gave features to the faces and substance to the arms and legs.

Caithness Glass, which was recently taken over by Royal Doulton, became almost synonymous with *Mastermind*, and I know that the long association meant a great deal to the young manufacturing venture in the far north of Scotland, struggling to make its way in a fiercely competitive world. The respect was mutual. To my certain knowledge, no winner of the Caithness Glass trophy has ever broken it, or sold it, or given it away. For all the winners, the trophies remain treasured mementoes of an intensely proud moment.

4

Lift-Off:
The First Hundred

When *Mastermind* began as a late-night programme for academic insomniacs it attracted a modest audience of 1.5 million; indeed, one critic opined that it seemed doomed to win the 'Bore of the Week Award'. Nevertheless, the viewing figures rose steadily over its run to a gratifying 6.5 million for the Final. The really spectacular change in the programme's fortunes, however, came early in the second series, in 1973, because of a fortuitous switch in scheduling.

It all happened because of a slightly *risqué* new comedy series written by Ray Galton and Alan Simpson called *Casanova '73* (subtitled *The Adventures of a 20th-century Libertine*). It starred the comic actor Leslie Phillips as a modern-day, married, smooth-talking womaniser called Henry Newhouse (which, of course, is *casa nova* in Italian). While *Mastermind* was going out at about 11pm on Monday evenings, *Casanova '73* started going out on Thursdays at 8pm, immediately after *Top of the Pops*, when presumably many young people were watching – a full hour before the traditional viewing 'watershed' at 9pm. There was an immediate protest from the Mary Whitehouse brigade: for '*risqué*' read 'smutty'. The third transmission was postponed, and in the fourth week *Casanova '73* was moved to a later slot, at 9.25 on Mondays, and *Mastermind* took its place at the prime viewing time of 8pm on Thursdays.

Mastermind continued in its Thursday peak spot for the rest of the 1973 series (and the rest of the 1970s). The viewing figures shot up to

12 million for the 1973 Final – much higher than *Casanova '73* had been getting. *Mastermind* had well and truly arrived as a major peak-time success. By the end of the second series it had become 'something of a cult', according to Vincent Mulchrone in the *Daily Mail*.

In a way, being pitchforked into a peak-time slot caused us real problems, because it gave the programme a new significance. To live up to 'cult status' the programme required more resources of time and care (and therefore a larger budget), more expertise, a more rigorously intellectual input. For my own part I was so busy on *Chronicle* that I was unable to devote to it the time it deserved; I would fly in from some far-flung part of the world on the morning of a programme recording and get my first look at the evening's scripts during the car-journey to the location, with Bill Wright at the wheel and Cherry Cole in the back seat going over the questions with me. Making *Mastermind* in the early days was a bit of a roller-coaster ride for everyone concerned.

All the time we were having to learn how to cope with the new challenges which came up. In the semi-finals in 1973, for instance, we had our first tie on both points and passes and had to have a tie-break.

The two contenders involved were Margery Elliott, a music teacher from Birmingham, who had won her heat with 'The Symphony Orchestra' and was now taking 'The Operas of Mozart'; and Dr Jeffrey Boss, a lecturer in cell biology at Bristol University, who had won his heat with 'Greek Mythology' and was now taking 'The Old Testament'.

Margery Elliott, who had been in the same year at Girton College, Cambridge, as Nancy Wilkinson, the 1972 winner, was a research chemist who had switched to music teaching as a career. At the halfway stage she had a lead of 5 points over Jeffrey Boss (14 against 9); but in the general knowledge round she added only 9, for a total of 23 (with 7 passes). Jeffrey, solemn, bearded and bespectacled, went off like a train, and then caused a lengthy and hilarious delay in the proceedings. Question 9 in his general knowledge round was, 'What is the capital of Mongolia?' Quick as a flash he riposted, 'Inner or Outer?' I was completely thrown by this, so I stopped the recording and went into a huddle with the production team. For about ten minutes the audience chatted as Jeffrey Boss sat inscrutably in the Black Chair, the lights glinting off his glasses, while the other three semi-finalists sat in silence, waiting. Eventually I resumed my seat and called for quiet, and then said to Jeffrey: 'What would you say if I said *Outer* Mongolia?' (expecting the answer 'Ulan Bator'). Whereupon Jeffrey replied, 'I would say "Pass". I don't know either of them.' The audience collapsed with laughter. The recording was restarted, and Jeffrey replied 'Pass'. I was sure that this interruption had cost him any chance he had of catching up on Margery's score, but he managed to muster the points to draw level with her on 23 (also with 7 passes).

The only way to settle the tie was by a play-off, with both contenders answering the same five questions. Jeffrey was escorted from the hall and secreted in the Gents' while Margery returned to the Black Chair. She got only one question right, while Jeffrey got two and thereby qualified for the Final.

Margery, deprived of a place in the Final, had caught the quiz bug by now. She reached the final of *Brain of Britain* on radio twice (1976 and 1992), she joined Mensa and, in 1978, became the first woman to win the Brain of Mensa quiz. Since then she has appeared on umpteen other quizzes, including *Fifteen to One*, *Jeopardy* and *Today's the Day*. Not content with that, she joined the Mastermind Club as soon as it was formed in 1978, and for fifteen years played a crucial role not just in its success but also in its very survival, as Secretary (1981–86), Acting Treasurer (1982), and Editor of the Club's magazine, *PASS* (1988–93).

1973: Patricia Owen

The 1973 winner was another woman, and another academic: Patricia Owen, a part-time lecturer in English and art at the Maria Grey College of Education in Isleworth. Born in London in 1925 of Australian parents, she went to school in Australia where she worked as a radio announcer while taking a degree in English at Sydney University. She returned to Britain to do a B.Litt. at St Hilda's College, Oxford, married a fellow academic, and taught for several years at what is now Baghdad University.

She only reached the Final through the *repêchage* round – the fourth semi-final, for the highest-scoring losers. But her win in the Final was a decisive one, against three male contenders. What made it all the more meritorious was that her semi-final and the Final were recorded on the same evening – something we never attempted to

Patricia Owen

do again, I'm glad to say. Patricia was totally unruffled by it all. She was only 'thrown' once, when I asked her, 'What was the exedra of Maximian?' She knew that 'exedra' meant 'throne', but my Scottish accent made 'Maximian' sound like 'MacSimeon', and she passed . . .

Patricia's win gave rise to an entertaining exchange of letters in *The Times*, started by a Mr Stephen Corrin of London:

> *Sir, I note that you devoted quite a deal of space to the result of the BBC television quiz* Mastermind. *Without wishing to diminish the happiness or underestimate the merit of the winner, I do think that the fine word 'mind' (for which it would be difficult to find an equivalent in any European language) is being debased in this context.*
>
> *Of the total range of mental, intellectual and perhaps even spiritual operations encompassed by the term, surely it is mainly*

memory which is being tested in a quiz in which the contestants are simply required to provide straight answers to a string of (admittedly difficult) questions in a given, restricted period of time? Perhaps the BBC might be persuaded to call the game Master Memory, *reserving 'mind' for more elevated purposes.*

Patricia replied with her only 'letter to *The Times*', and she has treasured the cutting:

Sir, Mr Corrin seems to be taking the title of 'Mastermind' more seriously than did any of the contenders that I met.

The term mind cannot, however, be reserved, as he suggests, for more elevated purposes. In English usage mind and memory are frequently coterminous: may I remind him of such collocations as to call to mind, to have in mind, time out of mind. The Concise Oxford Dictionary *brings to mind that remembrance is the first definition of mind.*

The quiz game tests the acquisition, storage and retrieval of information: all processes of the mind. It springs to mind that the game tests another human quality: presence of mind. During the quiz we had also to keep our minds on the job, mind our p's and q's and not mind too much whether we won or lost.

Therefore, Sir, I remain with undiminished happiness,
Yours faithfully,
Patricia Owen,
Mastermind of the United Kingdom.

It was not just the winners who were memorable, however. In the 1973 series we had an eminent theatre historian called Phyllis Hartnoll, who took part in Heat 7 offering as her specialised subject 'The History of the Theatre'. She did rather well on that – not surprisingly, because she was the editor of *The Oxford Companion to the Theatre*; but she came a cropper in the general knowledge round ('a humbling experience which no doubt did me a lot of good', as she was to write in *PASS* in 1982), and lost to Charles Key, the founder and first president of the Mastermind Club. When the Club was formed in 1978, Phyllis was one of the first to join; she was a regular attender at the annual functions, and won the Magnum (the in-house club quiz competition) in 1983.

Phyllis died in January 1997 at the age of ninety, having had a fascinating career as an editor, scholar and writer, and as a considerable
poet – at Oxford she had won the Newdigate Prize for English
Verse (the first woman to do so), and she also won the Oxford Prize
for Sacred Poetry (twice) and the Gold Medal of the Poetry Society.

One of the most unforgettable appearances in the early programmes,
however, was that of a brilliant young Oxford student from
Manchester, Susan Reynolds (now Halstead), who reached the Final
in 1974.

Susan was only nineteen years old, a classics undergraduate at
Lady Margaret Hall in Oxford. She was a quite exceptionally gifted
young woman. She could read when she was two years old, was a
typist at six, wrote poetry and short stories, acted (in both English
and Greek) and sang. By the time she went up to Oxford at the age
of seventeen she could read in twenty-two languages, and speak
half that number. She won prize after prize. She was to star in the
Lady Margaret Hall team on *University Challenge*. She was very shy,
very highly-strung, and talked more rapidly than anyone I had ever
met. Her ambition was to become the first female Fellow of All
Souls' College, and there seemed no reason whatsoever why she
should not fulfil it – except for the ill-health which had dogged her
childhood and which would wreak havoc with her university career.

Mastermind seemed a natural progression. She was selected on her
first application, despite doing a rather nervous audition. She was in
the first heat in the 1974 series, taking 'Greek Mythology', and
won without apparent effort ('as satisfying as a strenuous but exhilarating game of ball, with a swing and a rhythm of its own, bouncing
and catching the questions. No time to be anxious, and over so
quickly,' she said of the experience). From then on I had her marked
as a potential champion. In the semi-finals she took 'The Works of
Richard Wagner' and won again.

Then came the Final – and disaster. Susan was offering a third subject, 'British Ornithology'. The Final was being recorded in the
University of Manchester, and she felt practically on home ground,
happier and more confident than before. But when we met the
Finalists in the afternoon for briefing and rehearsal – no Susan. As the
time went by we began to be seriously concerned: had something
happened? Had nerves got the better of her? Had she chickened out

at the last moment? Eventually she arrived, dishevelled and as white as parchment, with a bruise on her forehead. She looked alarmingly unwell. I asked her what on earth was wrong. She told me that when she was dressing for the programme in her hotel room that afternoon she had had a bizarre accident. After she had put on the long-sleeved vanilla-coloured dress which her parents had given her for the occasion, she was stooping to put on her shoes when the wardrobe door swung open and struck her just above her left eye. I asked her if she felt well enough to go on with the show, even though it would have been like doing *Hamlet* without the Prince; but she was pluckily determined not to let everyone down by pulling out at the last minute. For Susan, I know, the rest of the evening was a blur of pain and giddy light-headedness. Afterwards she told me that all she was concentrating on was not to faint on camera.

She was grimly determined not to be a complete disappointment. Having scored a mere 5 on her specialised subject, she managed to add another 12 for general knowledge. The overall winning score that year was only 21 – much the lowest ever for a Final – but Susan's 17 was only enough to give her third equal place.

For Susan it was a tragedy of almost Homeric proportions, and we all felt desperately sorry for her. Letters from viewers poured in, too. Everyone was stunned, just as Susan had been. It created far more fame for her than for anyone else in the series – more than most champions have enjoyed, in fact.

Today Susan is still living in Oxford. She has been plagued by ill-health, but has won countless honours and prizes. She is a tutor in languages, literature, history and philosophy at the Oxford Overseas Study Course, and also works for Clio Press, writing abstracts of articles for journals in a wide range of languages. I shall always remember her, affectionately, as the greatest champion we never had.

1974: Elizabeth Horrocks

The champion in 1974 was the third consecutive woman to win the title, giving rise to good-humoured suggestions that the title of the programme should be changed to *Mistressmind* – 28-year-old Elizabeth Horrocks, a Welsh-born housewife and English teacher from Haslington, near Crewe in Cheshire. She had been challenged to enter by her husband, who had had to listen to her calling out the answers at the television set, and she decided that she ought to 'put her money where her mouth was'. She had a quick and quirky sense of humour. During a rehearsal session I misread a question: 'In the Old Testament, *what* [instead of *where*] was Moses when God spoke to him beside the burning bush?' Quick as a flash she replied, 'Surprised!'

In the programme proper, Elizabeth specialised in three literary subjects: 'The Plays of Shakespeare', 'The Works of J. R. R. Tolkien' and, for the Final, 'The Detective Stories of Dorothy L. Sayers'. In general, 1974 was not a high-scoring year, and Elizabeth won with scores of 24, 30, and finally 21.

Her victory in the 1974 Final in which Susan Reynolds crashed was a close-run thing: at the end of the contest she was tied on 21 points with Brian Wright, a civil servant from Shepherd's Bush in London, who was offering 'The Novels of Charles Dickens' as his specialised subject. Elizabeth had the fewer passes (7, against 11), and would have won anyway; but during the recording break before the presentation of the trophy there was a hurried consultation at my desk after Cherry Cole, sitting beside me as scorer and time-keeper, whispered to me that there had been a mistake in the scoring. It emerged that Brian Wright had been given a point for an incorrect answer to one of his general knowledge questions: 'Born in 1753, he was appointed architect to the Bank of England and to St James's Palace – who was he?' Brian had replied 'Soames', which I had mis-heard as 'Soane' (Sir John Soane, the correct answer), and accepted. I now asked Brian if he had indeed said 'Soames', and he sportingly agreed that he had. So a point was deducted from his score, thereby giving Elizabeth an outright win after all.

Elizabeth went on to take part in the first *Supermind* programme in 1975, a special challenge match which brought together the first four *Mastermind* champions. Each champion had to offer not one, but two, specialised subjects. Once again Elizabeth, who was taking 'The Life and Works of Jane Austen' and 'The Plays of Shakespeare', found herself in a tie for the lead, this time with the first champion, Nancy Wilkinson, with a tie on passes as well; there had to be a play-off, which Elizabeth lost 1–2.

Elizabeth has always been modest about her victory on *Mastermind*: she says she did not so much win the Final – the others threw it away. For several years afterwards, while she was bringing up

**Elizabeth Horrocks (second from left), with
fellow finalists Martin Gostelow, Brian Wright
and Susan Reynolds**

her two daughters, she would be asked to give talks on the
Mastermind experience at least once a month; and she tells me that it
may also have helped her to get her present job as a part-time
English teacher at Hyde Sixth-Form College (now Hyde Clarendon
College) in Tameside. The principal of the college, who was on the
selection board, was intrigued to see 'Mastermind Champion' on
her CV, and asked her about little else during her interview!

People everywhere were fascinated by the phenomenon that
women, although consistently outnumbered four to one by men on
the programme, should have won the first three titles. Why were
they doing so well? That question came up over and over again in
every press interview until I got heartily sick of it. At first I tried to
be flippant. I would say that it was probably because women had far
more time to read books and swot up on their general knowledge
while their menfolk were slaving away to keep them in idle luxury;
but I soon learned that irony is totally lost on earnest young journalists, when I found myself being quoted and cast as a chauvinistic
old misogynist. To be serious, I always had the impression that the
women contenders tended to be rather more relaxed on the programme than the men in the early days: they didn't feel that their

pride was at stake to the same extent, and treated it more as a game than the men did.

Because of the success of women on *Mastermind*, researchers in the psychology department at Reading University set up a special experiment. They wanted to test the theory that the left-hand side of the brain, which specialises in language control, is more highly developed in women than in men, whereas the right-hand side of the brain, which specialises in non-verbal functions, is more highly developed in men. Seventy-five undergraduates (thirty-eight women and thirty-seven men) were given two tests, against the clock. Try them out for yourselves and see how you get on.

The first test was a purely verbal one: 'Without speaking or writing, go through the alphabet mentally from A to Z and count up the number of letters containing the sound "ee".' The second test was a purely visual or spatial one: 'Without speaking or writing, go through the alphabet mentally from A to Z and count up the number of capital letters with a curve.' The results were that in the first test the women undergraduates were faster and made fewer mistakes, whereas in the second test the men were faster and made fewer mistakes. (The answer to the first test is eight; to the second, eleven.)

There were other, more complicated, tests. But the outcome remained the same: that the women were superior to men in most verbal or linguistic skills, which gave them a genetic advantage over men in a contest like *Mastermind* where the questions are all verbal. The conclusion was that the odds were on women winning *Mastermind*.

1975: John Hart

In the very next year, however, the female hold on the title was broken when the winner was John Hart, the senior classics master at Malvern College in Worcestershire. But other records were broken in 1975, too. There was a particularly wide spectrum of contenders, ranging from a lorry-driver from Rochester (Michael Munn) and a former coal-miner (Jack Tomlinson) to a member of the House of Lords (Viscount Tenby). In fact David Tenby, the grandson of Lloyd George and the first member of the House of Lords to take part in *Mastermind*, earned the dubious accolade of notching the lowest general knowledge score yet recorded (a mere 3), although he had done very well (16) on 'The American Civil War' as his specialised subject.

In David Tenby's heat was a Welsh contestant who came to us with a formidable reputation as a quiz prodigy: Antony Carr, a lecturer in Welsh history at the University College of Wales, in Bangor. As an eighteen-year-old schoolboy in 1956 he had been the youngest winner of radio's *What Do You Know?* and the winner of *Brain of Brains* the same year. In 1962 he had won the *Top Brain of Britain* title. On *Mastermind* he took 'The Life and Work of Mozart' as his specialised subject, and got through to the semi-finals on passes after tying on 26.

In the semi-finals he was pitted against another university lecturer who had made his mark in the heats: Francis Lambert, a specialist in Latin-American studies at Glasgow University. In his heat he had taken 'Cuba Since the Nineteenth Century' and broken the *Mastermind* scoring record with a massive 35 points. Aficionados of the programme were expecting a titanic battle in the second semi-final between 37-year-old Antony Carr and 33-year-old Francis Lambert.

In the event it was no contest. Francis, who was taking 'The History of Brazil Since Independence' against Antony's 'The Hundred Years War', strode to a majestic 37 points, breaking his own new record in the process and earning a place in the *Guinness Book of Records*.

Mastermind was Antony's last quiz. He is now Reader at the University College of Wales, and has published five scholarly books on the history of medieval Wales. How does he remember *Mastermind*? 'When I watch Mastermind now,' he says, 'the adrenaline still starts to flow at the sound of the theme music! But it was an enjoyable experience.' He has no great urge to try again, however: 'In the days when I competed, quizzes were fun, but people seem to take them far too seriously now. The whole business seems to be getting rather professional.'

Meanwhile Francis Lambert marched on to the Final, which was recorded in the Chaplaincy Centre in St Aldate's, Oxford. The burning question was: could anyone beat Francis Lambert? There were two schoolteachers and two university lecturers – the real 'Mastermind' stereotype of the old days. Two of them had been to the same school (the Dragon School at Oxford) – Francis Lambert and John Hart, who had moved purposefully to the Final with solid wins in the heats ('Athens in the Fifth Century BC') and the semi-finals ('Rome in the First Century BC'). The others were George Johnston, the

John Hart

vice-principal of Rainey Endowed School in Magherafelt in County Derry, who had been on *Brain of Britain* in 1961 and had reached this Final with 'French Literature 1600–1900' and 'The Music of Franz Liszt'; and Jacqueline Pearson, a lecturer in English literature at Manchester University; her specialised subjects had been 'English Drama 1593–1625' and 'The Life and Works of Christopher Marlowe'.

But now everything went wrong for Francis Lambert. He seemed curiously ill-at-ease and scored only 9 on his specialised round. The questions had been set by Hugh Thomas, a professor of history at Reading University and the doyen of Latin-American studies; but it was not the fault of the questions. Twenty years later he was to recall, 'It simply started to go bad. I felt it all slipping away from me, and could do nothing about it.' I can remember thinking during the questioning, 'When is Francis going to get into his stride?'

At the halfway stage he was lying 6 points behind John Hart, who had scored 15, and 3 behind George Johnston and Jacqueline Pearson. Now John, going first again, proceeded to add an effortless 14 on general knowledge to set the target at 29. George could only reach 26, and Jacqueline 24. Finally it was Francis's turn. Looking more and more agitated, he had a determined go at recovering his position and added 14, but it was nowhere near enough.

So it was John Hart who broke the mould and became the first male *Mastermind* champion. He told me he felt that Francis had taken it all much too seriously; he had ignored the closing piece of advice, which all contenders were given at the pre-programme briefing, to treat it not as an intelligence test but as fun. 'Fun' was what it certainly meant to John Hart. An hour after the recording of the Final, he took part in the first *Supermind* challenge – a light-hearted joust between the first four *Mastermind* champions. He had been so pleased to win the championship that he did not really care what happened on *Supermind*, and having celebrated with 'a glass or two of champagne' he was no longer on his best form, shall we say. He came in a cheerful fourth.

Apart from winning the Caithness Glass bowl, victory brought John an unexpected bonus – a two-week holiday with his wife the following spring at the invitation of the Union of Greek Shipowners; his win had made headlines in the Greek newspapers because he had taken 'Athens in the Fifth Century BC' in the Final, and this had earned him national hero status in Greece!

1976: Roger Pritchard

Another crop of surprises and pleasures and fascinating people came in 1976. We had our first London taxi-driver – no, not Fred Housego, but Robert Smith, who took 'The Viking Atlantic Voyages'; he was a voracious reader on all manner of subjects, and was going to take 'The Life of Lawrence of Arabia' and 'The Life of Toulouse-Lautrec' as his other specialised subjects. His particular interest in Vikings in America, however, had been aroused after a passenger left a book called *Viking America*, by James Robert Entline, on the seat of his cab one day.

Another of the contenders was the late lexicographer Dr John Sykes (1929–93), who described himself as 'a jackmind of all

Roger Pritchard

trades and a mastermind of none'. He had worked as a theoretical physicist at the Atomic Research Establishment, Harwell, then had become a translator of scientific books, coping with material in up to twenty languages; in 1970 he became editor of *The Concise Oxford Dictionary*. But his public fame rested on his extraordinary skill at solving crossword puzzles. He won *The Times* annual National Crossword Championship for four years in succession from 1972, and ten times in all before he retired from the fray in 1990; his record for finishing a *Times* puzzle in the championship was five minutes.

On *Mastermind* he sailed through his heat with 'Mathematics'. In the semi-finals he took 'Physics', and ran up against an all-too-familiar problem when 'my mouth refused say what my brain was telling it to say': to his chagrin he failed on a question which should have been meat and drink to a physicist – the correct definition of the acronym 'maser' ('Microwave Amplification by Stimulated Emission of Radiation'). However, he had the consolation of breaking the programme record for a general knowledge round with a dazzling 19 points.

The Final that year was fought out between a lorry-driver (David Wilson, from Sutton Coldfield), a teacher (Nicholas Spruytenburg, from Aldeburgh in Suffolk), a civil servant (Dr Roger Pritchard, from Weston-super-Mare), and a young postal officer (Amanda Hill, from Wallington in Surrey). It was the youngest Final yet, with an average age of thirty-three.

It was won by Roger Pritchard, who worked at the Department of the Environment in Bristol. Two years earlier he had won the *Brain of Britain* title; but he claims that his original application for *Mastermind* for the 1976 series was inspired by an excess of Christmas bravado (the Final was always broadcast during the Christmas break in those days). His specialised subjects were 'The Life of the Duke of Wellington' (because he had been given Elizabeth Longford's biography of him for Christmas, and could think of nothing better) and 'British Warships of the Twentieth Century'. Somewhat to his surprise he enjoyed it immensely, both as a contest and as a unique opportunity of seeing how a popular television programme was made. But he never took it very seriously, and I remember to this day his modest description of his feat – 'a magnificent inconsequentiality', he called it:

> *If you go into the programme imagining that it's very important and that you are going to win at all costs, I don't think you've got a chance. But if you go into it with the right attitude and treat it as a game, then I think anyone has a chance of winning, because there is a lot of luck in it, obviously.*

Inconsequential or not, for nearly twenty years he was the only person to have won both the *Brain of Britain* title and the *Mastermind* title, until even that record was emulated by Kevin Ashman in 1995, who held both titles simultaneously for a time.

Mastermind was the end of Roger's quiz career ('After all, how can you top that?'). He is now Head of the European Wildlife Division in the Department of the Environment, responsible for nature conservation policy – which, by an odd coincidence, means that I, as chairman of Scottish Natural Heritage, am in close contact with him again. It's a very small world.

1977: Sir David Hunt

The first hundred programmes ended with a glittering Jubilee Final in 1977, which was recorded in the magnificent setting of the Old Library in London's Guildhall. It produced one of the most popular of all our title-winners: the wise and genial retired ambassador Sir David Hunt, who was then sixty-four years old.

Sir David had had a distinguished war record. He had been private secretary to both Winston Churchill and Clement Attlee. He had worked in Uganda, Cyprus, Nigeria and latterly Brazil. But he very nearly came a cropper on *Mastermind*. He lost his heat by a short head because, as he admitted, he got so interested in the questions that he allowed himself the luxury of *discussion*. His subject was 'British Campaigns in North Africa in the Second World War'; and sometimes he would reply, 'Ah yes, that's a jolly interesting one – wasn't that so-and-so?', thus using up valuable time. Even so he qualified for the *repêchage* semi-final for the highest-scoring runners-up – and didn't make the same mistake again. This time he won with ease, taking 'The Allied Armies in Italy in the Second World War' (a subject on which he knew a thing or two, having served for more than two years as Field Marshal Alexander's principal intelligence officer in Italy). In the Final he romped home with a record-*equalling* overall score of 37 – 17 on his specialised subject ('The Roman Revolution, 60 BC to AD 14') and a record-*breaking* 20 on general knowledge. He went on to win the Champion of Champions tourney for the first ten *Mastermind* winners in 1982.

David Hunt dominates all memories of the Jubilee series in 1977. But others stay in the mind, too. The very first heat brought a fascinating blend of contenders: Sue Jenkins, a young student teacher

Sir David Hunt

from Marlow in Buckinghamshire who went on to the Final, specialising in 'Children's Literature' and 'France in the Seventeenth Century'; Ian Sewell, a printer from Oxford, taking 'The Old Testament', who had been billed in the *Radio Times* as 'the most fixated quizman in the first round' because he had been on *Brain of Britain* and *Brain of Sport*; Hugh Merrick, writer, mountaineer, translator and violinist, who at seventy-nine was the oldest contender ever to appear on *Mastermind*; and Martin Leadbetter, a fingerprint expert with the Hertfordshire Constabulary and a prolific composer. Because he was also co-editor of *Fingerprint Whorld,* the journal of the Fingerprint Society, he became the first editor of the Mastermind Club's in-house journal, *PASS*.

Another of the class of 1977 unwittingly occasioned the most unusual complaint which has ever been made about *Mastermind*. It was a letter from an outraged viewer claiming that I had committed a gross blasphemy on the programme: I had allegedly taken the Lord's name in vain by saying that Christ's baptismal name was Reginald! We were baffled by this, and searched carefully through all the programme videos. It turned out to have been the result of mishearing a question in the second heat. It concerned a contender called Patrick Hampshire, from Donaghadee in Northern Ireland, a 58-year-old wine merchant in London, taking 'The Life and Works of P. G. Wodehouse'. One of his questions had been 'What was Jeeves's Christian name?' Patrick answered, 'He didn't have one', but I corrected him: 'Yes he did: it was Reginald.' Ah, well.

But 1977 was David Hunt's year. After his win on *Mastermind* he became a regular television pundit on all manner of subjects. He appeared on programmes dealing with Attlee, Churchill and Macmillan, and the history of the Conservative party. He did programmes on battles he had taken part in, such as Crete and Monte Cassino, a series on 'Children's Diaries', and a preliminary talk on *Troilus and Cressida* for the BBC's complete cycle of Shakespeare's plays in 1985. Now a spry 84-year-old, he retains all his classical enthusiasms, and still does lecture tours in the USA. His interests, according to *Who's Who*, are 'reading, writing and rose-growing'; but *Who's Who* also records what he considers one of his proudest achievements: 'BBC TV Mastermind 1977 and Mastermind of Masterminds 1982'.

5

The Third Degree:
Setting the Questions

'Cocooned in the Mastermind chair, with the audience in darkness, all you are aware of is the bright tunnel of concentration which links you with Magnus. There is a strong sense, too, that he is positively willing you to do well, delighted when you answer correctly.'

MICHAEL DAVISON (1984), an editor for *Reader's Digest* Special Books

Over the twenty-five years of *Mastermind*, 1,231 willing victims, young and old, men and women, allowed themselves to be subjected to a grilling in the Black Chair. It involved preparing about 1,750 sets of specialised questions, and a corresponding number of general knowledge sets.

There were five questions which I was always being asked about the questioning on *Mastermind*: why do some people get more questions than others; who sets the questions; how fair are the questions; how are the subjects chosen; and do we ever make mistakes?

1. Why do some people get more questions than others?

Let me quote from the official statement which accompanied the programme notes sent to all *Mastermind* contestants:

All questions and their 'ideal' answers are meticulously timed during the course of their preparation. Therefore, if contestants react instantly and give the 'ideal' answer then all, in theory, should receive exactly

the same number of questions. Differences in the number of questions
actually received, however, are usually caused by slow reactions,
hesitation, or the giving of longer answers than are necessary.

This was not a PR bromide. It was for real. Once the early helter-skelter days were over, I would travel to the location the day before the programme recordings and go through all the question-packs with the producer or chief researcher, looking for potential problems. Were they phrased in the most straightforward and unambiguous way? Were they easy to comprehend when I read them at speed? Did they point the contender in the right direction from the first word? Was there more than one correct answer? Were there alternative answers which would be acceptable? And how on earth were the foreign words and names pronounced? (I confess a private shame here: for some unfathomable reason, I have never been able to pronounce French properly, and dreaded all French names which appeared on my cards. Aztec? Japanese? German? Italian? No problem. French? – Oh God.)

After we were satisfied that the questions were as nearly perfect as possible I would bring out the stopwatch and read out the questions, *and the optimum answers*, lickety-split at programme speed. I added the obligatory 'Corrects' with the appropriate breath pauses. If the time was up before I reached Question 20, some trimming had to be done. In the end, the questions were phrased and tuned and timed to such a pitch that if a contender were on form and answered correctly and without hesitation, he or she would receive the same number of questions as the others.

That was the theory, anyway. It didn't always work out that way, of course. An agonising pause for thought, followed by a despairing 'Pass', could seem like an age and could cost the equivalent of two questions – or even more. The viewer was left with the *impression* of excessive length, even though it was the responses, not the questions, which were long.

And when it *did* work, when the questions and answers flowed, when questioner and questioned started chiming, it was such an exhilarating feeling. There was a stride, a quickening rhythm, a gathering momentum which swept you both onwards, irresistibly; and at the end, as the bleeper went, you felt as if you had been running the race of your life. The score, whatever it was, came as a total surprise – you had both been oblivious to everything except this clenched concentration of mind and will.

There were only one or two such occasions when it *really* happened. I think of Chantal Thompson, the young trainee solicitor from Bristol, who seemed to have blown her chance of winning the 1990 Final in the ornate City Chambers of Glasgow. Chantal's father, retired banker Richard Thompson, had appeared on *Mastermind* in 1977 and family honour was at stake. Chantal's plane to Glasgow had developed landing-gear trouble and she arrived at the location very late and extremely flustered. Not surprisingly, perhaps, she scored only 12 on her specialised subject of 'The Life and Works of Cicero' and was trailing in last place at the halfway stage. In the general knowledge round, with nothing to lose, she just hurled herself at the questions. She felt she knew each question before it was asked; her confidence grew with every passing second; giving a wrong answer was inconceivable. She responded so swiftly and so surely that she beat the odds, beat the clock even, and added a blazing, record-equalling 22 to set a formidable target with 34. And she almost pulled it off: it took a very determined round by David Edwards to keep his nerve and pull ahead to win the title. Chantal may have lost the trophy, but she won all hearts with that magical performance when most other people would have thrown in the towel.

The other occasion was during the 1986 Final, recorded in the McEwan Hall of Edinburgh University. The favourite that year was Jennifer Keaveney, a careers officer at the University of Kent at Canterbury, who had earlier broken the *Mastermind* scoring record with 40 in her semi-final. In the Final she was up against some very high-scoring opponents, especially Hendy Farquhar-Smith, who had scored 37 in both the heats and the semi-finals. At the halfway stage in the Final Jennifer was trailing by a point, having scored 18 on 'The Life and Works of Elizabeth Gaskell'. In the general knowledge round, however, she simply took off. Concentrating with an almost frightening intensity, she streaked through 23 general knowledge questions and added 22 (with one pass) to equal her record-breaking feat with another 40 and clinch the title. Only then did her concentration break, and a most beautiful smile illuminated her face. Bryan Appleyard, reviewing the programme in *The Times* the following day, caught it very well: 'When she finds her range her head tilts slightly, all life seems to vanish from her face and the answers emerge as if she were merely the mouthpiece of some infinitely quick, infinitely informed computer.'

2. Who set the questions?

Specialised questions

For the first twenty years (1972–92) one man was responsible for co-ordinating all the specialised questions: Harold Boswell Taylor. A former headmaster, he was also a writer of school textbooks and a regular BBC broadcaster.

Boswell had already had a rich career by the time he joined the *Mastermind* team. He began writing for the BBC as a student at Birmingham University (his first success was a prize-winning short story, *Angle-snap*, which was read on the radio by the late Godfrey Baseley, the actor who originated *The Archers*). In all, he wrote more than two hundred feature programmes, stories and plays, and poetry anthologies for the BBC, including a series on village institutions and scripts for schools programmes. The most enduring programmes, perhaps, called *They Found the Secret*, told the dramas behind famous scientific inventions and discoveries, such as the development of the steam engine by James Watt ('The Man Who Harnessed Steam') and the breakthrough on vaccination by Edward Jenner ('Conqueror of Smallpox'). They were published in the 1950s by Macmillan as a series of booklets under the series title *They Served Mankind*, and were designed to bring scientific discovery to intelligent young readers.

His first experience of question-setting came with the television version of radio's *Top of the Form*. Soon he was writing all the questions and choosing the members of the teams. In 1965, when Bill Wright inherited *Television Top of the Form*, he inherited Boswell, too. It was the start of a partnership which was to last for the rest of Bill's life. Bill took over the school visits, but Boswell continued to write and research all the questions.

Boswell was also the editor for the Dolphin series of books for children (about a hundred altogether), published by Hodder & Stoughton, who also commissioned him to provide English versions of dictionaries originally published by Scott Foresman of Chicago, in association with *World Book Encyclopedia* – the largest selling encyclopedia in the world. Boswell became their schools consultant, and in 1962 he was appointed Research Director (later Editorial and Research Director) for the International Edition of *World Book Encyclopedia*. He had a London office but spent lengthy periods in Chicago.

Part of his work in Chicago was advising on questions for the *World Book College Bowl Quiz* programme, in order to give them an international dimension. The *College Bowl* team was keen to compete with other national teams, so the BBC agreed to host a *College Bowl* tour in Britain, playing against top school teams here. The *College Bowl* format was eventually bought by commercial TV and became *University Challenge*, which began in September 1962.

Bill Wright was very keen for *Television Top of the Form* to be international; Boswell, with all his experience, was recruited to take control of the organisation and question-setting. This was the genesis of *Transworld Top Team*, starting in 1967. Boswell wrote all the questions, and now he appeared on screen as adjudicator alongside the main presenter, Geoffrey Wheeler, with Mary Craig, who was the production assistant and researcher.

During this period Boswell learnt to tackle some of the problems of compiling programmes involving people with completely different educational training and national histories, customs, culture, environments – and even languages.

So when Bill Wright dreamed up the concept of *Mastermind*, Boswell Taylor was the obvious person to help with compiling the questions – particularly the specialised subjects. It was Boswell's task to track down the appropriate experts for the various specialisms and edit their questions into *Mastermind* style. He felt it was vital to have the questions written by people of some stature and prestige. This was difficult at first: *Mastermind* was a quiz, and in many academic eyes that condemned it. To start with, Boswell drew a complete blank: everyone he approached, even writers who had worked with him on other projects, lost interest the moment he mentioned the word 'quiz'.

The breakthrough came when Boswell turned to media people for help. The first catch was Patrick Moore, of *The Sky at Night*, who enthusiastically agreed to do any questions on astronomy and who never let the programme down (so I felt that it was peculiarly fitting that Patrick, the 'Old Man of the Sky', should be invited to present the trophy at the 1995 Final). Another expert recruit from the media was Dr David Butler, Fellow of Nuffield College and prolific writer on elections, who was the BBC's leading psephologist at the time (he had the original 'swingometer'); he set the questions for one of the subjects in the very first programme in 1972, 'British Politics Since 1900'. Stanley Sadie, the music critic of *The Times* who was working on *The New Grove Dictionary of Music and Musicians*, was another early recruit; Stanley put Boswell in touch with Michael Kennedy of the *Guardian*, who was editing a dictionary of music and helped Boswell to identify other appropriate music specialists. Boswell was also able to recruit John D. Bareham, a history lecturer at Exeter University, who had worked with him on a series of school textbooks.

For Boswell, finding the right question-setters became a bit like a treasure hunt. He avidly followed every lead and began to build up a network of people who could cover most of the standard subjects proposed by contenders on *Mastermind*. As the programme grew in popularity, Boswell found less and less difficulty in tracking down an appropriate question-setter, unless the subject was a particularly esoteric one.

When he first phoned a contact, he would just ask for *advice* about any hidden problems which the subject might reveal, and about finding a prestigious question-setter for a particular subject. In nine cases out of ten they would modestly offer themselves. Boswell would then ask for five questions to be sent in advance, because he wanted to see the parameters of the subject and how it was being tackled; he would rewrite them, if necessary, and send them back, explaining the difficulty of the process of getting the balance and the general level right, both within the particular set and against the other three sets in the programme – would the question-setter be prepared to accept this kind of editorial intervention? They were usually quite happy to accept.

It is worth remembering that most of the compilers had never been asked to set the sort of questions which were required for the specialised subjects on *Mastermind*. University dons tended to provide the 'Discuss' type of examination questions – usually verbose, lacking vitality and requiring essay-type answers ('What is the meaning of life?'). Boswell had to try to match subject to subject, question to question, so that every contender had an equal chance. He had to ensure that no one would be baffled by what a question meant. Some of the early sets which were submitted were impossible to use for one reason or another, and Boswell had to research the subject himself and write all the questions anew. It meant using his local mobile library service to an extravagant extent, but the librarians (at Banbury, Westgate in Oxford, Brackley, Towcester and Deddington, his local village) felt flattered to be involved with a prestigious BBC programme and spared no effort in tracking down the right books for him.

Over the years the list of names and addresses grew in size and importance. A sample of the people who wrote questions for us reads like a veritable *Who's Who* (see Appendix II). But one person who does *not* appear in the list is Tim Rice, who politely declined to write questions for us on pop music – not surprisingly, having been turned down as a *Mastermind* contender himself in 1973.

It wasn't always plain sailing. There was, for instance, the classic case of The Man Who Nearly Set His Own Questions. It happened during the 1973 series and involved a contender called John Coleby, a chemical engineering consultant from Buckley, in Clwyd, who had offered as his specialised subject 'The Life and Music of Liszt' and was (so the story went) inadvertently asked to set his own questions.

Alas, it isn't quite true. What happened was rather different. Boswell wrote to Shirley Barnet, the secretary of the Liszt Society, asking her to identify a question-setter. The following week, he received a very sensible set of questions from her, which had apparently been concocted at a committee meeting. Boswell never accepted 'committee' sets of questions: he always insisted on having a single question-setter. So he phoned Shirley Barnet and learned that one of the committee members had been the *Mastermind* contestant himself, John Coleby, although he had left the room during the deliberations about the questions. Boswell realised that he could not possibly use the questions under those circumstances, and went instead to someone with no connection with the Liszt Society to set a new batch of questions.

Later, the story was much improved and embroidered to the effect that we had actually invited John to set his own questions. John himself liked to claim that he had received a letter from the Liszt Society asking him to provide some questions for *Mastermind* as he was, in their opinion, the best authority on Liszt in the country, but that he had regretfully had to decline!

In the event, John did very well: he won his heat, and reached the Final, where he took Liszt again but lost to the eventual champion, Patricia Owen.

Boswell also tells a delightful story about a set he required on Queen Elizabeth of England. He identified a professor in Oxford and went to see him to explain the procedure. The professor was the archetypal unworldly, absent-minded don, and when the questions arrived they were hand-written in sepia ink on faded brown paper – but with no answers. When Boswell pointed this out, the reply was, 'But surely the contestants will be able to give the answers?' Boswell explained the procedure again and the professor asked him to return the questions because he hadn't made a copy of them (this was before the days of the ubiquitous photocopier); and this time the professor sent back the answers without the questions. Boswell had to send the answers back – and now the professor returned the questions with the answers written at the bottom, upside down, like a newspaper competition!

If there were a Caithness Glass trophy for *Mastermind* specialised question-setters, I would unhesitatingly award it to Alan Palmer, former head of history at Highgate School in London and author of nearly thirty books on modern British and European history; his latest, published in 1996, is *Who's Who in World Politics: From 1860 to the Present Day*. Boswell signed him up in 1976, on the advice of one of Alan's most distinguished pupils, Sir Martin Gilbert, Churchill's official biographer. The first two subjects he tackled were 'Tsar Nicholas II' and 'Bismarck'; thereafter he wrote more than 120 sets on subjects ranging all the way back to Richard II and geographically from 'The Occupation of the Channel Islands' to 'Twentieth-century China'.

Alan had considered applying for *Mastermind* himself in the early days, 'but was far too lazy to do anything about it'. Today he takes quiet pleasure in his exemplary record as a question-setter – although he admits to one blunder, in 1979, in a set on 'Elizabeth of Austria, the Hunting Empress'. One of his questions was 'What music did Johann Strauss compose for the wedding?', to which the answer he provided (having hurriedly misread a German account of Vienna in the year of her marriage) was 'The Annenpolka'. Oh dear! 'Common sense should have warned me that this was nonsense,' he told me ruefully. 'The Annenpolka probably celebrated someone called Anna, not Elizabeth; the correct answer was the "Myrtenkränze Waltz", whose title reflected the bride's traditional myrtle crown.' Fortunately the contender had no idea about the answer and passed (it was Elizabeth Compton, a farmer and housewife in Forfar, whose daughter, Alison Bell, took part in the 1990 series), but the error did not escape the notice of the secretary of the Johann Strauss Society of Great Britain, who sent Alan a stiff letter pointing it out.

The set of questions which Alan remembers best is the one he prepared on the Tower of London for Fred Housego, the London cab-driver who won the 1980 Final. Alan managed to stump him on only one: 'Who, in 1933, was labelled in the Press "the Officer in the Tower"?' (Lt. Baillie-Stewart). Not long afterwards he was at a publisher's party to celebrate the launch of one of his books; when *Mastermind* came up as a topic of conversation, Alan remarked that he had set the Tower of London questions – and from then on no one was interested in his book, only in Fred Housego!

I know how he felt. In every newspaper interview I do, in every casual conversation, Fred Housego's name comes up with monotonous regularity. Columnist Simon Hoggart, in a valedictory piece on the demise of *Mastermind* in the *Guardian* on 16 November 1996, recalled how he had gone to Iceland some years ago on 'a memorable press trip' for which I had acted as mentor and guide on all things Icelandic: 'Magnus was incredibly keen to fill us in on everything, so when one of our number said: "Magnus, there's one question I've always wanted to know," he eagerly said, "Yes?" The wretched hack asked: "What is Fred Housego really like?" and I thought he was going to cry.'

Boswell Taylor retired from the programme in 1992 after two decades of being one of its pillars: it was Boswell who had got it going and set its standards. Times were changing, however. Mary Craig, who had worked closely with Boswell and was the mainstay of *Mastermind* for fifteen years as assistant to the producers who succeeded Bill Wright (Roger Mackay, Peter Massey and David Mitchell), had left in 1989. New faces and new attitudes came on the scene, and Boswell found himself being marginalised. He was offered a rather nebulous position as 'consultant', but preferred to make a clean break – he didn't want what he considered to be a 'pottering' job; his unflagging energy required something more demanding than that. The very next morning a letter arrived from Hodder & Stoughton asking him to write fifteen books on teaching your own child – which he did, of course: Boswell has never missed a deadline in his long and distinguished career as writer, polymath and educator.

From 1992 the task of commissioning the specialist question-setters became largely the responsibility of Penelope Cowell (later Cowell Doe), who had been appointed assistant producer in 1990 as successor to Mary Craig and who would become producer from 1992–95. Dee Wallis now helped to identify the specialists and took over the whole operation when Penelope left.

General knowledge questions

Setting the general knowledge questions for Mastermind involved its own problems. In the early years Boswell Taylor wrote all the general knowledge questions himself, while Cherry Cole, the programme's first research assistant (1972–74), had the job of checking them. Cherry had never worked on a quiz programme before, and at the end of the first series she realised that it was impossible to research and check them all single-handed, so she recruited Diana Wilkinson, the wife of Phil Lewis, the head of the department, and an experienced BBC production secretary, to help with the research and provide additional questions of her own.

Setting general knowledge questions for a quiz is a very skilled business, and much depends on the phrasing. Robert Crampsey, the Scottish sports commentator who took part in the first series, did some question-setting for a schools quiz competition on Scottish Television and learned the hard way how fiendishly difficult it is to avoid questions which admit of more than one correct answer. An example he gives was one of his own favourite questions: 'In which sport do the winners go backwards?' The answer he had in mind was 'Tug of War' – but then realised that it could be sculling, or even backstroke swimming!

There are no worse questions than: 'What is the difference between . . .?', because there could be any number of differences; or

'What was the cause of . . .?', because causes are seldom simple or unambiguous. Di Wilkinson says:

> *Researching a topic thoroughly takes much longer than setting the*
> *questions themselves. The ultimate responsibility for phrasing a*
> *question lies with the researcher, not the setter. The important thing*
> *is to eliminate alternative answers and to get confirmation of the facts*
> *contained within the question itself as well as in the answer.*

When Mary Craig took over as production assistant in 1975 she introduced a more systematic method of working. She assembled an informal panel of people to submit questions which constantly top up the subject material of the various aspects of general knowledge we use. They formed a select group of tried and trusty question-setters and quiz-addicts; Mary would use questions from at least six panellists for any one series.

Bill Wright's wife, Sheila, was an early contributor. The actor John Witty (the 'distinguished gentleman' in the original 'Man with the Woolwich' ads) was also on the panel. Charles Key, the founder of the Mastermind Club in 1978, started sending in general knowledge questions soon after he was knocked out in the semi-finals of the 1973 series. Some of the other early Masterminders kept up their association with the programme by submitting general knowledge questions – people like the late Dr John Sykes (1976, semi-finalist), *The Times* crossword puzzle champion and editor of *The Concise Oxford Dictionary*. Another was the late Aylwin Fletcher (1979), a retired teacher from Chichester who had meticulously prepared no fewer than 5,000 possible general knowledge questions to help him revise for his *Mastermind* heat. It was all to no avail for Aylwin, alas: he wasn't asked a single one of the 5,000 questions he had so carefully swotted up and scored only 6; but when Bill Wright heard about it he invited Aylwin to send them in for future consideration.

The doyen of the general knowledge setters, however, was another former Masterminder, John George (1978), then Garioch Pursuivant to the Earldom of Mar and now HM Kintyre Pursuivant of Arms. He began setting general knowledge questions for *Mastermind* after just missing out on a place in the 1977 series; he sent in fifty questions, of which nearly forty were accepted by Bill

Wright. From then on he was a regular mainstay of the general knowledge panel; according to his own records, he supplied a total of 3,283 questions, of which about 2,000 were used. He also set specialised questions on heraldry.

3. How fair are the questions?

I find this very hard to answer. How on earth is one to judge the relative difficulty of such widely varied subjects as 'Aztec Mythology', 'The Life Cycle of the Honey-Bee', 'Institutions of the European Community', 'The Burial Grounds of London', 'Physics', 'The Sex Pistols and Punk Rock', 'The American Civil War' and 'The Plays of Shakespeare'?

We had a programme mantra: 'A difficult question is one to which you don't know the answer; and an easy question is one to which you do know the answer, but the other contestant gets asked it.' Boswell Taylor had a rule of thumb about the appropriate level of difficulty of a set. When he had been doing *Transworld Top Team* he and Bill Wright had decided on 'A' level as the standard of difficulty. For *Mastermind* it had to be higher than that; Boswell would tell his question-setters to aim at the level of people in their first year at university.

I always assumed that the questions in the Final should be harder than those in the earlier rounds. But not Boswell: he made the questions in the Final easier, not more difficult, to add to the pace of the programme and thereby its entertainment value; he also felt that there should be less chance of humiliation for a Finalist, because failure in a Final would feel much worse than in the earlier rounds. In the first round there was less need for maximum speed – it was more important that the camera could concentrate on the person *thinking* in public, to let *character* come through. The semi-finals should be a little faster, and the Final ought to be the fastest of all. And that's the way it was.

I was always the guinea-pig in our attempts to achieve a semblance of balance in the general knowledge sets for each programme. I had to answer the questions unseen to see how I coped with them; the intention was that I should score approximately the same for all four sets in each programme.

There was a certain pattern to each set. The first three questions were meant to be 'sitters', to give the contenders confidence (although sometimes they got them wrong, which had just the opposite effect). There would be questions about their home region, on geography, history, literature, mythology, music, current affairs and scientific terms or inventions. We would grade some of the questions as 'easy' or 'reasonably accessible':

> *'Which author did Hitler and Mussolini acclaim as the master prophet of right-wing authoritarianism?'* (Nietzsche)
> *'In Shakespeare, who is warned to beware jealousy, "The green-ey'd monster which doth mock / The meat it feeds on"?'* (Othello)
> *'What name is usually given to the tax imposed in Anglo-Saxon times to provide funds to buy off Viking invaders?'* (Danegeld)
> *'Isobars are lines joining places with the same atmospheric pressure; what are isotherms?'* (Lines joining places with the same temperature)

We would balance these with questions which we judged to be much more testing, such as:

> *'What name is given to the theory of mathematical structure developed by René Thom in which continuous input leads to sudden change such as the bursting of a bubble or the collapse of a bridge?'* (Catastrophe Theory)
> *'In Greek mythology, when the Olympian gods rebelled against Zeus, which 100-handed giant was summoned by Thetis to save him?'* (Briareos/Aegaeon)
> *'What collective term derived from Latin, meaning 'cradle', describes books printed before 1500?'* (Incunabula)
> *'On a weather chart, what is an isohyet?'* (A line joining places of equal rainfall/precipitation)

The programmes as broadcast always looked seamless and trouble-free. But the videos disguise a number of errors and retakes – usually as a result of successful challenges by contenders. This fail-safe was eventually built into the official rules which had to be signed and returned by all applicants:

If a contestant feels that any question or adjudication is unfair, or
wrong, then he/she has the right to 'challenge'. This right must,
however, be exercised immediately. *The programme recording will be*
halted and the matter discussed and resolved between contestant and
producer. No alteration to the scores or results can be made at the end
either of the round or of the contest. In all cases contestants must
accept that the decision of the Producer, as Adjudicator, is final.

The idea of being allowed to challenge wasn't built in from the
beginning, however. But once we had accepted the principle, they
came thick and fast, especially in the early days.

In those days, I am ashamed to say, I think I tended to regard a
challenge as a reflection on my spurious authority and the superior
knowledge bestowed on me by my question-cards. In the 1973
series, for instance, I was challenged by a schoolboy, Dorian
Llywelyn Smith, who as an eighteen-year-old pupil at Bishop Gore
Grammar School in Swansea was the youngest contender ever to
appear on *Mastermind*. He was already a mature young man of considerable intellectual ability, and had sailed through his audition for
the programme without the slightest difficulty.

On the night of the programme he argued over a musicological
technicality in one of the questions in his specialised subject 'Harps,
Harpists and Harp Music': 'How many E flats can a harp sound in
any one octave?' Dorian answered (correctly, as it turned out),
'One'; but, faithful to my cards, I contradicted him and said, 'No,
two – D sharp plays E flat.' Dorian disputed this because, although
D sharp and E flat are both played by the same black note on an
even-tempered keyboard, on a pedal harp you have to use different
strings. Because the production team had no books to hand, however, and no expert to give a ruling, the question was dropped.

Dorian was in the same heat as John Coleby, the 'Liszt' man, and
failed to make the semi-finals. But he went on to take a degree in
English at Fitzwilliam College, Cambridge. He then worked with
the VSO in aid projects in Egypt and Indonesia, before returning to
Wales to work in arts administration. In 1984 he started training as
a priest in Salamanca, in Spain, was ordained in 1990, and is now
known as Father Dorian Llywelyn.

There was a more successful challenge during the 1974 Final.
Martin Gostelow, a photographer from Dorset, was asked during his

general knowledge round: 'To which country did Hitler refer in September 1938 when he said that it was the last territorial claim he had to make in Europe?' Martin replied, 'The Sudetenland', but I said, 'No, Czechoslovakia' – whereupon Martin promptly challenged on the grounds that the Sudetenland was *in* Czechoslovakia. I accepted the correction with the words, 'It only goes to show what an ignorant bum I am!' (even though, on reflection, one could be pedantic and say that the Sudetenland was not a 'country' in the usual sense). The question and answer were retaken, and the challenge was erased.

In the 1977 series Martin Leadbetter, a police fingerprint expert and composer, managed to have a point reinstated during the recording break at the halfway stage of his heat. He was taking 'The Instruments of the Symphony Orchestra'. His questions had been set by Dr Stanley Sadie, who did all our music questions in those days. Martin scored only 6 points, but he was convinced that he should have been awarded a further point for a question which he claimed he had answered correctly. During the recording break in the middle of the programme he disputed my adjudication. The question was: 'How does a marimba differ structurally from a xylophone?' Martin had answered that the marimba had a larger compass than the xylophone, which is right, but it is only one of *several* differences. The producer agreed that the question had been ambiguous and added a point to Martin's first-round score.

After the programme, Martin raised an objection to another question for which he claimed he should have been awarded a point: 'Which instrument represents Till Eulenspiegel in Richard Strauss's symphonic poem of that name?' Martin answered 'the horn', but was told that the correct answer should have been 'the clarinet in D'. The trouble with the question, according to Martin, was that Strauss uses various instruments at different points in the score to describe Till's pranks and activities. The horn is used to describe Till's proud entry at the beginning of the work, whereas the clarinet in D is only used later, at a point where Till is in difficulty.

This time Bill Wright refused to yield. It left Martin feeling distinctly resentful. As Clive James wrote in his television column in the *Observer* the following Sunday: 'He knew all there was to know about musical instruments but found himself being asked about the pieces of music they were first used in. His little world crumbled.'

How such grievances could rankle! When Martin was editor of *PASS*, the second issue (June 1979) contained a lengthy article by him called 'In Camera', in which he recalled that he had been 'robbed' of a point in his heat. In fact, most of the Masterminders who wrote to me about their participation in the programme could barely remember any of the questions *they* got right – but they had extraordinary recall about the ones *we* got wrong!

4. How are the subjects chosen?

In his audience 'warm-ups' before recordings in the 1970s, Bill Wright used to tell of a letter he had once received:

> *Dear Mr Mastermind:*
> *Please can my Daddy come on your programme? He is having fits about it. His subject would be 'The History of Loganberries through the Ages'.*
> *Love, Amanda*

It always raised a laugh – not just because it was a charming letter from a little girl but because the very idea of accepting 'The History of Loganberries through the Ages' as a *Mastermind* specialised subject was unthinkable in those days. It was as unlikely as the archetypal rejected subjects which were always being quoted:

> 'Routes to Anywhere in Mainland Britain by Road from
>   Letchworth'
> 'Orthopaedic Bone Cement in Total Hip Replacement'
> 'The Development of the Self-service Petrol Station 1963–68'
> 'Cremation Practice and Law in Britain'
> 'The History of the Existentialist and Phenomenological
>   Philosophical Movement'
> 'The Banana Industry'
> 'The Managerial Career of Brian Clough'
> 'Meteorology for the Private Pilot Licence'
> 'Perfect Squares from 99 Squared = 9801'
> 'Diamonds are a Girl's Best Friend (as Everybody Knows)'

Over the twenty-five years of *Mastermind* there was a noticeable change not only in the acceptable and accepted subjects, but also in their range and scope. The early subjects used to be huge in their canvas. The first champion, Nancy Wilkinson, took 'French Literature' and 'The History of European Antiques'. Other subjects in the 1972 series included:

'The Visual Arts' (the first subject of all, taken by Alan Whitehead)
'Classical Greek Theatre' and 'The English Legal System' (semi-finalist Ivan Limmer)
'European History' (Nicholas Lane)
'European Architecture' (Michael Goldman)
'Modern History' and 'The History of Music' (finalist Joan Taylor)
'The American Civil War' (Robert Crampsey)
'The History of Medical Science' (Robert Holl-Allen)
'Politico-historical Geography' (semi-finalist the Rev. David Drake-Brockman)

Scottish primary school head teacher James MacGregor, a semi-finalist in 1972, took 'Dogs' and even 'Words', and Patricia Owen, the 1973 champion, grandly offered 'Byzantine Art' and 'Grand Opera' – just like that. Also in that year, Margery Elliott, a music teacher from Birmingham, took 'The Symphony Orchestra'; Dr Reginald Webster took 'Witchcraft' and 'Spanish Literature'; Phyllis Hartnoll, the editor of *The Oxford Companion to the Theatre*, took 'The History of the Theatre'; Eleanor Macnair, a scientific officer with the Admiralty (who would appear on *Mastermind* again in 1996), took 'Shakespeare's Plays'; and Christopher Monro, a clerk from Shrewsbury, took 'English Literature'.

The early Masterminders remember this breadth of subject rather proudly. Nancy Wilkinson recalls:

I have always felt that Bill Wright didn't want a 'memory-bank' type of programme. He wanted the sort of subject which distinguished between savoir *and* connaître: *being immersed in a subject (*savoir*), and just knowing the facts (*connaître*). He didn't want the sort of subject where you could simply mug up the facts and thereby know the answers to all the questions you could possibly be asked.*

I think some of the later subjects have been too dependent on knowing facts, and not enough on depth. Specialised subjects should not be as finite as some of them have become.

Penelope Cowell Doe tried to make the programme reflect more clearly the realities of what interested people – not to make the programme easier or more popular but, in a sense, more realistic. She put much greater emphasis on 'popular' subjects – not in order to bring *Mastermind* down-market, but because she felt that the time had come when popular subjects were admissible, like '*Dr Who*' and 'Warner Brothers Cartoons':

We had to look at the way the world was changing . . . Dr Who and other television programmes were becoming set subjects in university media courses – one could no longer say that it wasn't fit for Mastermind. *Also, the contestants themselves were changing. One of the assumptions made at the start of* Mastermind *was that everyone would know Shakespearean quotations and classical mythology – and people did, because they were educated in that way . . . but it was no longer so true of younger contestants, however good or well-educated they were.*

Certainly, nearly all the specialised subjects in the early days were connected with the arts and the humanities. Looking back on it now, people might be tempted to call it élitist, but I'm not sure that I would agree. It reflected the received (if rather conservative) idea of what was considered at the time to be worth knowing.

It was the series of five *International Mastermind* programmes (1979–83) which broke the mould, because the production team did not have the same control over the subjects offered by overseas participants. Thus we had 'The History of Rock Music from 1955' from the New Zealand Mastermind in 1979 (Mark Allan), 'The Life and Music of Bix Beiderbecke' from the Radio Telefís Éireann nominee in 1980 (Lewis Clohessy), and 'The Life and Music of Bob Dylan' from the Republic of Ireland champion, John Egan, in 1983.

From then on *Mastermind* itself began to accept similar subjects: 'Duke Elllington' (1984), 'Count Basie and his Orchestra' (1985), and 'Woody Herman' (1988). Also featured in the 1988 series was 'Pop Music 1955–79', taken by Howard Pizzey, a finance officer from

Staplehurst in Kent. In the 1990s we had 'The Beatles' (1993), 'Paul Simon' (1994), 'The Rolling Stones', 'Woody Guthrie' and 'John Lennon' (1995). When former punk Alan Whitaker, from Nancledra near Penzance in Cornwall, took 'The Sex Pistols and Punk Rock' in the first programme of the 1996 series, it raised a great stir in the media, as it was no doubt intended to do; but it was not so much because of the subject as because the BBC saw fit to bleep out the word 'bollocks' in a question about the Sex Pistols' first album, *Never Mind the Bollocks*. This well-meaning attempt to protect the delicate sensibilities of the *Mastermind* audience was thwarted, however, when the forbidden word appeared, uncensored, in the Teletext subtitles.

Sport was another subject which got short shrift in the 1970s, but came into its own in the 1980s and 1990s. So did films and the lives of film stars. Yet although *Mastermind* subjects tended to be middle-of-the-road and middle-brow, we also had several unusual, even arcane, subjects to tackle:

'*Aztec Mythology*' *in 1975 (George Earnshaw)*
'*The Life-cycle and Habits of the Honey-Bee*' *in 1976 (Lisa Duffin), and in 1996 (Ruth Burkhill)*
'*The* Moomin *Saga of Tove Jansson*' *in 1979 (John Old)*
'*Notable British Poisoners*' *in 1978 (Raymond Fell)*
'*Burial Grounds of London*' *in 1981 (Leslie Grout, the champion that year)*
'*The Vampire in British Fiction*' *in 1991 (Tina Rath)*
'*The Eleventh-century Japanese* Tale of Genji and Lady Murasaki' *in 1993 (Maureen Vlaar)*
'*The Buddhist Sage Nichiren*' *in 1994 (Stephen Wood)*

All these were a bit of a challenge, you might say. But the real problem was always with science questions. It has been alleged that there was an 'anti-science bias' on *Mastermind*, and to a certain extent this was true. Even if people chose to do a scientific specialist subject such as 'Cell Biology', which we did in 1972, or 'Physics', which cropped up twice in 1976, the nature of *Mastermind*, and the need to have a subject which was quantifiable and identifiable and uniquely packaged, meant that many of the questions related to the historical development of a particular branch of science or the story of the key scientists involved.

I was comforted to read, in the Preface to Bamber Gascoigne's superb 1993 book *Encyclopedia of Britain*, that Bamber himself had faced the same problem on *University Challenge*:

> *The most frequent complaint about* University Challenge *was that we had too few science questions. We tried to include more, and were usually rewarded with those looks of blank indignation unless there happened to be an appropriate scientist on the team (appropriate because a physicist would be flummoxed by any but an easy biology question, and vice versa). The reason, unacceptable to many scientists but I believe inescapably true, is that science can never be part of general knowledge in the same way as arts subjects. Scientific books are not comprehensible to the non-specialist. Anyone can read and may well find enjoyment in an author as serious as George Eliot; it is impossible to understand a treatise on physics of comparable importance without years of study.*

All I know is that science subjects were the ones I always feared the most, because the adjudication of the answers to 'definition' questions was a nightmare. It was an early attempt to get round this problem which gave rise to a memorable if faintly ludicrous episode in 1976.

It so happened that in two of the semi-finals two contenders were taking the same subject – 'Physics'. One was Dr John Sykes, the other was a mathematical physicist called Dr David Flower, from Slough. I had had considerable difficulties during the earlier semi-final at Durham University over the bout of 'Physics' with John Sykes; for David Flower's semi-final I seized a chance, however, because the question-setter was the professor of physics at Bristol University, Sir Charles Frank, and the programme was being recorded in Bristol. So we invited Professor Frank to attend the recording and placed him in my eye-line to my left so that he could send me signals about whether or not to accept an answer. It worked very well to start with. There was a hiccup over the second question, one of my *bête noire* definition questions: 'What is a nucleon?' (a neutron or a proton); I stopped the clock over David's answer and there was a lengthy discussion before Professor Frank adjudged it to have been correct. We re-recorded the first two questions and from then on I got a thumbs-up or a thumbs-down from Professor Frank whenever I looked to him for guidance. The last question, however, was an absolute stinker:

> *In the quantum-mechanical solution [bleep-bleep, 'I've started so I'll finish'] of physical problems, what are the conditions under which the WKB approximation may be adopted?*

David Flower thought carefully, and then replied:

> *When the change in wave-length of the wave function is small compared with the dimensions involved.*

The answer bore no resemblance to the definition on my card. In panic I looked at Professor Frank again for assistance; but this time the good professor merely shrugged his shoulders and held his hands wide open: it turned out that he had not set that particular question and decided he could not help! In despair, I accepted David's answer – much to the amusement of the audience, who had been monitoring all the helpful hand-signals I had been getting.

For the record, David Flower lost the semi-final on the passes rule to lorry-driver David Wilson. Yet it could so easily have gone the other way. Towards the end of his general knowledge round I asked him: 'Who was the composer of the *Tostquartette*?' David noticed Mary Craig's hand beginning to move towards the bleeper and thought to himself, 'If I guess "Haydn" and it's wrong, there won't be time for another question; if I pass, there will be.' So he passed, and got a question about umiaks (Eskimo canoes), which he got wrong; if he had guessed 'Haydn', he would have been right, and would have reached the Final to face the eventual champion, Roger Pritchard.

5. *Do we ever make mistakes?*

To this question I am tempted to say 'Pass', but honesty compels me to answer 'Did we not!' It's a subject which merits a chapter of its own . . .

6

Pardon My Blooper:
Blunders and Bloomers

There is nothing people like more than hearing about other people's blunders. During his audience warm-ups in the 1970s, Bill Wright would recount some of the innumerable fluffs and fumbles I was wont to commit. There was one occasion, he claimed, when I had thanked the University for their *hospital*, not their hospitality. He also insisted that at the end of one particular Final I announced, 'If you want to take part in next year's *Mastermind*, the address to write to for an application form will be on your *screams* at the end of the programme.' He also liked to recall occasional typing errors which had cropped up on my question-cards, for example 'How many pints are there in a *Magnus*?' (for Magnum). Another of his favourites was 'Which instrument did Vaughan Williams use to illustrate the Shepherd's *Pie*?' (for Pipe).

My slips of the tongue and spoonerisms and malapropisms became legendary in the office. My mispronunciations (especially of anything in French, which soon became an office joke) were embarrassingly legion; most of them were snipped out or replaced, but plain English had its problems, too. There are certain combinations of names and places which caused me endless worry in advance – like Martin Wyatt, in 1988, whose only sin was being 'a statistician from Oswaldtwistle'. (Go on, try it for yourself at speed.)

Sometimes I would only make my bloopers worse by trying to correct them. On one occasion I landed in the soup (or, rather, the

'Naked Ape' column in the *Guardian* in November 1981) for calling an unmarried contender 'Mrs'. She was Rosemary Meechan, from Kilsyth in Stirlingshire, who taught French and German at Kirkintilloch High School; thanking her at the end of the second round I called her *Mrs* Meechan, but quickly corrected myself: 'I think I elevated you to "Mrs" earlier, I apologise.' A viewer, Ian Powys from London, had it in the 'Naked Ape' column in a flash as a flagrant example of politically incorrect male chauvinism. I console myself, however, with the knowledge that it was one of my more ridiculous bloopers which gave rise to the funniest *Mastermind* sketch of all time – the celebrated skit by the Two Ronnies. More of that anon.

We didn't make all that many serious mistakes on *Mastermind*, but when we did we all felt it very badly. One of the names engraved on my memory is that of Dr Reginald Webster, one of the finalists in the 1973 series. He worked as an assistant psychiatrist in Whalley, Lancashire; but he was much better known as an experienced and popular broadcaster, a former member of the immensely popular *Ask Me Another* and *What Do You Know?*.

He was in the first heat of the 1973 series of *Mastermind* – and what a dreadful start we had. Reginald took as his specialised subject 'Witchcraft', on which he was a considerable authority; the questions, however, had been set by someone who was, shall we say, a rather lesser authority. I have been unable to track down a video of the programme; but appalled memory tells me that Reginald challenged practically every second question. There was something about the way he answered, and his arguments to justify his challenge, which convinced us that he knew what he was talking about better than we did; I also suspect he had realised very quickly that the research had been inadequate, and that he had us at his mercy. The upshot was that after numerous retakes he won his heat handsomely, and went on to win his semi-final with 'Spanish Literature'. Although the rules at the time allowed him to revert to his first-round specialised subject in the Final, he agreed that to take 'Witchcraft' again would have been too embarrassing all round; so he took 'The Geography of Spain' instead, and was runner-up to the champion, Patricia Owen.

In the 1973 series (how that series haunts me!) we also came close to making a truly ghastly blunder in Heat 9. One of the 'English

Literature' questions for Christopher Monro, a clerk from Shrewsbury, was: 'Of whom did Andrew Marvell write, "He nothing common did or mean / Upon that memorable scene"?' The answer on my card was 'Oliver Cromwell'. When I first saw the question on the morning of the recording, I felt distinctly uneasy about it – not just because of a vague memory of reading Marvell in my student days but because it seemed highly unlikely that anyone would write about Cromwell in that vein. I asked for the question to be checked, and the word came back – yes, it was fine, it came from Marvell's 'An Horatian Ode upon Cromwell's Return from Ireland'. I could not shake off my foreboding of error, and finally, half an hour before the recording, I telephoned home and asked my wife Mamie to check again for me. She looked up the poem, and quickly realised that it was a description, not of Cromwell, but of King Charles I at his execution. The question was rapidly changed to: 'What is the scene referred to in these words by Marvell: "He nothing common did or mean / Upon that memorable scene"?' Christopher Monro got it right: 'The execution of King Charles I.' It had been a close shave, and my blood still runs chill when I recall it.

The 1974 series had its share of crises too, I remember. On one occasion it led to a near walk-out by a contender – the only time it ever happened. It involved a choleric Celt called Dr Gerald MacKenzie, a country GP who was a veritable polymath, during the recording in the MacRobert Arts Centre of Stirling University of Heat 5 of that series. Gerald was offering 'The Life and Works of Beethoven' as his specialised subject (to be followed by 'The History of the Western Isles' if he reached the semi-finals).

It has to be said that the recording went badly from the outset. The session started with my recording an apology to a housewife from London, Olga Evans, who had taken part in the heat recorded two weeks earlier. She had taken 'The History and Geography of France from 1914'; but there had been a disastrous typing error which transposed the answers to two similar-looking questions. One of the questions was: 'Who was Prime Minister of France at the outbreak of the *First* World War?' Olga replied, 'Georges Clemenceau' (which was, of course, right); but my card said 'Paul Daladier'. The other question was: 'Who was Prime Minister of France at the outbreak of the *Second* World War?'; Olga replied (correctly again), 'Paul Daladier', but my card said 'Georges Clemenceau'! The mistake wasn't spotted at the time, but it was very soon afterwards: Bill Wright woke up with a start in the middle of the night with the awful realisation that the answers must have been transposed on the question-cards. So before the start of Heat 5 at Stirling University I recorded a humble-pie piece to camera that we were awarding Olga a further two points, and this was then tacked on to the edited version of Heat 4. Fortunately the lost points had not, as it happened, affected the result.

Gerald MacKenzie was desperately tired and feeling rather ill, and was far from his best. When he took the Black Chair, a fierce contretemps broke out over his specialised questions, with which Gerald disagreed violently; they had been set by Stanley Sadie, music critic of *The Times*. Gerald had been inattentive during the pre-programme briefing and had failed to pick up the fact that he had the right to challenge adjudications on the spot. Instead, after three or four questions and adjudications which went against him, his Celtic temper got the better of him and he exploded. He leapt from the chair and started to stalk off the set. I persuaded him to stay, for the sake of the recording, and he proceeded to deliver a lecture on Beethoven for what seemed like fifteen minutes, and which was greeted by joyous applause from the audience; Bill Wright was called in, the adjudications were adjusted and one of the questions was re-recorded, giving him a score of 12 (from 17 questions).

But the hostility simmered on. During the recording break at the halfway stage Gerald and I engaged in further acerbic exchanges. Not surprisingly, perhaps, he had an indifferent general knowledge round, but managed to come second in the final reckoning. At the customary hospitality session after the programme Gerald's dander was still up and he was determined to have a showdown with Bill Wright and myself; but as he made to accost us he was restrained by his wife, Doreen, who uttered the words which have become a classic in *Mastermind* folklore, 'Don't argue, Gerald; remember, you're a professional man'!

I'm glad to say that all was forgiven and forgotten as soon as the Mastermind Club was formed in 1978; Gerald played a prominent part in its foundation, and was President from 1984–90. More significantly, perhaps, he became the question-setter for the Club in-house quiz, the Magnum, which I have chaired practically since its inception, and we have become the firmest of friends.

In 1981 something went very badly wrong with a question in a specialised set on 'The Novels of Graham Greene'. The 'victim' of the mistake was Mrs Brenda Read, a computer systems designer from Bredon, near Tewkesbury. The 'Graham Greene Crisis', as I still call it, occurred as a result of Brenda's first question, which had not been written by our specialised question-setter but had been put in as an easy starter. The question was: 'In *Brighton Rock*, who assumed the identity of Kolley Kibber of *The Messenger*?' Brenda replied, '*Charles* Hale', but I refused to accept it, because my card said that the man's name was *Fred* Hale. Brenda blinked, and looked distinctly disconcerted; but mindful of the pre-programme briefing where the contestants had been advised that they *could* challenge an adjudication but only if they were absolutely sure of their ground, she said nothing.

During the recording break at the halfway stage, however, she queried the ruling because she was sure that she had been right: she claimed that although the man involved had been called 'Fred Hale' in the first chapter of the novel, in newspaper reports of the inquest after his murder it was revealed that his real name had been 'Charles Hale'. There was no copy of *Brighton Rock* to hand for a definitive ruling to be made, and Brenda was told that any change at that stage would involve a complete re-recording of her whole round (without the offending question), with all the disruption which this would entail. So Brenda acquiesced in the decision, albeit reluctantly.

At the end of the programme, however, that disputed question had assumed additional importance, because it made all the difference between winning or losing a place in the semi-finals; Brenda had tied for the lead with Godfrey Abbott, a surveyor from Bath, but with more passes, so Godfrey had been declared the winner. So Brenda now wrote to the producer asking if anything could be done. A thorough reading of *Brighton Rock* showed that Brenda had been right all along – such are the perils of being a quizmaster! If Brenda had been awarded that point she would have won her heat and gone into the semi-finals as an outright winner. Faced with this incontrovertible evidence of a blunder on our part, it was decided that Brenda should be given a compensatory additional place in the *repêchage* semi-final. She did not survive to the Final, but at least some justice had been seen to be done, albeit belatedly.

In the following heat there was perhaps an even more unfortunate misunderstanding, this time over the acceptable parameters of a specialised subject – 'The Peloponnesian War 421–404 BC'. The contestant was John Crawford, a rather dour-looking Scottish solicitor who worked for the Scottish Development Agency. His question-setter, Robin Seager, a tried and trusted member of Boswell Taylor's panel, had interpreted the subject more broadly – most historians date the outbreak of the war to 431 BC, not 421; so the set started off with a string of questions about events which took place in the decade leading up to 421 BC. John had not expected this, and failed to score on his first eight questions as a result. It was a desperately embarrassing situation all round. His saturnine features grew ever more thunderous as his score limped to a mere 8 (on a subject which he felt he knew extremely well); he scored only 9 in his general knowledge round, for a total of 17, and was clearly furious about the whole business. Indeed, before the programme was transmitted he complained bitterly to the *Scottish Daily Express* about the shabbiness with which he felt he had been treated. The whole episode left a bad taste in the mouth.

Questions about novels can be a real problem (as Margaret Drabble found when she set questions about her own novels and made several mistakes!). In the first semi-final of the 1987 series there was a research mistake on a question in a specialised round on 'The *Flashman* Novels of George MacDonald Fraser' by Mrs Jill McFatridge, which provoked a flood of correspondence. The question was: 'During their escape from Russia, why did Scud East desert Flashman when the sled overturned?' Jill replied, 'Because Flashman was pinned underneath the sled.' I pressed her for more information: 'But why did he *desert* him?' Jill replied, 'Because he had thrown Valla out before.' 'No,' I said, 'it was to take the news of the invasion of India by the Russians to Lord Raglan.' In fact, in the book, Scud had given that reason to Flashman; but in a later chapter, Flashman says: 'East would never have abandoned me if I hadn't heaved Valla out of the sled in the first place. He'd have stuck by me and the Christian old school code, and let his military duty go hang.' So Jill's answer had been correct after all.

It made no difference to the outcome, but it was another salutary lesson – firstly on the importance of reading the *entire* text of a novel, rather than just the episode involved, as we had found with *Brighton Rock*; and secondly, that 'Why?' questions are always dangerous – almost as dangerous as 'What was the first . . .?'!

There was another occasion, in the 1989 series, which caused a stramash in the media: I was accused of not so much a blooper as blatant favouritism towards one contender at the expense of another. It happened during a heat which was being recorded in Redbridge Community School in Southampton, in the presence of the head-mistress – who just happened to be the 1984 champion, Margaret Harris.

Two contenders were involved: Dawn Tozer, an art and design teacher at Portsmouth High School, who took as her specialised subject 'The Life and Works of Gwen John', and Mary Gibson, assistant librarian at the London School of Hygiene and Tropical Medicine, who was taking 'The Life of Mary Henrietta Kingsley', the Victorian explorer. It was a super competition: the two women had dazzling first rounds, both scoring 18, but Dawn had no passes and Mary had one pass. At the start of the general knowledge round, I gave my customary spiel about passes: 'Remember, according to the rules of *Mastermind*, if there is still a tie at the end of the second round, the contender with the fewer or fewest passes will be adjudged the winner.'

Since the previous year, the contenders were being called forward in the ascending order of their first-round scores. Mary produced a magnificent 17 (with no passes) to set the target at 35. I told Dawn that the target was 35 (with one pass), and that she had no passes as yet; like Mary, Dawn also produced a fine run of 17 to match the target of 35, with one question to go.

The bleeper went just as I was finishing the question: 'In 1856, building of the Royal Victoria Military Hospital was begun in which [*bleep bleep*] Hampshire village on Southampton water?' Dawn, after momentary reflection, said 'Pass'. Thinking that the intrusive bleeper might have blurred the point of the question, I reminded her: 'You may answer after the bell.' So Dawn had a go, but got it wrong – the correct answer was 'Netley'. However, by having a go she had avoided giving a 'Pass', as a result of which she had no passes.

So, on the passes rule, Dawn was declared the winner and went forward to the semi-finals. As the result was announced, Dawn com-miserated with Mary, who simply smiled. *Mastermind* was always notable for the sportsmanship with which contenders accepted defeat, whatever their private opinion of the adjudications. But as soon as the programme was transmitted, it created a tremendous furore. The BBC switchboard was apparently jammed for four hours by as many as a thousand calls (according to the *Sun*, anyway) from outraged viewers complaining that I had 'bent the rules' to help Dawn Tozer to win, by prompting her to have another go at a question after the bleeper, even though she had already said 'Pass'.

None of the contenders complained, however – especially not Mary Gibson. She knew that during the pre-programme briefing session and the rehearsals I had emphasised the importance of *not* passing after the bleeper – and that on many other programmes I had encouraged a contender to 'have a blurt' even after a pass. However, it had never happened before in such a close, cliff-hanging finish. The trouble was that I never used to look at the scores during the questioning – I would be far too busy with the questions themselves – and I, too, was taken aback by the furore. The only consolation was that Mary earned an indisputable place in the semi-final for the highest-scoring losers.

But it is mainly my own undisputed follies and *faux pas* which spring to mind when I look back fondly over the years of *Mastermind*.

In the *Mastermind International* of 1979 I managed to mishear an answer in one of Sir David Hunt's general knowledge questions: 'In a suit of armour, what part of the body was protected by a sabaton?' David replied, 'The feet', to which I responded, 'No, the foot'. David objected in a good-mannerly fashion, saying that he had indeed said 'feet'. There were murmurs of agreement from the audience. I said, 'I'm sorry – I thought you said the *seat*'; whereupon David commented, 'You would have had a job controlling your horse if you had armour on your seat!' This exchange was tactfully edited out of the broadcast version.

In a semi-final in the 1988 series, Kevin Perkins, a contracts liaison officer with Islington Borough Council in London, took 'The Detective Novels of Agatha Christie'. One of his questions was 'What did Miss Marple particularly notice about the hands of "the body in the library" which made her realise that the victim was not a showgirl but a schoolgirl?' When I read out the question, however, I got it the wrong way round – I said 'made her realise that the victim was not a schoolgirl but a showgirl'. The clue was the fact that the fingernails were bitten, and Kevin ignored the error and got the answer right. Normally we would do a retake at the end of the recording to cover up the mistake, but no one seemed to have spotted the error; right at the end, however, when everyone was preparing to close the programme, Kevin himself pointed out that I had read the question incorrectly, so a retake was done.

It is understandable, in the tension of the moment, that mistakes can occur. But some of my mistakes have been totally incomprehensible. In Heat 10 of the 1989 series, Malcolm Robertson, a composer from Lowestoft, Suffolk, who had scored a massive 19 on 'The Music of Aaron Copland', was asked in his general knowledge round: 'In Shakespeare, who gives his son the advice "neither a borrower nor a lender be"?' Malcolm replied, 'Hamlet'; whereupon I corrected him, saying, 'No: Polonius, his father.' It is beyond comprehension why I should have said such a thing: Hamlet's father was a spook on the battlements by then, as one of the scene-hands gleefully pointed out to me afterwards! None of the production team picked it up for a retake; but throughout the hospitality session afterwards people were coming up to me to nudge me in the ribs and say, 'What do you mean, "Hamlet's father"?' Mercifully the offending words were snipped out in the editing, and my blushes were saved; the edited programme had me saying, 'No, Polonius (ahem).'

But the blunders which delighted the audiences most were when, through a slip of the tongue, I would give away the answer in the question. For instance, in Heat 6 of the 1984 series I asked the eventual champion, Margaret Harris, in her general knowledge round, 'In early Greek open-air theatres, the audience sat in a raked semi-circle: what did they call the flat areas where the orchestra . . . where the *chorus* danced?' For the first time, Margaret smiled charmingly, and said, 'The orchestra'. 'Correct!' I cried – 'I gave that one away, didn't I?'

In Heat 1 of the 1990 series I managed to do it again. It happened at the end of the general knowledge round for Hilary Forrest, a history teacher from Manchester who had taken 'Life in the English Country House 1550–1830' and was in the lead at the halfway stage. When the bleeper interrupted during a question, I was a little thrown by it: 'The Turkish Van, the Abyssinian and the

British Blue are all breeds of which [*bleep bleep*] domestic ca . . . animal?' Before I had quite finished, Hilary chortled 'Cat! – I did know, honestly.' 'I think you knew the answer before I half-said it,' I conceded, and gave her the point. 'I shall be accused of gross favouritism for that,' I went on, 'but in fact it makes no difference to the outcome.'

It was this unfortunate tendency to give away the answer within the question which directly inspired the wonderful skit on *Mastermind* by the Two Ronnies. Comedians have always had their fun with *Mastermind*, from *Spitting Image* to John Cleese in *Fawlty Towers* berating his long-suffering screen wife, Sybil, with the withering comment, 'We'll put you on *Mastermind* – special subject, "The Bleedin' Obvious".' There have been funny sketches galore, by most of our notable comedians, such as Stanley Baxter, Frank Carson, and Little and Large; indeed one of the most enjoyable 'perks' of the programme, for me, was being invited to take part in a *Mastermind* sketch by Morecambe and Wise, whose outcome hinged on Eric answering 'Pass' to a question about the Khyber. But the Two Ronnies' sketch was in a class by itself.

I was walking along a corridor in Television Centre one day in 1980 when I was accosted by Ronnie Barker, who stopped right in front of me and said, 'Excuse me, sir, but did you say tomato?' He was referring to a question on the previous evening's programme when I had asked a question about fruit to which the answer was to be 'Tomato', but had blurted out the answer in the question itself ('The solanaceous plant *Lycopersicon esculentum* is a genus of which tomato?'). Ronnie Barker positively pounced on it. When I met him again, sixteen years later, at the BBC's 60th Birthday Gala knees-up in 1996, where he was being honoured with a special award for his prodigious services to comedy, he hadn't forgotten the episode; as I approached to add my congratulations his face lit up and he cried, 'Ah, it's the man who said tomato!'

He then told me that this had been the inspiration for the sketch, which he claimed was the funniest he and his namesake had ever done. After our chance meeting he had discovered that one of his scriptwriters, David Renwick (who now scripts *One Foot in the Grave*), was already working on a send-up based on a specialised subject, 'Answering the Question Before Last'. The question-master was Ronnie Barker; the contestant was Ronnie Corbett:

Good evening. Your name please? Good evening. *In the first heat, your chosen subject was 'Answering Questions Before They Were Asked'; this time you have chosen to 'Answer the Question Before Last'. Is that correct?* Charlie Smithers.

Your time starts now. What is palaeontology? Yes, absolutely correct.

What is the name of the directory which lists members of the Peerage? A study of old fossils.

Correct. Who are Len Murray and Sir Geoffrey Howe? Burke's.

Correct. What is the difference between a donkey and an ass? One's a trade union leader, the other's a member of the Cabinet.

Correct. Complete the quotation, 'To be or not to be.' They're both the same.

Correct. What is Bernard Manning famous for? That is the question.

Correct. Who is the present Archbishop of Canterbury? He is a fat man who tells blue jokes.

Correct. What do people kneel on in church? The Right Reverend Robert Runcie.

Correct. What do tarantulas prey on? Hassocks.

Correct. What would you use a rip-cord to pull open? Large flies.

Correct. What sort of a person lived in Bedlam? A parachute.

Correct. What is a jock-strap? A nutcase.

Correct. For what purpose would a decorator use methylene chloride? A form of athletic support.

Correct. What did Henri de Toulouse-Lautrec do? Paint strippers.

Correct. Who is Dean Martin? He's a kind of artist.

Yes – what sort of artist? Pass.

That's near enough. What make of vehicle is the standard London bus? A singer.

Correct. In 1892, Brandon Thomas wrote a famous long-running English farce – what was it? British Leyland.

Correct. Complete the following quotation – I've started, so I'll finish – about Mrs Thatcher: 'Her heart may be in the right place, but her . . .' Charley's Aunt.

Correct . . .

Some bloopers turn out for the best, after all.

7

The Riddle Class:
Who are the Quizlings?

'These are the few who air their knowledge,
Bright as the dew on morning grass,
Candidates all for a job at Delphi,
Eager to enter the riddle class.
Still there remains the unasked question:
How do you fathom people? – Pass.'

ROGER WODDIS

'What is a Mastermind?' That was the heading for a whimsical piece by the Editor (Martin Leadbetter) in the first issue of the Mastermind Club's in-house magazine *PASS*, in April 1979:

> *Somewhere in any standard English dictionary, between 'masochism' and 'matrimony' one can find the 'possessor of an outstanding intellect'; 'a chief, or superior mind'; 'a prominent mind'; 'a first-class mind'; or 'a chief controlling power behind a scheme'.*

When Mary Craig came up with the inspired title of *Mastermind* for the programme, none of us felt that we were in fact seeking to find, or to label, some supernaturally-gifted person of overwhelming intellectual prowess; we were seeking only to make a good television series – a series which certainly celebrated mental achievement but was fundamentally a parlour game played in public.

Yet viewers have tended to think of the people who appear on *Mastermind* as a sort of élite; in a way they are, because they have been selected from literally thousands of would-be Masterminders.

But basically they are ordinary people who are made extraordinary by the fact of being chosen to appear on the programme. Very few of them have achieved much in the public eye before or after, although there have been some outstanding exceptions like the retired diplomat Sir David Hunt, or London cabby Fred Housego, who has gone on to make a considerable mark as a television and radio broadcaster. For the most part Masterminders, however 'ordinary' in terms of material achievement, are special because of their capacity to know a great deal about a number of things and to recall it under pressure.

In the early days the contenders could be characterised by the epithet 'worthy': they tended to be middle-class people who read the quality broadsheets and wore tweeds for preference. As the years passed, however, public perceptions of Masterminders changed. In the local press they would be written about with deference and occasional awe; critics in the national press, however, tended to react against this by calling them 'boring' or 'tedious'. Robert Crampton, in *The Times* Saturday Magazine of 27 April 1996, brought a quizzical eye to bear on one of the annual social reunions of the Mastermind Club; but, like so many journalists, he went there with a preconceived stereotype of Masterminders as something they have never claimed to be – and then proceeded to shoot it down:

> *I don't know how 'bright and intelligent' they are and neither, I doubt, do they. They read a lot, certainly . . . but does that make them clever? I don't think they can know for sure, because so many of them are always trying to prove themselves . . . They are, in short, the remnants of an English professional middle class which was still thriving in 1972, its security relatively unadulterated and unthreatened by television, by social mobility, by the wealth of others, by travel, by failure, but which is now gasping for breath in 1996, diluted, smaller, unsure, looking around for reassurance.*

I am not sure if this rather shallow image of a 1970s class which has lost its way has any relevance or validity. Even if it has, it applies to only *some* Masterminders and *some* members of the Mastermind Club. Indeed, many of them enjoy mocking themselves.

Patricia Owen, who was a lecturer in English and art when she became champion in 1973, says:

Masterminders are basically intellectual snobs – we think we are a bit brighter than the average. We know we're a bit better informed than the average, otherwise we would not have been on the programme. We rather like that, and we've all got a competitive spirit, in a nice way – well, usually. A lot of people whose interests were not shared by their colleagues at work, or by their families, felt themselves validated by the programme, so that instead of being outsiders they had become people who had achieved something noteworthy.

Sue Jenkins, a student teacher and a finalist in 1977, who was a Mastermind Club committee member for fifteen years, says:

I think we are rather a peculiar bunch of people – you have to be, if you're the sort of person who goes in for quizzes. It has only a certain amount to do with brains. You can be incredibly clever on a certain subject, but you also have to have the type of brain which amasses information which is only useful for answering quiz questions.

Phillida Grantham (1981 and 1995), the current Secretary of the Mastermind Club, has a downright, no-nonsense attitude to it all: 'Many people are under the delusion that one needs a superior intellect to appear on *Mastermind*. Rubbish! What you need is a good memory, good recall in the face of mounting panic and, above all, guts.'

But what do we really *know* about the 1,231 quizlings who graced *Mastermind*? In 1989, Phillida Grantham, inspired by a French magazine's search for the typical citizen of France, conducted a survey of Mastermind Club members to find out more about 'Who We Are'. The members (about 360 at the time) were invited to fill in a long questionnaire; 129 replied – 84 men and 45 women.

What emerged was a portrait of the average Masterminder as a rather bright, well-educated, middle-class, middle-aged white-collar worker living in the south-east of England: an only child of professional parents; married (to a civil servant perhaps), with only a small family; by nature rather solitary and both introverted and extroverted; a regular churchgoer; a university or polytechnic graduate in one of the humanities who had done rather well at a fee-paying school; liable to offer literature, history or the lives of famous people as a specialised subject; likely to have gone in for other quizzes;

enjoyed the experience of the Black Chair a lot; interested in music, crosswords, other quiz programmes, chess, theatre, reading, history, gardening, squash, swimming and ornithology.

Oh yes – and probably a member of Mensa, too!

Occupations

An average can only give a stereotype, however. In Phillida's sample the 'top' occupation was teacher (28), followed by civil servant (17), doctor (6), librarian (5) and housewife (4). But the 1,231 Master-minders who took part in the programme represented a truly remarkable variety of jobs and occupations (and sometimes none at all): accountants and architects, actors and artists and airmen, bank managers and barmaids, ballet dancers and bricklayers, barristers and bus drivers, composers and clergymen (including a Benedictine monk), cooks and commissionaires, civil servants and computer pro-grammers, doctors and dentists and diplomats, editors and engineers, electricians and education officers, farmers and firemen, factory workers and foster-carers, greengrocers and geologists, heralds and housewives, hoteliers and housekeepers, insurance salesmen and insurance inspectors, journalists and journeymen, librarians and laundry-workers, lawyers and lorry-drivers and lexicographers, mid-wives and miners and musicians, nurses and neurosurgeons, an opera singer, policemen and postmen, publishers and private eyes, psychi-atrists and pharmacists, researchers and risk management consultants and railway workers, secretaries and students, shop-keepers and sci-entists, soldiers and seamen, teachers and tax inspectors, theatre directors and travel agents and taxi-drivers, university administrators and an under-sheriff, vets and a verger, writers and a weighbridge operator, youth workers and a zoo-keeper.

We even had our own modest equivalent of the celebrated 'sagger-maker's bottom-knocker' of *What's My Line?*. In 1977, Geoffrey Reynolds from Croydon appeared on the programme as an 'image intensifier tester'. He took 'The Life of Sir Francis Drake' to get through to the semi-finals; by then the BBC had received so many letters asking about his job that I had to ask him to explain precisely what it was: 'someone who tests a device for amplifying light so that you can see better in the dark'.

Age

Although the average age in the sample was forty-five and a half for men and forty-seven and a half for women, the range of ages of contestants was very wide. The youngest contestant was an eighteen-year-old schoolboy, Dorian Llywelyn Smith, in 1973, followed by nineteen-year-old Oxford undergraduate, Susan Reynolds, who crashed so spectacularly in the 1974 Final. There was also a clutch of 21-year-olds, led by another Oxford undergraduate, Kathryn Jones (now Johnson), who appeared in 1978 and 1995. Kathryn, who now works in the Department of Manuscripts at the British Library, failed to reach the semi-finals on both occasions; but she has proved herself a determined competitor in the Mastermind Club's annual in-house quiz, winning the Magnum trophy five times.

At the other end of the age scale, the oldest contestant was the late Hugh Merrick (1898–1980), author and mountaineer, who appeared in the first heat of the 1977 series at the age of seventy-nine; unfailingly genial and courteous, he looked twenty years younger, and although he failed to win his heat on *Mastermind*, he turned up on *Brain of Britain* two years later at the age of eighty-one! Barrister Philip Skottowe, from Reading, was seventy-six years old when he appeared in 1975 (he died in 1980). We also had at least three 75-year-olds. One was another author, Dorothy Middleton, who wrote and lectured on Africa; she was seventy-five when she appeared on the programme in 1987, taking 'The Exploration of Africa 1788–1888', and acquitted herself well – but she was up against a formidable civil servant from Winchester called Kevin Ashman, who would become champion on his return to the programme in 1995. Although Dorothy asked me not to mention it on the programme, what I also found interesting was that she was the sister of the man who was dubbed 'the best Prime Minister we never had', R. A. 'Rab' Butler. Also in 1987 we had another 75-year-old, the late Stanley Todd, a retired music teacher from Dunravens School in Streatham, who took 'Chamber Music 1750–1950' as his specialised subject. The third was Dr Patrick Welch (1990, semi-finalist), from Harlesden in north London, a retired lecturer in English and General Studies at Paddington Technical College, taking 'The Life and Times of Sir Robert Peel' and 'The Life and Career of H. H. Asquith'.

How important was age to being a successful Masterminder? The youngest champion was the ebullient part-time archivist from Portsmouth, Gavin Fuller, who was only twenty-four when he became the twenty-first *Mastermind* champion in 1993. Our oldest was the urbane former diplomat Sir David Hunt, who was sixty-four when he trounced three much younger competitors in the 1977 Jubilee Final; he went on to win the Champion of Champions just short of his sixty-ninth birthday in 1982.

So does age make a significant difference? The received wisdom claims that the memory and its retrieval systems are bound to deteriorate as you grow older; on the other hand, older people, merely by having lived longer, will have had the opportunity to amass more general knowledge than younger people – and, since *Mastermind* was so often won or lost on the general knowledge round, this should have given them a compensatory advantage.

In 1992, a hundred Masterminders were used as guinea-pigs in an attempt to shed more light on the subject. Dr Elizabeth Maylor, a research associate at the Age and Cognitive Performance Research Centre at the University of Manchester (now a research Fellow in the Department of Psychology at the University of Warwick), used volunteers from the Mastermind Club to conduct some research into the effect of age on the speed with which information can be retrieved from the memory, and the occurrence of mental blocks (TOTs, or 'tip-of-the-tongue' experiences). Through the Mastermind Club she wanted to explore the relationship.

She received ninety-seven replies to her questionnaire from Club members; they were aged between twenty-four and seventy-eight, and a third of them were aged fifty or over. She reported on her work in *PASS* and presented her preliminary findings to the London conference of the British Psychological Society in December 1992. Her conclusions were perhaps a little surprising – and, if you are in what the French so elegantly call 'the third age', rather comforting.

She found that there was no effect of age on the total number of questions attempted (a crude measure of speed) in either *Mastermind* round, nor on the proportion of passes to which contenders claimed to know the answer (TOTs state) in either round (approximately 35 per cent in all cases). She also found that in the specialised subjects round, the numbers of correct and incorrect answers were not affected by age; however, in the general knowledge round, the older contenders produced more correct, and fewer incorrect, answers than younger contenders did. The differences were statistically 'highly significant'.

The single most robust finding in the literature on the psychology of ageing is that people in their sixties take approximately one and a half times longer than people in their twenties to perform any mental task; however, where *Mastermind* is concerned, she found that older contestants performed better than younger contenders, even though the programme was one which placed a great deal of emphasis on speed.

Dr Maylor's overall conclusion from her findings was that it appears that decline in old age is not inevitable: in other words, whereas performance generally declines with age, there are some older people who can out-perform the best of the younger people, at least on a task which relies on knowledge accumulated over many years.

'It was very cheering to find that the bad effects of ageing are not inevitable,' she said. 'There is evidence from other studies that there are people who do not decline like the rest of us, and people who, by practice, can retain a high level of performance in certain areas although they might be declining in others.' She believed that her findings suggested that mental exercise, such as taking part in *Mastermind*, or reading or doing crosswords – maintaining a lively intellectual curiosity, in effect – paid off just as much as physical exercise does.

Education

Of Phillida Grantham's respondents, 93 had gained a university or polytechnic degree and nearly half had attended fee-paying schools. The same 93 claimed that they had been at or near the top of the class at school. But again the 'average' belies some of the most interesting aspects of the Masterminders who took part in the programme: two outstanding exceptions, champions both, left school with barely an 'O' level between them – taxi-driver Fred Housego (1980) and London Underground train-driver Christopher Hughes (1983).

Family

Of the 129 respondents to Phillida's survey, no fewer than 41 had been single children; single children, perhaps, tend to go in for more solitary hobbies like reading and have more adult company (and more parental pressure to do well?) than do children in large families. Yet one of the agreeable aspects of *Mastermind* was the number of family combinations we attracted. I can recall at least sixteen instances of family permutations on *Mastermind*: husband-and-wife (7), parent-and-child (7), brother-and-sister (1) and even a family trio!

Two husband-and-wife couples actually appeared in the same heat. The most spectacular example, in Heat 12 of the 1987 series, was the appearance of the Hancocks – Inspector Paul Hancock and his wife Christine Hancock. That contest went to a memorable play-off between them, which Paul won by a single point ('It's been Hancocks' half-hour,' I said at the time in a rare flash of inspiration). The Hancocks are now divorced, and happily ensconced with new partners, but they both assured me that their marital split-up had nothing to do with that epic struggle on *Mastermind*!

Dave Perkins, a tourism officer with Cheshire County Council, faced his wife, librarian Linda Morris, in Heat 3 of the 1989 series. Linda won the marital contest by a point, but failed on passes to reach the semi-final.

Five other husband-and-wife couples have appeared, but on separate programmes and in separate years. Sir Ashley Bramall, a retired London barrister who was a former Labour MP and chairman of the Greater London Council, took part in the 1976 series, and his wife, Lady Bramall (Gery), took part in the 1987 series. Kathryn Jones (now Johnson) first appeared as an Oxford undergraduate in the 1978 series. Her second husband, Stuart Johnson, reached the semi-finals in the 1993 series. Kathryn Johnson then took part again, in the 1995 series. Kate Williams appeared in the 1981 series, taking 'Bess of Hardwick' as her specialised subject. Fifteen years later her husband, John Garnon Williams, a former RAF helicopter pilot and now a historical cartographer, appeared in the 1996 series, taking 'Anglo-Saxon and Viking Place Names of England'. John Burke, a freelance author from Southwold in Suffolk, reached the semi-finals of the 1985 series; his wife, Jean, who worked as his secretary, reached the semi-finals two years later. Michael L. Taylor, a law lecturer at Thanet Technical College, first appeared in the 1988 series, losing in the first round to the champion, David Beamish; his wife, Kate, took part in the 1990 series. Michael Taylor took part again, in the 1995 series, where once again he lost (in the semi-final this time) to the champion, Kevin Ashman.

There have been several parent-and-child combinations. The Rev. Dr Michael Dewar, a clergyman in Northern Ireland, reached the semi-finals in the first series; twenty years later, in 1992, his elder son, David Dewar, a history teacher at Old Swinford Hospital School, Stourbridge, also reached the semi-finals. The Rev. John Gibson, a seventy-year-old 'semi-retired' part-time curate in the parish of Chilvers Coton near Nuneaton, took part in the 1975 series, losing in the heats to the future champion, John Hart; his son, classics teacher Christopher Gibson, reached the semi-finals of the 1985 series. Henry Pantin, a geologist with the British Geological Survey (now retired), was a semi-finalist in the 1976 series; his son, civil servant Andrew Daniel Pantin (now working in a medical library in Leeds), took part in the 1990 series. Elizabeth Compton, a farmer's wife in Angus, took part in the 1979 series; her daughter, Alison Bell, was in the 1990 series. They both scored exactly the same number of points – 24. Ann Hartland-Swann, a diplomat's wife, took part in the 1985 series; her son, Piers Hartland-Swann, took part in the 1988 series.

The 1986 champion was Jennifer Keaveney; but her father, retired civil servant Bernard Downing, had started applying for *Mastermind* before Jennifer, and eventually appeared in the 1992 series. The Billsons continued this reverse process. Mike Billson, a relief milk roundsman in Oxford, was a finalist in the 1987 series; his father, the late Tom Billson, took part the following year.

I also have fond memories of a brother-and-sister combination in the 1988 series. Mary Hunt, a retired nursing auxiliary at the Queen Victoria Hospital at East Grinstead in Sussex, lost in her heat; but in the other heat which was recorded at Hatfield Polytechnic that evening her brother won through to the semi-finals. He was actor Alan Foss, who had starred the previous year in a memorable April Fool version of *Mastermind* written by Stephen Fry.

But the sibling record on *Mastermind* goes to a family trio, the Thompsons of Taunton in Somerset, all of whom had 'form' as quizzers before *Mastermind*. Richard Thompson, a retired banker, appeared in Heat 8 of the 1977 series; he took 'The Mahrattas and Their Wars 1657–1848', and came second. His daughter, trainee solicitor Chantal Thompson, was a finalist in the 1990 series and produced that breathtaking general knowledge round of 22 which nearly snatched the title. Her twin brother, Major Peter Thompson, appeared in the 1994 series.

Why did they take part in Mastermind?

Phillida Grantham's 1989 survey produced a crop of fairly predictable answers: they had done it for fun, or as a response to family nagging, or as a challenge to themselves, or because they were bored with an otherwise ordinary life. One or two respondents were honest enough to say 'hubris', or 'conceit'; others said 'to be seen on TV', or 'I like quizzing and I'm good'. One even admitted, 'because I'm a bighead'.

Paul Campion, 1983 semi-finalist, says: 'What an odd lot we were, with nothing whatever in common except that we took on a challenge and succeeded ("success" here means that we actually took part without chickening out, not that we necessarily did well). Our knowledge is quite amazingly assorted, mostly useless, but it is important to us, and *Mastermind* has, to quite a degree, immortalised our achievement. What a hell of a lot of fun it was!'

I have always felt that it took a rather exceptional kind of bravery, even foolhardiness, to volunteer for the Black Chair. I did it once myself, in response to a challenge which I felt I could not refuse. It happened during the TV Christmas season of 1980. After Russell Harty had been physically attacked on his show by Grace Jones, Sue Lawley on *Nationwide* invited viewers to write in to say which other TV personality they would most like to see getting a taste of his or her own medicine.

Simon Warr, who was a housemaster at the Royal Hospital School near Ipswich, wrote the best letter, nominating me for the ordeal, and as a prize he was picked to put me in the hot seat, on 3 December 1980. He had done a little broadcasting before, but he claims that he was terrified at the prospect. I'll bet he wasn't half as petrified as I was. For my specialised subject I took 'Viking Archaeology', because I had been working for the previous two years on a major television series called *Vikings!* and reckoned I would have a chance of getting at least a few of the questions right. The questions were set by a friend of mine, Professor Peter Sawyer, who had been an academic consultant on the series. Let's just say that he knew rather more about the subject than I did. I managed to get through the twenty questions within the two minutes and raise a score of 14 or 15, I think. I must have been mad to agree to do it.

But it had one very important effect: it made me sympathise more than ever with the people who took the Black Chair over the years, for whatever reason (which they were probably already regretting). Some were numb with nerves, some were in despair, most of them were tense. I take my hat off to them all.

Masterminders, even the most modest, were courting some sort of public recognition for their talents. But how does one explain the motives of those people who appeared on *Mastermind* when the last thing they wanted was to be publicly recognised?

In 1983 there was a spectacular story about a man from the north-east of England who was spotted on *Mastermind* by the local press just after he had been jailed for embezzlement. He was a retired sub-postmaster from Burton in Lonsdale, in North Yorkshire, who took part in Heat 6 which was recorded at Loughborough University of Technology on 3 November 1982. His specialised subject was 'British History 1714–1815' and he came joint second on 23, just one point behind the winner (Robert Woodcock). None of the *Mastermind* team knew his secret – that soon after he had applied for *Mastermind* he had been charged with the theft of more than £5,000 from his sub-post office at Culcheth, near Warrington. He went for trial and was given a sentence of nine months' imprisonment (with six months suspended) on the Friday before his programme was transmitted on a Sunday in February 1983. When the programme was broadcast the local press ran the story of his trial and sentence, and the story was gleefully taken up by the national media as well. On 16 February, Mac of the *Daily Mail* published a cartoon of a convict sitting in the Black Chair being carted out of Television Centre by the Old Bill, with myself in hot pursuit waving my question cards and crying, 'I've started, so I'll finish!' The original of that cartoon was acquired and presented to me by producer Roger Mackay and the *Mastermind* team, and I treasure it still.

He hadn't won a place in the semi-final – that would have put us in a distinctly embarrassing position. But it was impossible not to feel a pang of sympathy for him. It was revealed at his trial that he had 'borrowed' the money over a period of two years to pay two large tax bills, and was awaiting the proceeds from the sale of his house to pay back the missing money when the theft was discovered. The money had, in fact, all been repaid before the trial.

Even more bizarre was the case, also in 1983, of the unfrocked priest who was exposed as a bigamist after appearing on *Mastermind*. In Heat 11, which was recorded in the clerical setting of Christ Church College, Canterbury, there was a contender calling himself 'The Rev. Robert Peters', who took as his specialised subject 'The Life and Times of Archbishop William Temple'. 'Peters' had told us that he was a Church of England priest, that he was a Doctor of Divinity with a degree from Manchester University, and that he was Director of Theological Studies at University College, Buckland, near Oxford. He had made a very good showing at the audition; he was bald and bulky and bespectacled, and confident to the point of arrogance. On the programme, however, he scored only 7 on his specialised subject and 12 on his general knowledge round, and came joint third on 19, well behind the winner, John Edmond, a computer systems project manager from Watford.

After the transmission of the programme, late in March, we received phone calls and letters claiming that he had been kicked out of the Church of England for bigamy. It was not a situation with which we were particularly familiar and we responded as non-committally as we could. However, it was all done for us by the media. In the *News of the World* the following Sunday it was revealed that 'Peters' was, indeed, an unfrocked parson who had been thrown out of the Church of England in 1953 after a bigamy scandal. His real name was Robert Parkins, and he had become a priest in 1942; he had married Hilda Brunton, but in 1946 had bigamously married Margaret Gladdish. After the unfrocking he had gone to Australia, Canada and the USA, where he changed his name to 'Peters' and got various jobs by claiming he had a string of degrees to his name. In 1956 he had lied his way into a research job at Magdalen College, Oxford, and a post as director of theological studies at University College.

In 1957 he was found charging students £130 a time for worthless certificates in theology at St Aidan's College, Shropshire. In 1959 came his second bigamous marriage, to a New Zealand girl called Marie Baillie. What on earth could have possessed him to apply for *Mastermind*? Did he, by then, think he was unassailable? Talk about hubris!

There was another case of dubious identity, in 1985: a very different sort of story, poignant rather than piquant. I always called it 'The Case of the Woman Who Appeared Twice'.

It happened at a time when the rules of *Mastermind* did not allow contenders who had already sat in the Black Chair to reapply at a later date (that rule wasn't changed until the 1995 series). In January 1985 a woman called Mrs Sheila Altree, a school laboratory technician from Okehampton in Devon, had to be disqualified. She had just won Heat 2 at Bristol Polytechnic, taking as her specialised subject 'The Ghost Stories of M. R. James', and qualified for the semi-finals. However, a contender who had appeared with her in an earlier series recognised her when she appeared on screen the second time (even though she had then not been called Sheila Altree) and telephoned to ask if he could reapply himself since we had obviously changed the rules!

It transpired that Sheila had, indeed, appeared on *Mastermind* before, in Heat 5 of the 1980 series, as Sheila Denyer, a laundry worker from Devon, answering questions on 'The Bible'; she was great value, very interesting, a bit out of the way, a TV 'personality'. She had scored 24 and come second, and had only just missed a place in the fourth semi-final for the highest-scoring losers.

No one on the production team had recognised her the second time round. She had been auditioned by a new producer, she had changed her face, her husband, her name, her address, her job, her hairstyle – and in her application form she claimed that she had never appeared on TV before and had neither applied to, nor appeared on, *Mastermind*.

There was consternation in the *Mastermind* office. The two application forms were checked, and the handwriting seemed to tally. A videotape of the earlier programme was unearthed; the two programmes were put on screen side by side, and there was no doubt that the two women were one and the same person. She would obviously have to be disqualified.

Peter Massey, the producer, had the unenviable task of ringing her at her school. The school secretary assumed that it was to congratulate her on her performance; but Sheila's first words when she came to the telephone were, 'You're not going to disqualify me, are you?' When Peter challenged her on why she had done it, she denied that she had been deceitful: she had married again, and was a different and happier woman. She said she was a new person and that this had justified what she had done.

There was really no choice but to disqualify her, and replace her with the runner-up in her heat – Corporal Ian McKillop, serving with the RAMC at Aldershot.

In his letter confirming the disqualification, Peter Massey wrote:

Following our telephone conversation this lunch-time, I write with great sadness to inform you that I have decided that it would not be right for you to take any further part in the present series of Mastermind.

My reasons are, as we discussed, that it is a rule of the programme that people who have appeared are not permitted to take part again. It gives me no satisfaction to point out to you that on your application form you answered No to each of the following questions:

1. Have you ever appeared on TV?
2. Have you applied for Mastermind *before?*
3. Have you had a Mastermind *audition before?*

I accepted your application in good faith, and although you have given me your reasons for giving these particular answers, I am afraid I cannot accept them.

In her first application form, as Sheila Denyer for the 1980 series, she had written under the 'Career History' heading: 'Rolling Stone – Marriage 1964. Divorce 1973. Now free and happy with 2 children and new fiancé.' In her second application form, for 1985, she wrote, under 'Career History', 'Chequered!'. (It turned out that she had been a night janitor in a morgue.)

She felt genuinely aggrieved about our decision. She told a reporter from the *Evening Standard* in January 1985:

The BBC should have turned a blind eye to the problem. When I entered six years ago I was still married to my first husband and was Mrs Sheila Denyer. Now I am Mrs Sheila Altree and I am a different person. There was nothing wrong with having a second go. When the man from the BBC phoned me, I felt he was accusing me of cheating. But I do not see it that way at all. I think of it as a misunderstanding. After I was told I went for a long walk up onto the moors with my dog and I just cried my eyes out.

Perhaps I'm just a big softie, but I always felt a bit unhappy about that episode. So when the *Mastermind* rule was changed to allow 'recidivists' to reapply, I persuaded the producer (now David Mitchell) to make contact with her and offer her the chance of another audition, for a 'legitimate' second appearance. Sheila accepted at once, made out her application form, was auditioned and was accepted for the 1997 series. There seemed to me to be a proper poetic justice in it, to tie up a loose knot of unfinished business before the programme came to an end (this time she reached the semi-finals).

The recognition factor was clearly important to some aspirant Masterminders, at least, as a compensation for perceived failure or a vindication of perceived success. Why else should a private detective (who would presumably prefer to remain fairly anonymous) risk becoming a very public one by appearing on *Mastermind*? It certainly didn't put off Eric Forrester, a private eye from Glasgow; what's more, he did it twice, in 1987 and 1995. By a curious coincidence, his 1987 appearance, broadcast on 11 January 1987, was featured on *Crimewatch* as a vital clue establishing the time at which a crime had taken place. *Crimewatch* was appealing for information about a serious assault on an elderly pensioner in his home as he was watching *Mastermind*, which pinpointed the time of the crime; and to jog viewers' memories the producer used a clip from the programme showing Eric in the Black Chair. However, there was no mention of the fact that Eric was a private eye; nor, mercifully, was there any reference to the fact that, to his intense embarrassment, Eric had got a question about Perry Mason wrong in his general knowledge round!

An article in the *Radio Times* before the 1983 Final summed up rather well, I thought, this whole question of why people wanted to appear on *Mastermind*:

They don't even do it for subsequent fame, for few go on to be media celebrities . . . In fact, most winners subside into the lives they lived before they opted for the one-off spotlight. One of the finalists said, 'If I win, I shall be happy to be anonymous again. The point about this competition is that it gives others an indication that reading and knowledge, and intellectual experience, are enriching to their lives. Getting a prize is a mantelpiece job.'

Mantelpiece job or not, there are some *Masterminders* whose life-interests, their lives, indeed, have been changed, or at least reinforced, by appearing on *Mastermind*. Fred Housego, the 1980 champion, who went on to become a broadcaster and media personality, is the obvious example who always springs to mind. But there were others whose lives were greatly affected.

Paul Campion, head of the Piano Department at Harrods, was a contender in 1983; for him, one single lucky guess in his general knowledge round (the question was about the River Amazon) changed the whole course of his life, because that correct answer was sufficient to take him into the semi-finals and give him the opportunity to use his second specialised subject, 'The Life of Kathleen Ferrier'. His appearance in the semi-finals elicited a letter from Kathleen Ferrier's sister, Winifred (Paul had not realised she was still alive), and they became firm friends until her death in 1995 at the age of ninety-one. Winifred introduced him to other relatives and colleagues of Kathleen Ferrier who had been influential on her life and extraordinary singing career. It was all such a revelation that Paul started researching into Ferrier's surviving recordings as a subject for a book: *Ferrier – A Career Recorded*, published in 1992. It was followed by another, *Glyndebourne Recorded*. This was the kind of work he had always wanted to do. He gave up his job at Harrods and now has a successful career as a writer and lecturer – all thanks to *Mastermind* and a lucky guess. Luck continued to attend him when he won £6,400 on *The $64,000 Question* show in 1990, but that's another story.

Dr Joan Bridgman (1987) feels that her life, too, was profoundly affected by the programme. She had earned an honours degree in English at Bedford College, London University, but had failed to break into academia. She worked in an insurance office. She had to leave the company when she got married and drifted into teaching when her two children were old enough to go to school. And she started working on a thesis for a postgraduate degree.

She moved into teacher training at Maria Grey College at Twickenham. She went to the West Country, working part-time at the West London Institute of Higher Education (as it then was), until she broke her leg, which prevented her from driving to London. At a low ebb, she decided to apply for *Mastermind* to give herself a goal apart from her thesis, which was on 'The Publishing History and Literary Context of *Watership Down*' and which seemed pretty pointless without a lecturing job to go with it. She did well, taking 'The Life and Works of Samuel Beckett', but not well enough to beat the champion, Jeremy Bradbrooke. But that didn't matter:

> *The turning point of my life was filling up that application form for* Mastermind.
> *First there is the membership of the Club itself. It is a very special club. I have never before met so many nice people gathered together with whom one can have such an instant rapport, yet whose backgrounds are so very diverse and interesting. We meet once a year and I feel a real sense of fellowship with the Club membership and with the production team, who entertain us with the latest special subjects at a good dinner or lunch every year.*
> *Secondly, soon after the programme, my M.Phil., which I had been working on for some years, was converted to a Ph.D. in 1990. On the strength of this I now teach two courses for the Open University, as well as at least one semester a year at Brunel University where I teach English on the modular degree course.*

Joan broke her leg again after the programme. She was also diagnosed as having cancer. With that behind her, she has been determined to live life to the full and do everything humanly possible. For the past five years she has travelled to academic conferences in the USA and given papers on myth and other research interests, and published numerous articles and book reviews.

It is humbling to think that Joan should attribute so much of this success to *Mastermind*: 'This is a kind of "thank you",' she wrote, 'for what the programme must have done for so many of us – what is achievable, even if we only try and fail. As Samuel Beckett put it: "Fail again, fail better".'

8

'The Professionals'

'Why tease me with pedantic themes,
Predicaments and enthymemes,*
My mental storehouse vainly stowing
With heaps of knowledge not worth knowing?'

ANACREON, translated by Thomas Love Peacock

Throughout the *Mastermind* era a new quiz culture was developing in Britain. Not that *Mastermind* created it, as such – Bamber Gascoigne's *University Challenge*, which had begun in 1962, and radio favourites like *What Do You Know?* (1953–67), the forerunner of *Brain of Britain*, have much more right to such a claim – but *Mastermind* certainly reflected it and helped to reinforce a rapidly developing national pastime. Today, pub quiz teams are as common as darts teams, if not more so, and there are pub quiz leagues up and down the country. The Civil Service, for example, has a quiz league with several divisions, with promotion and relegation and knock-out competitions galore.

The best-known quiz league is the Merseyside League, which began in 1959. It is an extraordinary organisation which started in six pubs in Bootle and by 1982 covered an area of 1,000 square miles, with some 18 leagues, 250 teams and about 1,500 players. It was the catchment area for several distinguished Masterminders, particularly in the late 1980s: people like chartered surveyor Michael Formby and history teacher Phil McDonald, who both took part in the electrifying *Mastermind* Final of 1986, when Jennifer Keaveney equalled her scoring record of 40; and planning manager Philip Gray, from Prescot, who was in the David Beamish final of 1988.

*Condensed syllogisms.

The oldest quiz league in the world, however (and I am assured that this claim has been accepted for a future *Guinness Book of Records*), is the York City branch of the CIU (the Club and Institute Union, the official name for the association of working men's clubs), which was founded in 1946. The York CIU league has four divisions, and it provided *Mastermind* with one of our semi-finalists in 1993: Steve Hayes, a railwayman from Dringhouses near York, who plays for the York Railway Institute quiz team in Division 1 of the league. He won his heat with 'The History of the Grand National' but came a cropper in the semi-finals against Barrie Douce.

Among what Roger Woddis so felicitously called 'the riddle class' there is now a very distinct sub-class – a sort of semi-professional group one might go so far as to call 'the professionals'. For some, quizzes have become a consuming hobby, almost a way of life; some are addicts; for a very few it can make a reasonably lucrative sideline.

A few years ago, Mike O'Sullivan (1987) did a survey of *other* television or radio quizzes in which his fellow Masterminders had appeared. Mike, who once worked for the housing department of the Greater London Council (he took early retirement in 1989), was pitchforked as a reserve at eight days' notice into the 200th programme of *Mastermind*, recorded at the University of Kent at Canterbury, where he and Peter Chitty were only just beaten by Margaret Spiller. As soon as he was elected to the Club committee in 1991 he sent out his questionnaire to all the Club members. Nearly a third sent them back for processing – 124 in all. The results were quite staggering: by 1991, no fewer than 91 Club members had made 240 appearances on 68 quiz programmes!

Top of the league for other quizzes was *Fifteen to One* (Channel 4) with appearances by 48 Masterminders, followed by *Brain of Britain* (BBC Radio) with 40. Next came the three versions of *Sale of the Century* (Anglia, Australian TV and Sky) with 15, followed by *Winner Takes All* (Yorkshire) with 12 and *University Challenge* (Granada) also with 12. No fewer than eight Masterminders had won the top prize of £6,400 on *The $64,000 Question* (Central): Kate Vernon-Parry (1984) and Mike O'Sullivan himself in 1990, followed in 1991 by Paul Campion (1983), Stewart Cross (1987), Margaret Fleming (1988), Sheila Ramsden (1977), Julie Tedds (1989 and 1996) and Perry Thomas (1990). Another winner in 1991 was a future Masterminder, Tim Westcott (1994).

In his article in *The Times* Saturday Magazine in April 1996, Robert Crampton likened some of the members of the Club to the kind of professional pool-table hustler portrayed on film by Paul Newman, and singled out Geoffrey Thomas (1994 semi-finalist) as an exemplar:

> *Geoff and his fellow Masterminders make unlikely Paul-Newman-as-Fast-Eddies at first glance, but that is what in effect many of them are, hustling public bars, function rooms and TV studios up and down the country. Geoff says it: 'Sad, really, that a grown man has nothing better to do than sit swotting facts.'*

He makes an interesting case-study, Geoff Thomas. A self-confessed quiz freak, he was a lecturer in modern languages at Mid-Cheshire College, Northwich, in Cheshire; he took early retirement in 1991, thus having time to apply for radio and TV quizzes (but not game-shows which, despite their dazzling prizes, he considers 'demeaning for serious quiz freaks'). He took part in *Brain of Britain* in 1991 ('with no particular distinction'). In 1993 he won a midi hi-fi system in the grand final of Ed Stewart's accumulator phone-in quiz on Radio 2 ('a bit downmarket').

On the development of his addiction to quizzes, he says:

> *I have always been interested in the curious habit of acquiring bits of factual information, starting early with sporting arcana. At an early age I was encouraged by my elder brother to chant, mantra-like, the line-up of Manchester City's FA Cup-winning team of 1934.*
>
> *As a member of Lancashire CCC I have long sat among a group of cricket buffs posing obscure cricket questions: 'Who is the only Test cricketer to have climbed Mt Kilimanjaro twice?' (Bob Crisp, South Africa); 'Who performed the "double" eight times and never played in a Test?' (Frank Tarrant, Middlesex); 'Which two England captains appeared in the 1939 Alexander Korda film* The Four Feathers*?' (C. Aubrey Smith and A. C. Maclaren). This, I imagine, led to amassing facts of a general nature and, like most quizzers, I have a childish desire to show off. Quizzes are, after all, ego trips.*

When he applied for *Mastermind* he realised that there was no sub-stitute for sheer hard work if he was to do well. He made sure that he had all the reference books he needed, especially the *Guinness*

Book of Answers, *Brewer's Dictionary of Phrase and Fable*, the *Chambers Biographical Dictionary*, and Bamber Gascoigne's *Encyclopedia of Britain*. That was all for general knowledge – which, he asserts, *can* be mugged up, despite many people saying that it can't. (It should be said, however, that hosts of Masterminders never found that necessary, and did extremely well by relying solely on their general reading and their wide range of interests.)

On *Mastermind* in the 1994 series Geoff took the 'The Life of K. S. Ranjitsinhji', the great cricketer; after months of preparation he was still swotting furiously throughout the morning of the big day – and it paid off with a handsome win on 35. In the first semi-final, recorded in Haddo House Hall, he was involved in a tie-break on 34, and this time he lost 3–4.

Geoff was deeply disappointed – having got so far he desperately wanted to reach the Final:

> *Scarcely a day has passed when I have not relived with some anguish the questions which I did not get right – such is the power and magic of the programme which it still exerts after two and a half years. 'Which was the first country to win the World Cup three times' – and I said* Italy*! Swotting for three months, and I said* Italy*! [It should have been Brazil.]*

What do people like Geoff do after *Mastermind*? In 1995 he won Radio 4's *Counterpoint* quiz – the programme to find the 'musical Brain of Britain'. He also plays in the Northwich and District Quiz League in a team called 'The Lion and Railway', which has been undisputed league champion for the past two seasons; he finds, though, that if he drops into a pub running a pub-based quiz for the regulars, he is *persona non grata* as often as not ('It's not fair, he's been on *Mastermind*'). Undeterred, he appeared on BBC2's *Today's the Day* – and won the 1997 Final. When the quiz bug bites, it bites hard.

It's a curiously tight network, this sub-class of semi-professionals. Take the case of Londoner Christopher Cooke, a former computer systems adviser with Barclays Bank who has now set up his own business, selling kits for scale models made from card. His first foray into the quiz world was in *Brain of Britain* in 1978, where he was beaten in the semi-finals by Major Arthur Douch, who would himself take part in the 1980 series of *Mastermind*; on the same programme he also met Ingram Wilcox, who would lose to Fred Housego in the 1980 Final. During his own stint on *Mastermind* in 1980, Christopher took part in the 150th programme in the MacRobert Arts Centre at the University of Stirling. There he lost narrowly to another of Fred's opponents in the Final, civil servant Samuel Mortimer.

After *Mastermind*, Christopher appeared on several quizzes, 'mostly mercenary', including a 'Supermind' competition organised by Thomson Local Directories in 1981. After an initial postal round, he took part in the finals at Richmond Town Hall, with David Jacobs as the question-master. The specialised round was pre-set: 'The London Borough of Richmond'. Christopher won the Final, the title of 'Richmond Supermind', and some Thomson holiday vouchers. He won money on *Jeopardy* in 1982 and on *Winner Takes All* in 1984; he won even more money and a holiday in Shetland on STV's *Now You See It* in 1985, and some tumblers and a glass jewellery box on BBC's *Four Square* in 1989. In 1988 he appeared on *Brain of Britain* again, where he competed in the semi-finals against Owen Gunnell (1986 finalist) and Rachel Leonard (1984). He reached the Final with Ian Meadows, the 1985 *Mastermind* champion, and Robert Gleeson (1978 finalist), but came fourth. He also appeared on *Fifteen to One*, in which he reached two Grand Finals (where he met Ingram Wilcox again) and won the Top of the Finals Board Trophy.

Anthony V. Martin, a semi-finalist in 1978, is another addict – and in his case it ran in the family. His father, Leslie Martin, who was a Directing Actuary in the Government Actuaries Department, appeared on *Criss Cross Quiz*, *Brain of Britain* and *Fifteen to One*, where he lost in a Final to his son! Anthony had read Classics at Keble College, Oxford, and was a reserve for the college team for *University Challenge*. He then trained as a librarian at Loughborough University and started working for the borough of Knowsley on Merseyside. One of his jobs as an assistant librarian at Kirkby Library was tracing requested books and supplying them for the library's readers. One reader from Knowsley Village ordered several books on George Stephenson, the railway pioneer; a year later, in 1977, this reader turned up on *Mastermind* answering questions on 'The Life and Work of George Stephenson' – it was none other than Peter Richardson, the most professional of 'the professionals' (see below).

Anthony thought to himself that if one of his readers could do this, why shouldn't he? He had been watching *Mastermind* for several years and used to do quite well at answering the general knowledge questions at home. Now he applied for the 1978 series, and was accepted after an audition in Manchester. In the event he lost in the *repêchage* semi-final to the eventual champion, Rosemary James.

On the morning after the transmission of the programme, however, there on the doorstep of Kirkby Library was Peter Richardson with an invitation to join his Rainford quiz team ('Rex Lions', formerly 'The Golden Lion') in the Merseyside Quiz League. Anthony was a mainstay of the team until he left the area in 1994; in addition to his literary and classical expertise, he showed astonishing knowledge of soap operas and children's TV programmes. The team also included Colin Pilkington (1992).

After Kirkby Library, Anthony worked at Prescot Library. The *Final Five* programme before the 1988 Final featured Philip Gray walking to Prescot Library to change his books. Anthony also provided some old books for Eileen Eaves, retired Head of Drama and sixth-form tutor at St Mary's College in Wallasey, who took 'The Life and Career of Sarah Siddons' in the 1988 series and reached the *repêchage* semi-final. Anthony himself took part in *Brain of Britain* in 1988 and appeared, with considerable success, in several series of *Fifteen to One*: he became overall series champion three times – a record unbeaten so far even by other Masterminders. He met a number of Masterminders in the finals, including Kevin Ashman (1987 and 1995 champion), Glenys Hopkins (1992) and Eleanor Macnair (1973 and 1996).

A remarkable nest of quizzers is to be found on the third Wednesday evening of every month at the Grape Street Wine Bar in London. These are the Masterminder regulars – people of a wide range of ages and occupations who between them provide a kind of quiz exchange: it is a veritable quiz training ground, which produces a bewildering array of quiz teams of ever-shifting membership.

Most of them take part in the South London Quiz League, which plays to an extremely high standard and consists of eighteen teams in two separate divisions. Andrew Curtis (1995 semi-finalist), who had never tried a quiz before he entered for *Mastermind*, plays with Trevor Montague (1995), Robert Jones (1995 finalist), Ray Ward (1978 semi-finalist) and Tim Westcott (1994) for a team called 'The

Rue St George', a wine bar in Croydon. Kevin Ashman, Dr Ken
Emond (1992 semi-finalist), Gavin Fuller (1993 champion), Phillida
Grantham (1981 and 1995) and Paul Henderson (1987 semi-finalist)
play for a team called 'The Allsorts'. Each team consists of four
players, although in practice many consist of 'squads' from which a
team for the evening is drawn. Both teams are currently in Division
1; in 1996, 'The Allsorts' beat 'The Rue St George' in the Charity
Shield by one point.

Trevor Montague is the catalyst for other quiz activities. In 1995
he assembled a scratch team called 'I've Started, So I'll Finish' for the
Quizmail Shield, consisting of himself, Andrew Curtis, Phillida
Grantham and Peter Chitty (1987), with Kevin Ashman and Gavin
Fuller as 'guest stars'; they won the Shield and prize money of
£250. In 1996 he gathered a team including himself, Andrew Curtis
and Tim Westcott for a quiz organised by the White Hart hotel
chain; they won the national final and a holiday for two in Barbados.

There is also a very occasional quiz team of nebulous membership
called 'Kensington Gore' whose core members are Barrie Douce,
Glenys Davies, Gavin Fuller and David Tombs (the name alludes to
their shared experience in the 1993 Final). Andrew Curtis and Gavin
Fuller also take part in a monthly postal quiz run by The Red Lion
pub in Barnes; their team is called 'The Brains of Morbius' (an allusion
to their shared interest in *Dr Who*). The postal quiz attracts several other
Masterminders, including Trevor Montague ('London Irish') and
Kevin Ashman, whose team, 'The Regicides', always seems to win.

There's no stopping them once they've started.

Most people would suppose that Kevin Ashman, the all-but-invin-
cible 1995 champion, was the most 'professional' Masterminder of
all; but he repudiates any such suggestion. Certainly, he takes major
competitions very seriously, and wins them with astonishing regularity; but he thinks the use of terms like 'semi-professional' or
'professional' misleading or inappropriate (unless they are used
humorously) because they imply some degree of ability to make a
living by 'quizzing', which simply cannot be done in this country.

Another Masterminder, Peter Richardson (1977 semi-finalist), a
production manager of photo-chemicals for Kodak in Kirkby, has
always been one of the most determined and successful quizzers in
the Mastermind Club – someone who, like Kevin Ashman, is

prepared to do a lot of studying to win a specific competition. Over many years he and Kevin have enjoyed a ding-dong struggle for supremacy in the Mastermind Club in-house competitions, the Magnum (Kevin leads by 5 wins to 4) and the Mugnum (Kevin leads 3–0).

Peter is perhaps the nearest to what can be called a 'professional' quiz player. That is what Robert Robinson, chairman of *Brain of Britain*, called him once – and he did not intend it as a compliment. In a four-part series in *PASS* (July 1992 onwards), Peter explained why he had no objection to the title of 'professional quiz-player':

> *When I call myself a professional I don't mean that I play for the money, although if there are valuable prizes to be won I have no objection. I mean rather that my approach is professional in playing to win and going to considerable lengths to give myself the best chance by thorough preparation and careful study of the game and of its rules.*
>
> *Storing up potentially useful answers, however you set about it, is a fairly obvious step and I'm sure we've all done it, and not only for our specialist rounds. On the simplest level we commit great slabs of boring fact to memory. For instance, I know every capital and every currency in the world. I take no pride or pleasure in this, but question-setters keep asking for them and if you want to win you can't afford to miss sitters like that.*
>
> *What seems to separate the professional from the dilettante is the close study of the game and of its rules, listening to tapes of earlier rounds and previous series to get into the mind of the question-setter and so guide preparation, and to become accustomed to the style of the questions and the question-master and to practise responding, and thinking out how to maximise the chance of success before and during the game, without actually cheating – more, without doing anything which may upset the other players unfairly.*

'Professional' could be defined as playing to win money and big prizes, but that is not strictly accurate. Peter cannot think of any game on which he has won prizes which he would not happily have played for nothing, or just for expenses: 'We do it because it's fun; and if a big prize comes with winning, so much the better, but it's not the motivation.'

His first foray into broadcast quizzes was on Radio 2's *Treble Chance* in 1971. He played in a team of three from Southport, and they all studied hard, reading the *Daily Telegraph* for three months because they had been told that this was the paper from which the question-setter and presenter, Michael Tuke-Hastings, culled all his topical questions. The team won the Final and Peter was the top scorer. On the train home he came to the conclusion that he was perhaps of national standard: that he didn't suffer from nerves and did well under pressure, that he was very fast on a buzzer and that he enjoyed broadcasting. So he sat down and applied for *Brain of Britain* and *Sale of the Century*.

In 1973, on *Brain of Britain*, he reached the Final, which turned out to be one of the closest and highest-scoring finals ever; Peter lost out on the very last question; he was to appear on *Brain of Britain* again in 1987, when he came second in the Final, and was joint winner of the subsequent *Masterbrain* competition.

In 1976 came *Sale of the Century*; it was while studying for that series that Peter fully recognised the importance of being quick on the buzzer:

> *It's no good waiting until you know the answer before pressing the buzzer. It's not even enough to buzz when you have heard the full question. You have to buzz just before the question becomes plain, banking on the fact that no question-master can stop talking instantly.*

Peter waltzed through to the Final and was so confident that he hired an estate car in advance to cart home his winnings. Despite this invitation to hubris he won the Final and goods to the value of £3,000 – gold jewellery, cutlery, a bicycle and hi-fi set – plus a Mini.

After this highly profitable venture in commercial quizzing he 'returned to respectability' with *Mastermind* in 1977. Oddly enough, he did not do very well on *Mastermind*: he won his heat with 25 points overall, taking 'The Life and Work of George Stephenson', but in his semi-final he came in last with 'Tolkien's Fiction' and a low score of 21 overall.

The Krypton Factor followed in 1979. He trained hard for the obstacle course round – too hard, because he pulled a muscle and was only restored to a semblance of fitness by the legendary Joe Fagan at

Anfield (later to be manager of Liverpool Football Club). He fared no better in the intelligence round, but he won the title of 'Superperson' almost entirely on the final buzzer round (of course!) on general knowledge. As a result of this the rules were changed in the *Krypton Factor All-Champions* tournament in 1980, limiting the buzzer general knowledge round to half a dozen questions, and Peter came second.

In 1981 he lost on *Winner Takes All*. In 1982 he lost on *Countdown* on the very last conundrum. In 1983 on *Jeopardy* he won £1,000. In 1986 he took part in *Masterteam* in a team of Masterminders, but lost to a team which contained a pop music specialist ('not my scene at all').

Then came the big-time. In 1987 he took part in the big-money *Sale of the Century* World Championship in Melbourne. This lavish show, according to Peter, is the most intellectually demanding game of them all – not because of the difficulty of the questions, but because of the incredible buzzer-work of the old Australian hands. He didn't reach the Final but his takings as runner-up in the UK section were £1,200, as against the Final winner's £50,000. He tried again in 1988 and once again failed to reach the Final, but his takings were £1,800 as runner-up in the UK section. At his third attempt, in 1989, he reached the Final at last (by beating his old Mastermind Club rival Kevin Ashman in the UK semi-final). His winnings this time were £11,000. He missed out on a further £14,000 by picking the wrong 'Cashbox' – and laughed cheerfully (it really was just a game). The winner took home £85,000!

Thereafter he appeared twice on *Fifteen to One*, and in 1982 he won BBC Scotland's *Catchword*. Finally, in 1996 he appeared on the *Great British Quiz*, where his team lost in the semi-final by a single question and failed to win a trip to the Great Barrier Reef. But he was pleased to discover that at the age of sixty-seven he was still really fast on the buzzer . . .

The story goes (although it is in all probability apocryphal) that when a new TV quiz series called *Going for Gold* was announced, almost every member of the Mastermind Club gathered for a mass audition at a venue in London's Regent Street! True or not, it tells a great deal about the popular image of the Masterminders: amateur or dilettante, professional or semi-professional – but above all, addicts every one.

9

Champions All: 1978–89

'This is a country, after all, where the Grand Final of a programme like
Mastermind *is frequently won by cab drivers and footplate-men. I have
never been able to decide whether that is deeply impressive or just
appalling — whether this a country where engine drivers know about
Tintoretto and Leibniz, or a country where people who know about
Tintoretto and Leibniz end up driving engines. All I know is that it exists
here more than anywhere else I know.'*

BILL BRYSON, *Notes from a Small Island*

In 1961 a sixteen-year-old schoolboy left Kynaston Comprehensive
School for Boys, in St John's Wood, London, with one 'O' level
('The British Constitution') and this somewhat ambivalent form
master's report: 'Appears satisfied with a minimum effort. He has
done well in some subjects, but I think his general interests are too
powerful for him to be an academic. However, he is possibly the
most civilised member of the class.' In addition, for History, his
report read: 'Not yet working really seriously.'

After a spell as a clerk in an advertising agency the young man followed his father into the Post Office as a postman; but after the Post
Office strike in 1971 he decided to try to become a taxi-driver. This
meant doing 'the knowledge', a fiercely difficult course on London's
street geography based on the 'Blue Book' (which is actually pink) of
468 runs, starting with 'Manor House to Gibson Square' (Finsbury
Park to Islington). He took to it with enthusiasm, and within eighteen
months he was driving a cab based at Heathrow Airport. He developed what someone called 'a massive intimacy with London's history':
he would read voraciously during quiet periods on the rank, and now
has a huge library of history books at his home in Croxley Green in
Hertfordshire. He is also a Blue Badge London Tourist Guide.

His name, of course, is Fred Housego, the 'gabby cabby' who won the *Mastermind* title in 1980 and thereby changed the perception of *Mastermind* as an essentially élitist programme. His win was seen to break the mould: here was the ordinary man-in-the-street taking on the professional knowledge-brokers and 'beating them at their own game', as Bryan Cowgill had put it. For many viewers it gave *Mastermind* a new lease of life for the 1980s.

It should not be forgotten, however, that the 1970s had ended on an astonishing high in terms of viewing figures. After the switch of transmission times to a prime slot on Thursday evenings in 1973, each series averaged about 10 million, peaking at 13 or 14 million. The all-time high for viewing figures came in the autumn of 1979, when ITV was on strike for five weeks; during that period the figures were 16, 18 and 19 million (twice), climaxing in a chart-topping 20 million on Wednesday, 17 October 1979.

This was particularly pleasing because, after Sir David Hunt's victory in the Jubilee Final of 1977, some people feared that the programme had peaked and could only go downhill. Not a bit of it!

1978: Rosemary James

Rosemary James was a 33-year-old teacher of Latin and classical studies at The Mount School in York when she appeared on *Mastermind*. Taking 'The Mythology of the Greeks and Romans' as her specialised subject she was beaten in her heat, on passes, by Ray Ward, a librarian with Sheffield City Libraries, taking 'Manned Space Flight'; but she qualified for the semi-final for the highest-scoring losers, won that with ease taking 'The Life and Works of Frederick Rolfe' (Baron Corvo) and went into the Final at Heriot-Watt University, Edinburgh, as the favourite. Her win in the Final meant that women had edged ahead again in the championship stakes, with four wins against three by men.

Winning the championship qualified Rosemary for the first *Mastermind International*, which was recorded in the Old Library at London's Guildhall. There were seven champions in the tourney, including Barbara-Anne Eddy, a Canadian student from Vancouver who had won *The $128,000 Question* in the USA; Godwin Anaba, a blind 21-year-old student of politics at the University College of

Rosemary James, with Bill Cotton, then Controller BBC1

Wales, Aberystwyth, the current Nigerian Mastermind; Mark Allan, a 21-year-old relief worker from Dunedin, the current New Zealand Mastermind, taking 'The History of Rock Music Since 1955'; John Mulcahy, from County Cork in Ireland, winner of the 1978 *Top Score* contest on Radio Telefis Éireann; and Sir David Hunt, the 'Jubilee Mastermind' of 1977.

The winner was John Mulcahy, hotly pursued to the tape by Sir David Hunt, with Rosemary James trailing. The Irish press had assumed that the recording was a live broadcast and published the result next morning. It was all good fun, I suppose, but I felt distinctly uncomfortable at what I considered the dilution of the simplicity and directness of *Mastermind* itself.

The following year also had its share of memories. In the first heat at York University we had a very catholic selection of contestants: a keeper at Chester Zoo (Richard Green, the winner), a fireman from Darlington (Paul Elliott), an English lecturer at Hull College of Higher Education (Albert Preston), and a barmaid from Harrogate (Diane Harris, a former ballet dancer). We also recorded two programmes in our first military establishment – the Royal Military Academy at Sandhurst. But the location I recall with the greatest pleasure was Trinity College, Dublin, one of the oldest and greatest universities in western Europe. It was our first recording in the Republic of Ireland – but what made it particularly memorable was the fact that the recording coincided with my fiftieth birthday, and Radio Telefis Éireann marked the occasion by presenting me with a handsome facsimile edition of the *Book of Kells*, the beautiful eighth-century illuminated manuscript of the Gospels which resides in Trinity College Library.

1979: Philip Jenkins

In 1979 *Mastermind* achieved the highest-ever viewing figures for a Final (17 million). Also, Dr Philip Jenkins, a 27-year-old at Cambridge leading a research project into the history of English Civil Law from 1790 to 1914, became the youngest champion yet. He had already gained a double first at Clare College in history and Anglo-Saxon, Norse and Celtic studies, and was one of the most intellectually brilliant of all our *Mastermind* winners.

On *Mastermind* he had offered 'The Development of Christianity AD 30–150' for the heats and 'The Vikings in Scotland and Ireland AD 800–1150' for the semi-finals, because he reckoned that these subjects would appeal to Bill Wright and myself at his audition. He was right! The Final was recorded in the Painted Hall of the Royal Naval College, Greenwich – the Navy's university, in effect: a complex of eighteenth-century buildings designed by Sir Christopher Wren as a naval hospital. The historic Painted Hall with its magnificent ceiling is a remarkable work by Sir James Thornhill, celebrating Britain's greatness based on maritime power and the Protestant succession through the 'Glorious Revolution' of 1688. It was a wonderfully prestigious location, but it presented considerable technical problems: the BBC had to indemnify the college for millions of pounds because of possible damage to the paintings from the heat from the lamps, and that made the lighting extraordinarily difficult to organise. The acoustics were appalling, too. But that location really *was* worth it, in the end – it looked absolutely superb on screen.

Philip Jenkins

For the Final, Philip offered a third subject, 'The History of Wales 400–1100' (he had worked out that there was only one contemporary historical source for the early period, the Romano-British sixth-century historian Gildas, which made revision that much easier), and coasted to a decisive win. Soon after his victory he left Britain for Pennsylvania State University, where he is now Professor of History and Religious Studies. Winning the title had no impact on his academic career (in the USA they had never heard of

Mastermind, and were amazed to hear about a TV quiz which didn't give thousands of dollars in prize money), but he says that it was important for his self-image. He enjoyed the experience so much that he was happy to make 'a sentimental pilgrimage' of 4,000 miles from Pennsylvania to take part in the 1982 champions tournament. I treasure the comment he made about the *Mastermind* experience: 'It was taking part in something which was much more than just a television show: it's a national institution – it's rather like inviting a horse to participate in Trooping the Colour!'

1980: Fred Housego

This was Fred Housego's year. But it was also a deeply harrowing year for all of us on the programme because of Bill Wright's increasing incapacity through motor neurone disease, and his death just after the last heats at the University of Aberdeen. There was, indeed, a very touching moment in the Final when Bill Cotton, then Controller BBC1, invited Bill's widow, Sheila, to hand over the trophy on behalf of the BBC.

Memories of that traumatic year tend to focus on the Final itself, which was recorded in the historic Porter Tun Room, built by Whitbreads the brewers in Chiswell Street in London. The massive, unsupported king-post timber roof, completed in 1784, is the major feature of the room. The programme was recorded in the Overlord Room, which was originally the downstairs part of this massive fermenting chamber; it now houses the great Overlord Embroidery which commemorates the invasion of Normandy in 1944.

And what a Final it was! Besides Fred Housego, the other finalists were John Keogh from Bootle, a postgraduate student at Liverpool University; Ingram Wilcox, a civil servant from Bath; and the late Sam Mortimer, a civil servant from Watford. At that time contenders came forward for their general knowledge round in their original order of seating. Fred was in the lead (with 'The Tower of London') after the first round with 18, and had set the overall target at 33 after his general knowledge round. Sam Mortimer, going last on 14, started well, getting seventeen of his first questions right to reach 31; but he failed to get any of the remaining six questions right (such was his speed of response that he got through twenty-three questions!) and ended on 31, to a loud murmur of sympathy from the audience.

But it was Fred Housego who claimed the limelight. Within a month of his win he starred on *This Is Your Life*. Eamonn Andrews, heavily disguised in deerstalker, beard and dark glasses, pretended to be an overseas traveller at Waterloo who was to be driven by Fred in his taxi to the LWT Television Theatre. Fred proceeded to tell the disguised Eamonn all about the landmarks on his journey across the river. The programme brought together a colourful array of Fred's family, friends and colleagues, whose Cockney humour permeated the whole show and reinforced and reflected the chirpiness of Fred Housego himself. I had the pleasure of being invited along to give my own tribute:

> It was the fairy-tale Final of all time. The whole nation was wanting Fred to win, and the whole nation didn't think he could make it – and I was one of them.

Fred had become a household name overnight and a new career in the media beckoned. He had said that his win on *Mastermind* would be a 'nine-day wonder' and that he would soon become an ordinary taxi-driver again. But in no time at all he went on to become a broadcaster in his own right. On radio he was soon appearing in Ned Sherrin's *Week Ending* and revelling in its bantering, combative atmosphere. He then became a regular team member on Richard Baker's Monday morning radio programme *Start the Week* (typically, he quipped that it was only because he was expected to take all the participants home afterwards in his taxi). In the spring of 1981 he was invited to do road reports on Michael Aspel's new *Six O'Clock Show* on ITV. In the summer he made a series of history programmes for BBC2 called *History on Your Doorstep*. Much as he enjoyed it, he now feels he wasn't quite ready to undertake such a series, and wishes he had come to it rather later, when he had learned more of the basic skills of presenting and interviewing. He then worked for Radio London as a morning news presenter and presenter of weekend live music programmes. He went back to the cabs for a while; then in 1991 he became a traffic correspondent and feature presenter on LBC, and presenter and producer of *The Comedy Hour*. He now presents a mid-week live phone-in programme, *Through the Night*, for

**Fred Housego, with wife Pat and daughters
Kate and Abigail**

four nights a week on LNT 1152 and continues to do *The Comedy Hour* at weekends.

For Fred Housego, more than any other Masterminder, becoming champion meant a real change in his career and his life. And yet he very nearly missed out on his great chance: just before his first-round heat was due to be transmitted he collapsed with a suspected heart attack, and ended up watching himself on television from a bed in an Intensive Care Unit. It turned out that he was suffering from pericarditis and he recovered just in time to take part in his semi-final.

In 1995 Fred made the headlines again, but not in a way he would have chosen. He was charged with driving a car while over the limit. He pleaded guilty, apologised without reservation and presented no mitigating circumstances in his defence. His main concern was that his highly publicised fall from grace might reflect badly on the taxi-driving profession as a whole. He lost his licence for a year. On the day he got it back (30 May 1996) he went straight to the Public Carriage Office in Penton Street for his taxi-driver's badge. It could have been withheld, requiring him to take 'the knowledge' again; instead he was given his old badge back, with a severe warning about being 'a fit and proper person' in future. It was a distressing and, to Fred, deeply shameful episode, but he comported himself with great dignity throughout.

Looking back on it all, Fred – still the same cheery, happy-go-lucky Fred Housego – says:

> *People still say to me, 'Aren't you a bit disillusioned that you're not doing so much television now?' Not for a minute! Not a second do I regret. It has all been great fun. And I say to anybody who wins* Mastermind, *'Get out there, grab it with both hands – the bus doesn't come past twice.'*

Fred Housego was the first of a long line of memorable champions in the 1980s. I look back on them all with affection and respect: Leslie Grout (1981), Christopher Hughes (1983), Margaret Harris (1984), Ian Meadows (1985), Jennifer Keaveney (1986), Dr Jeremy Bradbrooke (1987), David Beamish (1988) and brave Mary-Elizabeth Raw (1989) struggling against the ravages of multiple sclerosis to come out on top. Each of them was special, each was different. Each earned a place in the *Mastermind* hall of fame.

1981: Leslie Grout

Leslie Grout, from Windsor, a teacher at Ottershaw Middle School in Surrey, had six applications to appear on *Mastermind* turned down because we were always inundated with more applications from teachers than we could use. It was not that Leslie was rejected because he was considered to be inadequate and not worth auditioning; it was just that we could have filled the programme a hundred times over, on paper, with young-to-middle-aged, personable, likeable, well-educated, well-informed teachers of similar background from the south of England – just like Leslie himself. He eventually decided to have one last try, for the 1981 series. This time he was auditioned (by Roger Mackay) and accepted, and went on to win the championship.

Leslie Grout was Windsor through and through. He had been born there and had grown up in the shadow of two great historic buildings, Windsor Castle and St George's Chapel. His father, Bill Grout, worked for the Crown Estates on Windsor Great Park for fifty-one

Leslie Grout

years. Leslie had become a member of the Friends of the Chapel, a worldwide body of people who supported the Chapel financially; in 1973 he had become a Sunday lay steward as well, which encouraged him to start an extensive library of books on the Chapel.

The specialised subjects he offered were St George's Chapel, Windsor (of course) and, less predictably, 'Burial Grounds of

London'; he had been going round the classic London cemeteries like Highgate and Kensal Green and Norwood for years, taking pictures, long before they became 'fashionable'. Roger Mackay's reaction was 'Well, it's different, isn't it?', and Leslie thinks that this was probably the deciding factor in his acceptance.

In the heats he defeated Phillida Grantham, who was then a youth worker in Earl's Court and was offering 'Wines of Europe'. He only just squeaked through the semi-finals with his 'Burial Grounds of London', winning on a pass count. In the Final he was able to revert to St George's Chapel for his specialised subject, and held off a stiff challenge by Ian Barton, head of the classics department at St David's College, Lampeter, who was taking 'Roman Emperors of the First and Second Centuries' (Ian was to have a second go at the title, in 1995, but then he would get no further than the semi-finals).

Leslie's win on *Mastermind* qualified him to represent the UK in *International Mastermind 1982*, which was recorded in New Zealand. He won handsomely with 'Windsor Castle' as his specialised subject – the first UK champion to win the international title – thereby ensuring that the next year's international competition would be held in Britain.

Leslie immediately joined the Mastermind Club and has been a regular attender at annual functions ever since; apart from Patricia Owen and Rosemary James he was the only champion to be a 'regular' member of the Club until Gavin Fuller (1993) and champion-to-be Kevin Ashman (1995). In 1987 Leslie won the Club quiz, the Magnum, the first champion to do so. Of his outstanding record on the programme, he says modestly that *Mastermind* has not made his fortune, but has made him very fortunate. It is a very felicitous summation.

1982: Sir David Hunt, Champion of Champions

This was a sort of intercalary year for *Mastermind*. It had been decided to switch the schedule of transmissions from late autumn to early spring (from October 1981 to January 1983) and, since 1981 had been the tenth series, it seemed a good idea to fill the empty year and celebrate the tenth anniversary with a tournament featuring the first

Sir David Hunt, Champion of Champions

ten Mastermind champions (six men and four women) in a special *ludus ludorum*. It took the form of three programmes shown on consecutive evenings over the May Bank Holiday weekend: two qualifying 'heats' with five champions in each, with the best two from each heat going forward to a Final. And just to prove that they were true polymaths, the champions all had to offer different subjects from the ones they had chosen in their earlier appearances.

All three programmes were recorded in the handsome Old Library in London's Guildhall. There had been a library at Guildhall since medieval times, established with money left by two wealthy City merchants – William Berry, and the even more celebrated Mayor of London, Dick Whittington. The present building dates back only to the 1870s; a stained-glass window commemorates the introduction of printing into England and depicts William Caxton at his printing press.

In the first heat the winners were Philip Jenkins, the 1979 champion (who had flown back from Pennsylvania for the occasion), taking 'The History of England AD 500–800', and Sir David Hunt (1977), taking 'The History of Cyprus'. The winners of the second heat were Rosemary James (1978), taking 'Norse Mythology', and Patricia Owen (1973), taking 'The Art and Architecture of Constantinople AD 330–1453'.

In the Final, Philip Jenkins, who was now taking 'European History AD 500–800', scored a first-round 17 for a 1-point lead over Rosemary James, who was offering 'The Life and Works of Frederick William Rolfe'; David Hunt ('Alexander the Great') lagged in third place on 13, a point ahead of Patricia Owen ('The Life and Works of Giuseppe Verdi'). In the general knowledge round Philip, Rosemary and Patricia levelled out at 23, while David Hunt surged effortlessly past the winning post with 28. It had been a most enjoyable contest; and all the participants, I believe, were content with a result which left three of them in a triple tie for second place.

I must confess that I had harboured a private suspicion at the time that the BBC was using the occasion as an excuse to end *Mastermind*: ten series, and a champions' tournament – all very neat. But I was wrong. *Mastermind* still had many years to go and there was a long gallery of champions still to come, starting with the second 'people's champion', Christopher Hughes.

1983: Christopher Hughes

Christopher Hughes was a London Transport Underground train-driver on the Piccadilly line (Cockfosters to Heathrow). He was a bachelor, living with his 77-year-old Scots mother at Ponders End in Middlesex (she died in 1993 at the age of eighty-seven). I have always found Chris the most enigmatic of all the *Mastermind* champions: a big, burly man, brimming with intelligence and unfulfilled potential. *Mastermind* certainly affected his life – and not necessarily for the better.

Chris was an only child and had an unsettled childhood. His father had a variety of jobs after the war, which resulted in frequent changes of home until he joined London Transport as a cleaner on London Underground. Chris went to junior school in Enfield, where he passed his '11-plus' without difficulty. His stay at Enfield Grammar School was much less comfortable; he became a serious under-achiever and more or less absconded at the age of fifteen. He was shunted to Tottenham Technical College to sit his 'O' levels, which he duly passed in maths, physics, chemistry and English language.

He considers his education 'a disaster'. He feels that Enfield Grammar School (and the education system) had no interest in him because he was living just outside the boundaries of the catchment area: 'I was in a perpetual state of war with the school authorities – perhaps I was a bit of a devil. The only intellectual challenge was arguing with them.'

As a boy, Chris had always wanted to be a train-driver: 'My first memories of steam are looking over the side of my pram in Welwyn Garden City when I was eighteen months old. We used to cross the railway tracks on the way to the shops, and I can still remember seeing the last Ivatt Atlantics on the Cambridge Buffet Express.' At the age of sixteen he got himself a job as an engine cleaner with the Eastern Region of British Railways, at Hornsey, and within a month he was promoted to fireman. That got him on to the footplate just in time to do a bit of shovel-swinging – at one time, under training, he handled the throttle of *The Flying Scotsman*. But by the summer of 1965 the Age of Steam in Chris's sector came to an end (it officially ended in Britain in August 1968). In 1974 he went to work as an Underground train-driver.

He had always had a rare ability to soak up general knowledge, coupled with an excellent retrieval system. In 1973 he had been on Hughie Green's *The Sky's the Limit* in Newcastle and won £100. In 1981, after doing a quiz in *TV Times* (scoring 38 out of 40), he applied for Eamonn Andrews' new satellite-linked *Top of the World* series. He won one week's programme (taking 'The Chicago Gangs During Prohibition' as his specialised subject), but was then knocked

Christopher Hughes

out by an Australian vicar. This whetted his appetite and he applied for *Mastermind*. He was auditioned by Roger Mackay and was accepted for the 1983 series. He was thirty-five years old at the time.

Chris won *Mastermind* with deceptive ease, taking as his specialised subjects 'British Steam Locomotives 1900–63' (of course!) and 'The *Flashman* Novels of George MacDonald Fraser'. He went on to win *International Mastermind 1983* with similar ease. It was the last of the internationals and was recorded in the Sheldonian Theatre, Oxford. Nancy Banks-Smith wrote of Chris in the *Guardian* on 30 August 1983: 'What we have here is definitely a Mycroft Holmes, possibly a Nero Wolfe.'

After winning *Mastermind* and *International Mastermind*, Chris Hughes was a media favourite for a while, just as Fred Housego had been. He told an *Evening Standard* reporter before the Final, 'I would like to think that a *Mastermind* title would be a second chance in life.'

It was, for a time. But it didn't last – nor did his job on the railways. His bosses at London Transport were unimpressed with his win and were not inclined to allow him to make anything of it. He was refused unpaid leave to make a TV documentary on the history of the Great Western Railway for TVS. Instead, he was sent for aptitude tests at the Industrial Training Research Unit at Cambridge; as a result, London Transport insisted that he should become a computer programmer. Chris had no interest in computers (not because he was a technophobe but because he believes that computers are one of the blind alleys of history!), so he turned down the offer (this was splashed in the *Daily Mail* on 10 June 1983). This kind of publicity annoyed London Transport. Offers of broadcasting work were now coming in, and in October 1983 Chris decided that it was time to strike out on his own as a freelance broadcaster.

For a couple of years things went quite well. He was offered a lot of work and proved that he was no slouch at it. In 1985 he presented the fifty-minute documentary on the history of the Great Western Railway for TVS, entitled *Days of Steam: 1835 from Paddington – A Journey with Christopher Hughes*. Chris talked about the old days of the GWR and showed a group of youngsters how the locomotives worked. He told the story of Isambard Kingdom Brunel (whose seated statue can be seen at Paddington Station), who built the first broad-gauge London to Bristol line. It was a fascinating, compelling and wonderfully informative documentary. Byron Rogers wrote of it in the *Sunday Times* on 23 June 1985: 'Last week a new TV star was born . . . It will tell you a lot about television to see what use is made of him in the future.'

Chris also featured on *QED* in a programme subtitled 'The Quest for Mastermind's Brain', narrated by Anthony Clare; it explored how the brain looks and how it works, with Chris investigating the world of brain research. In 1984, with John Junkin, he was one of the team captains on *Loose Ends*, a light-hearted panel game series chaired by Tim Brooke-Taylor. He had a spot for a time on Radio 2 with Ken Bruce. He published a book, *The Great Railway Quiz*, in 1985.

By the end of 1985, however, the media work had dried up. Chris went on the dole for a time before taking on some casual work, driving a van for a local delivery firm. After that he applied for a post as a clerical officer with the National TV Licence Records Office in Islington. But this turned out to be what he considered a 'snooping job' and after three months he resigned.

He was now at a very low ebb. On *Did You See?* in 1987 he said of his *Mastermind* experience:

> *It changed me from being a Tube train-driver grinding up and down the Piccadilly Line to being something of a minor personality in the television world. I wouldn't have missed it for the world. There are some aspects of the aftermath I might have regretted, but you take your chances in this world when they come. Things haven't worked out as well as I might have wished, but I'm not bitter about it. The sad fact remains that at the moment I am unemployed.*

Not long afterwards his mother spotted a small advertisement in the local paper from British Railways, wanting station staff in the Broxbourne area, near Hertford. He applied at once and was accepted back with alacrity as a leading railman, in charge of looking after the station and the booking office at Stamford Hill. Since 1989 he has been a driver again, working on the Paddington to Reading line.

1984: Margaret Harris

Margaret Harris was deputy head teacher at Woolston Comprehensive School in Southampton when she won her championship in 1984; later she became Head of Redbridge Community School in Southampton. She won it with a record score of 38 points – a record she held until 1986, when Jennifer Keaveney broke it, twice, with 40. Yet she had come second in her first-round heat, taking 'The Life and Work of Cecil Rhodes', and only managed to progress further through the semi-final for the highest-scoring losers. She was beaten by Primrose Wood, from Paignton in Devon, a chartered physiotherapist at Stepscross School for Physically Handicapped Children in Torquay, taking 'The Lord Peter Wimsey Novels of Dorothy L. Sayers'. Primrose scored 31, and Margaret 'only' 29.

The result gave Margaret a salutary shock, and she resolved to study much harder for the *repêchage* semi-final at the Royal Military College of Science at Shrivenham, in Oxfordshire, where she was offering 'The Postal History and Philately of Southern Africa'. In the event, such was her concentration that when the staging behind the contestants collapsed during the recording, and a section of the audience disappeared from view, she did not even notice the commotion. The recording had to be stopped and Margaret had to do a retake of some of her questions, but nothing was going to stop her now.

The Final was recorded, for the first time in the history of *Mastermind*, on board an aircraft-carrier, HMS *Hermes*, berthed in the naval dockyard in Portsmouth. *Hermes* was the largest aircraft-carrier in the Royal Navy (28,000 tonnes) and then in the twilight of her career. She had been the command and operational centre for the Falklands Task Force in the spring of 1982. The programme was recorded in the low-ceilinged hangar which had been cleared of aircraft apart from a hulking Sea King helicopter.

There was a somewhat inauspicious start to proceedings: Margaret Harris managed to get herself lost in the maze of the dockyard on her way, which caused us all considerable concern when she failed to turn up on time for the afternoon rehearsal. At the recording itself, John Gilpin, the stage manager, 'did a Magnusson' by welcoming the audience on board HMS *Ark Royal*! And no sooner had the first round begun before the wretched scoring system broke down yet again, after the very first question. Dr Kate Vernon–Parry, a hospital anaesthetist from Carlton Forest near Worksop in Nottinghamshire, had just answered her first question on 'The Life and Works of Arthur Ransome' when the machine jammed; there was a delay of twenty minutes while it was repaired, and I had to dig deep into my stock of feeble jokes to keep the audience diverted if not amused.

Once again, however, Margaret was utterly determined not to let anything deflect her. Concentrating with furious intensity she swept into the lead with an impressive 20 on 'The Life and Work of Cecil Rhodes', comfortably ahead of Dr Richard Joby, a lecturer in economics at Paston Sixth Form College in North Walsham in Norfolk (11); Kate Vernon–Parry (15); and Jill Goodwin, from Southgate in

**Margaret Harris, with MM and Alasdair Milne, then
Director-General of the BBC**

North London, an insurance clerk in the City, who was taking 'The
Lives of Charles II and James II' (18).

There were to be no slip-ups in the general knowledge round
either. Margaret finished off the task to which she had set her mind
with a decisive 18, to reach 38. No one could stay with her, not
even Jill Goodwin, whose 35 would have been enough to win many
another Final.

The recording of the first two semi-finals of the 1996 series at Blackpool Tower Circus provided me with the opportunity to fulfil a secret life-long ambition: to be a ringmaster for an evening (p. 191). It was for publicity purposes only, alas; it would have been fun to record the programmes themselves dressed in scarlet, as a not-so-subtle reminder of my role on *Mastermind*, but wiser counsels prevailed.

Two of the early Masterminders, who both reached the 1973 Final. In the first programme of the series the late Dr Reginald Webster (top), an experienced broadcaster who had been a regular on *Ask Me Another*, taught us a salutary lesson about the importance of researching the specialised questions ourselves, however eminent the question-setter (p. 73). John Coleby (right) became known as The Man Who Nearly Set His Own Questions, on 'The Life and Music of Liszt'(pp. 57–8).

Susan Reynolds, the brilliant young Oxford student who swept into the 1974 Final, only to crash to defeat after a pre-programme accident with the door of her hotel wardrobe (pp. 38-9).

Sue Jenkins, a finalist in the 1977 series. She was a founder-member of the Mastermind Club in 1978, and ran the Club's Mugnum competition from 1985 to 1993 (pp. 213–15).

The 1980 Final, triumphantly won by Fred Housego, was shadowed by the death of the programme's 'onlie begetter' and first producer, Bill Wright. The Caithness Glass trophy was handed over by Bill's widow, Sheila.

The intercalary year for *Mastermind*, 1982, saw a competition between the first ten champions. Left to right: Philip Jenkins (1979), Nancy Wilkinson (1972), Roger Pritchard (1976), Elizabeth Horrocks (1974), Sir David Hunt (1977, the winner), John Hart (1975), Patricia Owen (1973), Leslie Grout (1981), Rosemary James (1978), and Fred Housego (1980).

The gloriously ornate McEwan Hall of the University of Edinburgh was the setting in 1986 for one of our most spectacular finals. It was won with a record-breaking score of 40 by Jennifer Keaveney, a careers officer at the University of Kent (pp. 53–4 and 135). In those days there used to be five finalists – here, from left to right, they are: Michael Formby, Owen Gunnell, Hendy Farquhar-Smith, Jennifer Keaveney and Philip McDonald.

"I'LL TAKE *CARNAL KNOWLEDGE*, PLEASE."

Mastermind has inspired countless cartoons over the years. This simple drawing by Nick Baker in *Punch* in the late 1970s' is one of my favourites – the original now graces the wall of my study.

'I've started, so I'll finish...'

This cartoon by Mac, published in the *Daily Mail* in February 1983, was inspired by the case of the retired sub-postmaster who was jailed for embezzlement only a few days before the programme in which he had taken part was transmitted (p. 93).

Civil servant Gill Doubleday (now Woon), a finalist in 1989, was inspired to apply for *Mastermind* by the example of the 1986 champion, Jennifer Keaveney, who had been a contemporary at school. In the Final she lost to Mary-Elizabeth Raw by a single point.

Chantal Thompson, then a trainee solicitor in Bristol, now working as a solicitor in London, gave an electrifying performance in her general knowledge round in the 1990 Final, which all but won her the title (p. 53). Two other members of the Thompson family are also Masterminders: her father, retired banker Richard Thompson (1977), and her twin brother, Peter, who appeared in the 1994 series (pp. 91–2).

The third semi-final of the 1993 series, recorded in the Assembly Rooms of the City of Bath, became a nightmare for everyone concerned – especially John Colverson and Glenys Davies, pictured here. As a result of a series of long technical breakdowns, and challenges to some of the questions, Glenys was accused of gamesmanship and even of cheating (pp. 180–83).

The 1995 Final, recorded in the General Assembly Hall of the Church of Scotland in Edinburgh, was a resplendent affair, with myself and the contenders wearing dinner jackets. From left to right: Melvyn Kinsey, Kevin Ashman (the winner), MM, Henry Boettinger and Robert Jones.

Bill Wright (1921–80) was the man who, literally, dreamed up the idea of *Mastermind*, with its menacing inquisitorial style and Black Chair.

Bill Wright's 'Girl Friday' was his PA, Mary Craig, with whom he made a string of television quiz programmes before *Mastermind*. It was Mary who thought up the title, and who became famous as the 'Dark Lady' who sat beside me on set as scorer and timekeeper.

Peter Massey had the longest association with *Mastermind* of any of its directors and producers: he directed the pilot programme in September 1971, and was director for five series (1974–78), producer for six series (1985–88 and 1990–91), and executive producer for one series (1992).

Keeping the score on *Mastermind* was always fraught with difficulties in the early years, but my life was revolutionised in the 1992 series by the introduction of a computerised system we called 'Archimedes' (pp. 26–7). Peter Byram (left), special facilities manager at the BBC, devised the new system, which was usually operated by Bob Richardson (right).

For the last fifteen years of *Mastermind* the senior researcher was Dee Wallis (seated); for the last two series she was also the assistant producer. Latterly the team of researchers consisted of Saira Dunnakey (left) and Elizabeth Salmon (right).

One of the historic photographs in the *Mastermind* archives is the picture taken at the inaugural meeting of the Mastermind Club, at the Café Royal in London in September 1978 (p. 203). Fifty-seven founder-members posed for the photograph, with Bill Wright sitting in the Black Chair. All these years later, I can no longer identify all the people in the photograph, alas. The front row is fairly clear, with, from left to right: Margaret Askew (now Sillwood, 1975), Dr David Delvin (1976), Charles Key (1973), Lance Haward (1976), Hazel Martin (now Prowse, 1977), Gena Davies (1975), Alan Blackburn (1975), ??, Sue Jenkins (1977) and Oonagh Lahr (1974). I can also spot other familiar faces, like Margery Elliott (1973), Maggie Garratt (1976), Hugh Merrick (1977), Anna Goldstein (1976), June Maggs (1976), Archie Orton (1973), John George (1978) and Pauline Fowling (now Wells, 1975). But the rest? If any readers can fill in any of the gaps, I would love to hear from them.

The twenty-first series of *Mastermind* was celebrated by a gathering of old and new hands who have worked on the programme over the years. Back row: John Gilpin, Neil Ardley, Bridget Ardley, John Wilson, Dennis Butcher, Doreen Munden, Peter Greenyer, John Wiggins, Elizabeth Salmon, Brenda Haugh. Middle row: Caroline Fletcher, Stephen Potter, Jacky Cox, Damaris Pitcher, Anne Foster, Andrea Conway, Lorraine Silberstein, Andy Dimond, Rosemary Traynor, Alison Woolnaugh, Sally Daley, Geoff Higgs, Martin L. Bell, Debbie Hylton, Cherry Cole, Toni Charlton. Front row, seated: David Mitchell, Mary Craig, Penelope Cowell Doe, MM, Sheila Wright, Roger Mackay, Dee Wallis, Peter Massey.

Tony Dart (1981, 1997) became President of the Mastermind Club in 1990, after salvaging its finances as Treasurer from 1983 to 1989.

Gerald MacKenzie (1974) was President of the Club from 1984 to 1990, and is now Life Honorary Vice-President.

Phillida Grantham (1981, 1995) has been Club Secretary since 1991.

Christine Moorcroft (1988, 1996) has been Editor of *PASS* since 1996.

Margery Elliott (1973) has been one of the Club stalwarts, serving as Secretary (1981–86), Acting Treasurer (1982) and Editor of *PASS* (1988–93).

Paul Henderson (1987) has been Treasurer since 1989.

Peter Chitty (1987) has been Membership Secretary since 1992.

John Widdowson (1977), who died in 1993, was Secretary of the Club from 1986 to 1991.

Three core members of the production team: Julie Corcoran, the last production secretary; David Mitchell (seated), who was director, producer and finally, in 1996–97, producer/director; and John Gilpin, who was assistant stage manager in the pilot programmes in 1971 and the regular floor manager 1982–97.

Mike Jennings, one of our veteran stage hands. He used to be a 'show-working supervisor'; in the latter years of the programme he played a humbler part with undiminished commitment and enthusiasm (p. 233). Mike, for me, represents all the unsung members of the BBC scene crews and camera crews and riggers who worked for the programme.

1985: Ian Meadows

Ian Meadows was dubbed a 'drop-out' when he won the title because, even though he was then working as a hospital driver at Groby Road Hospital in Leicester, he had taken a degree in history at Trinity College, Cambridge. Like Chris Hughes, Ian was a champion who had never achieved the heights of which he was capable – except when he won *Mastermind*. He is also the only Masterminder I know of who experimented with hypnosis to improve his chances on the programme!

Ian was born in Leicester, the son of a pattern-maker. He was always a loner: a loner at school, and a loner at university. He had worked his way through comprehensive school to earn a Cambridge entrance which entitled him to a place at Trinity College, the grandest and the largest college in Cambridge. He felt very out of place, and although he worked hard to achieve the kind of degree in history which would offer him the chance of taking a Ph.D. and becoming an academic, when he came to his final exams he failed to get the good 2:1 which would have opened the door to that sort of future. With that, he felt that his life had collapsed; furthermore, when he came to thinking about other jobs which might be available, he realised that all his education had not in fact equipped him to do anything in the wider world.

It meant ten years of drifting from job to job, always trying to develop a research project (on 'The History of Smoking') which would revive his dream of becoming an academic. He worked as a hospital porter, then as a museum cataloguer, but all the time he felt that his inner drive for life, for success, was running out. Finally, after a particularly barren period, both financially and emotionally, he returned to the place where he realised he had been happiest – working as a porter at Groby Road Hospital in Leicester. And there, in Leicester, he found something like peace of mind: an acceptance, at least, of the renunciation of his cherished illusion about an academic career. Hospital portering might be a career cul-de-sac for some, but paradoxically Ian found it acceptable. He found room for recreation in the hospital grounds, he had time to learn to drive and move to van-driving, and this gave him even more time to himself, which he filled by reading voraciously, to swot for quizzes, to improve his mind (or cram it with useless information, depending on one's point of view). 'Without the stress of striving for unattainable goals,' he wrote to me, 'life drifted by quite pleasantly.'

It was in that fairly relaxed state of mind that he applied for the 1985 series of *Mastermind*. He had been interested in quizzes at school but had shrunk from trying to break into the all-conquering *University Challenge* team at Trinity College when he was there. He was accepted for *Mastermind* at his first audition: as a hospital van-driver he felt that, to some at least, he might have the novelty value of some of the eighteenth-century 'peasant poets' like John Clare and Robert Burns. He worked very hard at his specialised subjects – 'The English Civil War 1642–47' and 'The History of Astronomy/Cosmology up to 1700' (a relic of a course he had done at university on the history of science). But the harder he worked, the more nervous he became. This was his first serious quiz and, with his Cambridge débâcle in mind, he feared that the whole thing might be a disaster. At the suggestion of his brother-in-law, a dentist, he decided to try hypnosis. Ian doesn't know whether the hypnosis sessions helped him or not, but at the time he felt better because he was doing something positive about his mental state, not simply being its victim.

Whatever the cause, Ian skated through his heat and the semifinals with relative ease. The Final was recorded in Cambridge, at Robinson College, and should have been tailor-made for Ian. Robinson College, the newest of Cambridge's academic institutions, is the archetypal story of local boy makes good. Sir David Robinson, the founder, left school to work in his father's bicycle shop and went on to amass a huge fortune in the motor and television trades. But for Ian it was not a happy homecoming: he no longer knew anyone there, and the place had memories of loneliness, stress, and above all, failure. But he also knew that, on form, he was the favourite.

It was the thirteenth Final of *Mastermind* – and for Ian it turned out to be lucky at last. He was now reverting to 'The English Civil War 1642–47'. He was as taut as a coiled spring throughout, and when I announced his winning score of 30, he thumped the arms of the Black Chair; later he actually kissed the Caithness Glass trophy when it was presented to him. Some commentators did not like this kind of behaviour, and compared it to the aftermath of a Cup Final;

Ian Meadows, with MM

but, knowing what it meant to Ian Meadows at that moment, it is easy to understand:

> *Well, what should I have done? Custom seems to dictate that winners look sheepish and, in some cases, more nervous, now that the contest is over. For the first time I had the leisure to think about all these people watching – well, I had to do something. I suppose I fell back on to the stereotypes of male triumphalism . . .*

But for Ian Meadows there was to be disappointment. His victory did not give his career the new kick-start for which he had hoped. He had the chance, admittedly – he was offered the opportunity of doing his Ph.D. at Leicester University; however, the authorities wanted him to do something on his area of specialised expertise on *Mastermind* (the Civil War), while he wanted to do 'The History of Smoking'. Consequently he vacillated, and meanwhile their interest cooled. It seemed to him a parable of his life.

He went in for other quizzes, doing very well but never quite well enough, always just missing out on the top prize. And that, too, he felt, became a parable of his life.

In 1989 he took a postgraduate Certificate of Education and worked as a supply teacher for a couple of years, but realised that he did not enjoy teaching. In 1991 he turned his back on classrooms and joined the Inland Revenue in Nottingham, working in the pensions schemes office. The job mainly involved working from files, on his own rather than as part of a team. The job, he says, suits his studious and rather unsociable temperament; whenever he feels bored or dissatisfied with the job he thinks of going back to teaching and, hey presto, the fit passes.

The story of Ian Meadows and his victory in *Mastermind* has had no happy ending, alas:

> *I would like, at this midpoint of life, to be able to look back at a soaring edifice of achievement. Instead, I can only see a glittering but slender minaret, striking up through a thick blanket of obscure, low cloud which covers everything else. On a day-to-day basis, life is okay; it is only when I reflect on it (as you have invited me to do) that I find that the whole thing could have been managed rather better.*

1986: Jennifer Keaveney

There was a major extension for *Mastermind* in 1986: the number of contenders was increased from forty-eight to sixty-four, involving twenty-two programmes – sixteen heats, five semi-finals and a Final. It produced the first blind contender to appear on *Mastermind*: Leslie Pye, who has been blind from birth, the Head of Braille Book

Production at the National Library for the Blind at Stockport. His heat was recorded in the Royal Northern College of Music in Manchester; he took 'The Life and Works of Johannes Brahms' as his specialised subject, and scored 28 to come second to an eventual finalist, Michael Formby. After he retired, Les reappeared on *Mastermind* in 1996 at the age of seventy-two with his guide-dog, Jonathan, and took 'Manchester United to 1968'; on that occasion he came third, with an overall score of 26, to a future semi-finalist, Margaret Thomas.

The year also produced a really memorable winner. Jennifer Keaveney was born in Orpington in Kent, the eldest of three daughters. Her mother was a teacher and school librarian; her father, Bernard Downing, was a civil servant who would later take part in *Mastermind* himself. It was, not unexpectedly, a home which was full of books and where reading was a way of life. Jennifer read voraciously – anything she could lay her hands on.

Jennifer attended Newstead Wood Girls' School, where she took part in her first quiz: she captained the school team in a 'Top of the Form' competition to raise money for a local charity; another member of the team would also become a *Mastermind* Finalist – Gill Doubleday (now Woon), in 1989. From school Jennifer went to the University of Hull to read English; she was a member of the college's *University Challenge* team which reached the semi-finals in 1978. It was her first experience of appearing on television, but she found the atmosphere of *University Challenge* – with its audience of vociferous and partisan students – less of an aid to concentration than the solemn hush of a *Mastermind* recording. At Hull she also met her future husband, Arthur Keaveney, who is now a senior lecturer in classics at the University of Kent at Canterbury and a well-known classical historian.

After leaving Hull, Jennifer worked as a trainee librarian at Chelsea College, London, before returning north for a year to take a postgraduate diploma in librarianship at Newcastle. By this time Arthur had obtained a lectureship at the University of Kent, and after their wedding in 1980 Jennifer started work as a library assistant there. Four years later she changed direction and moved sideways to become a careers information officer. She still works in the university's Careers Advisory Service.

Jennifer had enjoyed watching the programme for a number of

Jennifer Keaveney

years, pitting her wits from her armchair against the contestants on the box. Her real reason for applying, however, was curiosity – not to see how she would get on in the programme 'for real' (she never expected to get that far), but to see something of the way the programme was made. She was auditioned by Peter Massey, and remembers her chagrin at failing to get one of the literary test questions right: the author of *The Man of Mode* – a play she had studied at university (George Etherege).

She chose her specialised subjects ('The Life and Works of Elizabeth Gaskell' and 'The Novels of Edith Nesbit', of *The Railway Children* fame) because she had enjoyed reading them before and knew she would enjoy them enough to study them in the depth required. She did a great deal of preparation on her specialised subjects – reading, making notes, composing questions and rehearsing them (with Arthur entering into the role of question-master with relish). She decided she would just have to trust to luck for the general knowledge questions.

I have already described her spectacular win in the Final, when she broke the scoring record for the second time with 40. Winning *Mastermind* did not change Jennifer's life, although she says that it made it extremely interesting for a while. She became involved with one or two other quizzes: with one of the runners-up, Philip McDonald, she took part with the winner and runner-up of *Brain of Britain* in *Masterbrain*, and the two Masterminders came first and second; she also took part in a Radio Kent quiz against the winner of *The Krypton Factor*, which she won. She was invited to the 'Women of the Year' lunch at the Savoy in London, and returned to her old school to present 'A' level prizes and certificates (including one to her younger sister, Alison).

It is a pleasant irony that Jennifer's father, Bernard Downing, appeared on the programme some years later, in 1992; he is now a freelance lecturer in adult education, from Maidstone in Kent. In fact he had first applied for the programme *before* his daughter appeared in the 1986 series; it was only on his third application that Bernard was auditioned and finally accepted. Jennifer was in the audience in the Historic Dockyard Church in Chatham to see her father try his luck with 'The Life and Reign of George II'. He did well, but not quite well enough to defeat Richard Ford, director of a greetings-card company and a marketing consultant in London, who went on to that year's Final.

1987: Jeremy Bradbrooke

Folklore has it that the winner of the fifteenth series of *Mastermind*, Dr Jeremy Bradbrooke, a GP in Trowbridge in Wiltshire, wore Union Jack underpants for luck; and he needed it, because the 1987 series attracted the largest number of applications ever received – a phenomenal total of nearly 8,000 aspirant Masterminders. About 500 people were auditioned to find the 64 contenders required.

It was a series of tremendously high scoring and unforgettable moments. It was memorable for, among other highlights, the husband-and-wife head-to-head between Inspector Paul Hancock and Christine Hancock in Heat 12, which Paul won on a play-off against his wife.

Heat 9 in the series was the 250th edition of *Mastermind*, won by Margaret Spiller. To celebrate that milestone there was an 'unscheduled' *Mastermind* for good measure – a brilliant April Fool's spoof written by Stephen Fry for four actors and recorded 'for real' on the same evening as Heat 9 at Christ's Hospital School, Horsham, in its modern Elizabethan-style theatre-in-the-round. The spoof relied for its effect on a completely deadpan performance; only towards the end did the uneasy suspicion begin to arise that all was not what it seemed.

The programme purported to come from the Hayek Institute of Intercultural Humanist Studies at Brandiston, in Norfolk; and in honour of the 250th programme it presented 'four of our faithful reservists who wait in the wings in case we have a last-minute cancellation – this programme is theirs'. They were, allegedly: a plumber from Fant, Hampshire, 'Jim Maynard' (actor John Peters), taking 'The Eighty Years' War'; a classical librarian from Plymhead, West Sussex, 'Margaret Exall' (actress Janet Whiteside), taking 'The Life and Novels of C. P. Armitage'; the retired Member of Parliament for North Hayden, 'Stephen Dyer' (actor Alan Foss), taking 'Australasian Fauna'; and a fashion consultant from London, 'Peter Lovering' (actor John Hudson), taking 'The Life and Work of Karl Gloping', the physicist.

Its brilliance lay in the way in which it caught unerringly the style of the questions and my own rather pompous mannerisms:

[on 'Australasian Fauna']
'What is unusual about a Firebush beetle?'
'It has eight legs.'
'Yes . . .?'
'It's an arachnid.'
*'A member of the spider family – correct. When was the last
   higgerdoe seen in New Zealand?'*

'In the 1890s.'

'Can you be more specific?'

'February 1896.'

'Correct.'

[On 'The Life and Work of Karl Gloping']

'What aspect of differential spectroscopy in MASER emissions led to Gloping's theory of unrelated probability in quantised wavicle transformations?'

'The Seager leakage of alpha particles.'

'Er – correct. What labour-saving device did Gloping install in his house in Cambridge in 1938?

'A home-made microwave.'

'Correct – made from old radar dishes, believe it or not.'

Unerringly, in the general knowledge rounds, Stephen Fry also homed in on my now-legendary weakness over French pronunciation:

'Which novel opens with the words, "Le vingt-quatre février mille huit cent quinze, la vigie de Notre-Dame-de-la-Garde signala le troit-mâts le Pharaon, venant de Smyrne, Trieste et Naples"?'

'I'm sorry, could you repeat that, please?'

'Certainly – stop the watch. Which novel opens with the words, "Le vingt-quatre février mille huit cent quinze, la vigie de Notre-Dame-de-la-Garde signala le troit-mâts le Pharaon, venant de Smyrne, Trieste et Naples"? Start the watch.'

'The Three Musketeers.'

'No, The Count of Monte Cristo.'

The result (as if it mattered!) was a win for 'Margaret Exall' after some 'final adjustments to the scores, taking into account the number of passes'. It was enormous fun to make and I think it ought to have become one of the great BBC classic April Fools, like Richard Dimbleby's 'spaghetti trees'. Unfortunately it was transmitted, unannounced, in the Terry Wogan show on 1 April as a special, and in consequence most of our regular *Mastermind* audience missed it. Those who tuned in to Terry Wogan that evening were either baffled or annoyed. The BBC Duty Office received nearly a hundred calls from irate viewers complaining that they had missed their favourite programme and that it was all a scandalous waste of their licence fee. Some had been genuinely fooled by it: one wrote in asking for details of the novels of C. P. Armitage so that he could read them for himself, while another wanted to establish a family relationship with the winner, 'Margaret Exall', because she had the same name.

I recall clearly all those who took part in it – in particular, the actor who took the part of 'Stephen Dyer' ('Australasian Fauna'): the late Alan Foss. Unbeknownst to me, he had already applied for *Mastermind* proper in his own right as a polymath, and his name was working its way through the machinery which would distil 64 *bona fide* contenders from the list of 5,000 applicants.

When he appeared on *Mastermind* proper in 1988, his heat was recorded at Hatfield Polytechnic on the same evening as his sister, Mary Hunt, was taking part in another heat, taking 'The Silent Films of the 1920s' as her special subject. Alan took as his specialised subject 'The Life and Works of P. G. Wodehouse' – 'Plum' Wodehouse. In my mind's eye he seemed to become the spoof 'Stephen Dyer' again, taking a huge, infectious, plummy pleasure in absurd Wodehousian names like Market Snodsbury and Battling Bilson.

Alan won his heat with ease and went on to the semi-finals. This time he took 'The Life and Works of Frank Richards'; and as he settled, comfortably ample, into the Black Chair, he seemed to become not 'Stephen Dyer' but Billy Bunter himself: all that chubbily cherubic delight in the ridiculous names of his friends at Greyfriars, like Samson Quincy Fffield; all those dismayed, naughty-boy responses when he got a question wrong.

Alan came fourth in his semi-final. He died a year later, and I was privileged to deliver the address at his memorial service at the 'Actors' Church' (St Paul's, Covent Garden) in London. He had done *Mastermind* proud. His proper appearances had been no spoof; he had always taken his enthusiasms seriously – his encyclopedic knowledge of cricket, his wide reading, his skill at doing *The Times* crossword but, above all, his enjoyment of the theatre trade which he had practised with such amiable lack of theatricality.

But back to 1987. Like so many other people, Dr Jeremy Bradbrooke had enjoyed watching *Mastermind* from the security of an armchair, until one of his daughters suggested that he ought to enter

Jeremy Bradbrooke

the competition himself. From then on, the idea of Daddy appearing on *Mastermind* became a bit of a family joke; he certainly never expected to reach the Final. The subjects he chose were distinctly warlike: 'The Franco-Prussian War 1870–71', 'The Anglo-American War 1812–15', and 'The Crimean War', because he had always been fascinated by history. He enjoyed the studying involved; it gave him a good excuse to indulge his hobby, and it made a change from work. So that he could continue his revising between house-calls, he made a cassette of relevant facts and figures to which he could listen in his car.

In Jeremy's heat, which was recorded at the College of St Mark and St John in Plymouth, he defeated Joan Bridgman, a lecturer in English from High Littleton near Bath, taking 'The Life and Works of Samuel Beckett'. Joan ruefully recalls how one can go to pieces in the general knowledge round. She was asked a question on London to which the answer was 'County Hall'. Joan worked in London, she frequently passed the place, she had friends who worked there, it is an imposing edifice on the banks of the Thames – yet she could not name it. 'It's too easy,' she thought to herself, 'they can't possibly mean that.' From then on she could think of nothing but County Hall, and passed on her last six questions. 'The ability to forget a mistake, to put it behind you instantly and move on to the next problem with no looking back, is a vital skill and a salutary lesson I have never forgotten. The quiz is not just a test of memory and instant recall; it is ultimately a test of coolness and of not caring too much.'

In the next heat, also recorded in Plymouth, we saw another potential champion go to pieces: Geoffrey Dearnley, the retired headmaster of the village school at Woodbury Salterton, near Exeter. He had been tremendous in the rehearsals, and everyone thought he was a certain winner. In his specialised round, however, he simply froze on the very first question and could not utter a word. I stopped the recording and started the round again, but by then his confidence had been destroyed and he scored only 6. In his general knowledge round he came storming back with 17, but the match had been won and lost long before then.

Jeremy's semi-final was recorded in the ancient tranquillity of Lincoln Cathedral with its superb Bishop's Eye Window, its frame filled with flowing tracery and surviving remnants of medieval glass. It is a place steeped in history: the Cathedral's origins go all the way back to William the Conqueror, 900 years ago; early Parliaments took place in the chapter house; and the medieval library contains one of the only four surviving contemporary exemplars of Magna Carta. The recordings took place in the centre of the Cathedral, at the crossing of the great transept and the nave; and the abiding memory of them is that it was bitterly cold. Cold? It was freezing in there. I only hope that Jeremy's Union Jack underpants were thermal; indeed, one of the contenders went back to his hotel and put his pyjamas on under his suit to avoid hypothermia! It was so cold that the pace of the whole programme slowed down and became sluggish – even my question rate, as I felt my mouth going numb. The producer, Peter Massey, had elected to position himself inside the Cathedral, in the chancel, because the scanner van was so far away; he became so paralysed with cold (he claims!) that he was incapable of communicating with me via my earpiece.

It was the first time that *Mastermind* had been recorded in a cathedral, and the lighting for such a huge place presented a real challenge to our engineering manager, Dennis Butcher. The reason we were there at all was that one of the 1986 finalists (Michael Formby, from Aintree, a chartered surveyor with Liverpool City Council) had taken 'The History and Architecture of Lincoln Cathedral' as his specialised subject in the semi-finals, and as a result the Dean and Chapter were inspired to invite us to record two of our semi-finals there the following year.

Jeremy edged to a close win with 'The Anglo-American War 1812–15' to move forward to the Final, which was held in Britannia Royal Naval College in Dartmouth. Although we were on *terra firma*, technically we were on board ship, on the quarter-deck of HMS *Dartmouth*; in fact the Edwardian hall was built some eighty years ago as part of the permanent shore-based college which replaced the old wooden-hulled training ships which were moored in the River Dart.

Once again there were five finalists, and on previous form the main threat to Jeremy was going to be Mike Billson, a relief milk roundsman from Oxford. He had won his heat with 'The American Indian Wars 1860–90' and his semi-final with 'The Life of Manfred von Richthofen 1892–1918'. Informal in jeans and shirt, he was now reverting to 'The American Indian Wars 1860–90'. Jeremy, who was the only one of the Finalists to offer a new subject ('The Crimean War 1854–56'), was equal to the challenge, however, and won by a couple of points on 33.

1988: David Beamish

Anyone called David Beamish must have grown heartily sick of being called 'my beamish boy' all his life and hearing coy references to slaying the Jabberwock and choruses of 'O frabjous day! Callooh!

Callay!' But there was something undoubtedly beamish about David when he turned up for his *Mastermind* heat in the Keep of Colchester Castle to take part in his first-ever quiz. There was an appealing diffidence about him, an air of vulnerability, underlined by his engaging habit of hanging half a question-mark on the end of his answers, as if he doubted that he could possibly be right.

David appeared on *Mastermind* as a clerk in the House of Lords — his first post after leaving St John's College, Cambridge, with a degree in law. During the series he became the Establishment Officer responsible for personnel matters; he was promoted to Clerk of the Journals (1993–95), and is now Their Lordships' Principal Clerk of Committees.

There was a major change in the format of the programme in 1988 — the order in which contenders returned to the Chair for the general knowledge round was altered, in order to reflect the state of play in the programme. Instead of doing the second round in their original seating order, they were now called forward in the ascending order of their first-round scores, which meant that the leader in the first round would go last in the second. It ensured that the game would not be finished as a contest if the first contender were to be so far ahead after the start of the specialised round that none of the others could possibly catch up.

David had been badgered into taking part by his mother. He had been interested in *Mastermind* since watching the first series as a student in Cambridge, where he had been a near-miss for the St John's College team on *University Challenge*. From then on his mother urged him to apply for *Mastermind*. David resisted the suggestion because he had no particular subject on which he felt himself to be any kind of expert. In 1982, however, the BBC showed a serial about the life of Nancy Astor, which inspired David to read a biography of her; it then occurred to him that her life could make a good *Mastermind* specialised subject.

He applied for the 1987 series, but was rejected after an audition and decided not to reapply. In the following year, however, he was telephoned and asked to come for another interview: a new batch of twenty questions had been prepared for that year's interviews, and Peter Massey wanted to check the standard by trying them out on some 'near misses' from the previous year before using them on new applicants. David agreed, and this time he was accepted immediately.

David Beamish

David worked very hard on his specialised subject. He coupled his reading of books about Nancy Astor with copious note-taking, including, for example, a chronological list of events of her life. He also wrote out some potential questions and their answers. These he later recorded on cassettes, leaving a short pause before the answers, so that when he played the tape he could attempt the answer before it was given on the tape. He played the tapes again as he drove to Colchester for his first heat.

By the time he arrived in the Keep of Colchester Castle he was clearly in a Jabberwock-slaying mood. It was just as well. It was an extremely high-scoring heat – all the contenders scored 30 or more – but David simply slaughtered the opposition. Sitting in the first seat he established a commanding lead with his specialised subject, and in the second round he administered the *coup de grâce* with a crushing 39, all but equalling Jennifer Keaveney's two-year-old record.

He had deliberately avoided having any passes, and this was to stand him in good stead in his semi-final, which was recorded in the New Hall of Middlesex Polytechnic at Trent Park. This time he was taking 'The British Royal Family 1714–1910' because he had read and enjoyed biographies of Queen Victoria and Edward VII. Once again he was up against stern opposition, in particular Mark Turner, a barrister at the Manchester bar, who was offering 'The Life and Times of Edward II 1284–1327'. At the halfway stage he held a lead of two points with 18. But in the general knowledge round, Mark Turner put in a dazzling 20 to set the target at 36 – normally quite enough to earn a place in the Final. David was last to the Chair, and now his determination not to pass paid off again. With his very last question he squeezed past the winning post with 37 points, but it had been a very close-run thing.

In the Final, which was recorded in the MacRobert Arts Centre of the University of Stirling, he still did not have it all his own way. At the halfway stage he was being headed by Margaret Fleming, a tax inspector with the Inland Revenue in Brighton. She was taking 'The Life and Novels of Virginia Woolf', and scored 19 – a point ahead of David Beamish, who had reverted to 'The Life and Times of Nancy Astor 1879–1964'. The other three finalists were not far behind: Roy Bailey, from Great Shefford near Newbury in Berkshire, a film and video producer with his own production company; Philip Gray, from Prescot on Merseyside, a planning manager with Pilkington Reinforcements; and Barry McCartney, from Sudbury in Suffolk, a teacher at Stoke-by-Nayland Middle School, whom David had already defeated in the heats.

In the general knowledge round, with the contenders coming forward in the ascending order of their specialised subject scores, Roy Bailey reached 29. Philip Gray then set the early target at 32. Barry McCartney, his eyes tightly closed throughout in concentration, added only 11 for a total of 27. David Beamish, diffident as ever but determined as ever, put in his challenge with 17 to raise the target to 35. It was now up to Margaret Fleming to make her bid for glory, but she stumbled over some of the early questions and could add only 14 to fall short on 33.

So the 'beamish boy' won the title; what's more, he had completed all his six sessions in the Black Chair without a single pass. As *Mastermind* champion he took part in *Masterbrain*, on which the winner and runner-up of *Brain of Britain* play a special challenge match with the champion and runner up of *Mastermind*. He took 'The Life and Works of Beatrix Potter' as his specialised subject, and he and Margaret Fleming came first and second respectively. Since then he has 'retired' from quiz contests, apart from charity team quizzes and the annual quiz of the Surrey Association of Church Bell Ringers!

Winning the title brought David little in terms of public recognition, although Mrs Thatcher invited him to a reception at 10 Downing Street (she 'didn't exactly speak' to him, however). David was also invited to the North of England Open Air Museum at Beamish, in County Durham, to launch a restored Blackpool tramcar which had been built in 1901, and ceremoniously broke a bottle of Beamish stout over the bumper. But for him the main effect of winning *Mastermind* was that it boosted his self-confidence: if he was ever faced with a daunting prospect, he would say to himself, 'If I can survive *Mastermind* unscathed and undefeated, I can do that!'

1989: Mary-Elizabeth Raw

The 1980s ended for *Mastermind* as they had begun, with a tremendous burst of publicity for a new champion: Mary-Elizabeth Raw, a veterinary surgeon from Weston-super-Mare who is confined to a wheelchair because of severe multiple sclerosis. It was the first time in the history of *Mastermind* that a contender did not use the Black Chair; instead, the Chair was removed during a recording break so that the stage manager, John Gilpin, could wheel Mary-Elizabeth into place.

Mary-Elizabeth will no doubt be displeased with me for mentioning her disability in the same breath as her victory; she always resented the fact that the media took as much interest in the wheelchair as in the person who occupied it. But the fact remains that the public was deeply impressed by the way she had overcome such harrowing handicaps of health and mobility and proved so triumphantly that having a disabled body does not mean having a disabled mind. In her book about her experiences, . . . *And No Passes*, there is scarcely a page without a reference to her physical problems. It all served to make her victory even more special, even more meritorious. As I wrote in my Foreword to her book:

> *Her win was as much a triumph over adversity as a victory over her fellow contestants. She pushed herself to the very limits of endurance – and proved to the watching world that physical disability, however debilitating, can be conquered by courage and application and will-power . . . It is the story of a brave woman who set her formidable mind and indomitable will to winning a title she feared she might be too handicapped to win. By doing so, she bestowed on it a significance which transcends its own very modest claims.* Mastermind *seeks to celebrate the human mind and its astonishing capacity; with her poignant victory, Mary-Elizabeth Raw celebrated humanity itself.*

Mary-Elizabeth Raw is a veterinary surgeon, with postgraduate qualifications in veterinary radiology and neurology, and a Fellow of the Royal College of Veterinary Surgeons. She had wanted to be a vet ever since she was a small child; by the time she appeared on *Mastermind*, however, she was unable to earn her living as a practising vet, but she did some second opinion work from time to time on a purely voluntary basis, using a specially adapted word processor for writing. She is still a regular contributor to various veterinary publications and is a joint editor of the *Veterinary Annual*.

She saw *Mastermind* on television for the first time in 1974, and from then on she was determined to take part, knowing that it was the ultimate quiz challenge. She applied for the programme in 1975, but by that time she was very tottery on her legs and Bill Wright asked her to reapply when she was in better health. She applied again in 1985, but again failed to get a place after an audition in Bristol. She applied once more in 1986, but she had had a bout of serious ill-health and failed to do herself justice. She decided to wait until she could say that she had been a year with no major upsets and applied again for the 1989 series. This time Peter Massey accepted her, provided that she felt fit enough to accept the invitation.

As her first specialised subject she had chosen King Charles I ('this cultivated, devout, irritating and at times devious man') because of a lifelong interest which had started when she was four years old, on a visit with her parents to an ancient hostelry in Southwell, Nottinghamshire, called The Saracen's Head. It was there that Charles had surrendered himself to the Scots in May 1646, and the hotel displayed a facsimile of the king's execution warrant. Her father later became Headmaster of King Charles I School in Kidderminster – the only school in the country to be named after the king. During the days of his rule, Charles had granted a charter to Kidderminster in 1637 on condition that the existing grammar school would bear his name; the school's founders' day is the Friday nearest to 19 November, the king's birthday.

Mary-Elizabeth was in the first heat of the 1989 series, which was recorded in the Taliesin Art Centre of the University College of Swansea. The set had a curiously unfamiliar feel. David Mitchell was now producing the programme, and for the first time in the history of *Mastermind* I was seen sitting alone at the quiz-master's table; Mary Craig, who had for so long been the 'Dark Lady' in shot beside me as scorer and timekeeper, was now sitting at the side of the set, off-camera. I felt oddly alone and vulnerable without her, but there was no time for nostalgia as the first heat of 1989 swung into explosive action.

In the specialised subjects round, Wayne Stainthorpe, a steelworks crane-driver from Porthcawl in Mid-Glamorgan, was taking 'The Family *Anatidae* – Swans, Geese and Ducks of Britain and Europe' as his specialised subject in honour of the centenary year of the Royal Society for the Protection of Birds. He scored an imperious 19. Mary-Elizabeth, sitting fourth, promptly matched it. In the second round Wayne added 17 on general knowledge to set a formidable target of 36 to beat. Once again Mary-Elizabeth rose to the challenge, and more, reeling off twenty-one correct answers for a record-equalling 40. As she returned to her place, the audience erupted into the most tumultuous applause I can remember hearing on *Mastermind*.

She was not to achieve quite the same heights again. In her semi-final, which was recorded in the King's Hall of the University of

Newcastle upon Tyne, she took as her specialised subject 'The Life of Albert, the Prince Consort' ('an intriguing man with a great knowledge of the arts and science'). She had had a long and wretched journey through vile March weather and was looking ill and exhausted. Nevertheless she saw off the opposition with a solid 34, two ahead of her closest rival, Dr Ian Verber, a paediatrician at St George's Hospital, Tooting, who had achieved only a moderate score (11) on his specialised subject of 'The Geography of the National Parks of England and Wales' but had come back strongly with a blazing 21 in his general knowledge round.

And so to the Final, which was recorded in the Arts Centre of the University of Warwick in Coventry. By this time the media were well alerted to the possibility of a dramatic 'wheelchair win', as they called it, and the place was swarming with press people and camera crews. I cannot remember a Final with quite the same atmosphere of heightened expectancy both before and during the recording.

Mary-Elizabeth's four opponents were a mixed and fascinating bunch, as always: Tom Bean, a young stock and arable farmer from the parish of Pebworth, Evesham, in Worcestershire, who had a fine private collection of books and was taking a new specialised subject for the Final, 'The Life and Works of Edward Lear'; Myra Knight, from Glasgow, a housewife and former primary school teacher, who was reverting to 'The City of Glasgow from Earliest Times'; Gill Doubleday, from Blackheath in London, a civil servant in a department with the resounding title of 'the Department of Trade and Industry (Exports to Europe branch, France desk)' which always made the audience chuckle – she was now reverting to 'The Life and Works of John Bunyan'; and Dick Jones, a policy research officer with the Institution of Electrical Engineers in London and a veteran of several other quiz programmes, who was reverting to 'The History of the Conservative Party 1832–1940'. Mary-Elizabeth herself was reverting to 'The Life and Reign of Charles I'.

At the halfway stage Mary-Elizabeth, with 18, had a lead of two points over Myra Knight; Dick Jones, who was suffering from a viral infection, had crashed, alas, and was out of it with only 8. In the general knowledge round, despite a sympathetic burst of applause as he returned to the Chair, he became more and more demoralised and added only another 9 to reach 17. Tom Bean, who was on 13, failed to score on his first six questions and his smile grew a little

Mary-Elizabeth Raw, with MM

strained as he struggled to make 10 points and reach 23 ('Down in flames, I fear,' he announced ruefully as he left the Chair).

The real battle was now on. Gill Doubleday, on 14, made a tremendous run of twelve correct answers before missing her stride, and added a rousing 18 to set the target at 32. Myra Knight made occasional mistakes but reached 31 before getting her last three questions wrong. So it was now up to Mary-Elizabeth Raw to make the final charge for victory. She raced to 30, started slowing down, but rallied and reached 33. She had won the *Mastermind* title. And she too, like David Beamish, had achieved it without a single pass (hence the title of her book, *. . . And No Passes*).

The Caithness Glass trophy was presented by the champion who had inaugurated the 1980s for *Mastermind*, Fred Housego:

> *I never thought I would be nervous again in the presence of*
> *Magnus, the music and the Black Chair — but I was. Every year,*
> Mastermind *always presents us with a nerve-racking finish and a*
> *very worthy champion indeed, and this year, 1989, is no exception.*
> *There is little for me to say to Mary-Elizabeth Raw except*
> *congratulations, and just a couple of words — enjoy your new-found*
> *fame!*

Enjoy it she certainly did. Her book details a whole year of being fêted and feasted, including a reception at 10 Downing Street (Margaret Thatcher *did* speak to this champion — at considerable length), of speeches and guest appearances all over the country. No one, not Sir David Hunt, not Christopher Hughes, not even Fred Housego himself, inspired quite such a sustained period of interest as Mary-Elizabeth Raw did.

The 1980s have been called, by some commentators, 'The Golden Age of *Mastermind*'. For myself I don't much care for such a facile label, because it implies that other decades and other years were forged from baser metal, and with that I cannot agree. The programme certainly held its high place in public esteem throughout the 1980s, with audiences averaging a steady 10 million viewers. But I have never been much of a ratings man; what always mattered to me was the quality of the product we were making for television — and I do not believe that this quality was any 'better', or more special, than it was, say, in the 1990s, as we shall see.

10

Per Ardua . . .
Highs and Lows

'Though confident once
In your specialist choice,
A tic or a cough
And your tremulous voice
Betray you to millions;
And right from the start
Six passes, wrong answers –
Your game falls apart.'

MARTIN NEWELL, 'Disastermind'
Published in the *Independent* on 29 May 1996,
the day of the first heat of that year's series

It is in the nature of things that champions are remembered long after the runners-up, however gallant, are forgotten. But *Mastermind* was always a little different: on *Mastermind*, failure was sometimes as memorable as success. Indeed, as the American comedian Earl Wilson once put it, 'Success is simply a matter of luck – ask any failure.'

One Masterminder in particular had greatness thrust upon him for his scoring feats: Welsh-born Arfor Wyn Hughes, who was Head of Art and Design at the Manor School in Cheadle Hulme, near Stockport, when he appeared in the first heat of the 1990 series. But he earned his celebrity not for being a Mastermind but as 'Disastermind'; for Arfor Wyn Hughes, the dream of winning the title of champion turned into a nightmare – a case of *per ardua ad disastra*.

From long and sometimes poignant experience, we advised applicants *not* to offer their 'professional' subjects. The scope and range of the questions might not suit them and they might end up with egg on their faces through no fault of their own. Arfor, alas, ignored this well-meant advice and insisted on taking as his specialised subject 'Impressionist and Post-Impressionist Painting 1830–1914'.

The recording took place in the Great Hall of the University of Lancaster, which was celebrating the twenty-fifth anniversary of its royal charter. I was feeling very chipper as I introduced the first programme of the eighteenth series:

> *As always there has been no shortage of brave-hearted applicants to fill the sixty-four places available on the programme, and to take their chance in our faithful old Black Chair, which has been with us, man and boy, chair and stool, for all these seventeen years.*

That programme is still etched on my memory. The other contenders were a policeman (Detective Constable Anthony Wilkinson, publications officer with the Manchester police); a teacher (Hilary Forrest, head of Humanities at Urmston Grammar School in Trafford); and a retired chief copy-taker with the *Yorkshire Post* (Jack Clark).

To start with, everything went well. In the afternoon rehearsals, when as always we used old sets of general knowledge questions, Arfor came out on top. There was no hint of anything untoward about to happen. There was a slight early hiccup, no more: Jack Clark, who was seventy-one at the time and becoming a little deaf, was taking 'The Diary of Samuel Pepys 1660–69' – a subject he knew well, having played the part of Pepys in amateur theatre productions (indeed, he went on to write delightful articles in *PASS* on the annual reunions in authentic Pepysian style). One of his questions was, 'Which phrase in the diary, repeated again and again, suggests that the diary was written late at night?' Jack looked blank – but it was such an obviously easy question that I stopped the watch, suspecting that Jack hadn't heard it properly. I repeated the question, and comprehension dawned: '"And so to bed"!' As Jack told me afterwards, 'That phrase of all phrases! If I hadn't answered that one, I would never have smiled again.'

Then it was Arfor's turn – and everything went wrong. To everyone's dismay he managed only 5 on his specialised subject. I was practically in despair – it always felt dreadful seeing a contender beginning to disintegrate. And although he was given an encouraging round of applause as he returned to the Chair he added only another 7 to reach 12 – 16 points behind the winner, Hilary Forrest.

The media had a field day, of course. Eventually the interest died down, but in 1992 it was given a second lease of life when Arfor sportingly appeared in a BBC2 programme called *TV Hell*, hosted by Angus Deayton and Paul Merton. Arfor had no qualms about agreeing to take part: one of his pragmatic mottoes in life is: 'If you fly with the crows, expect to get shot.' In a ten-minute section dubbed 'Disastermind' (repeated in September 1993) he was billed as currently holding the title of 'Lowest Living Mastermind Scorer' and became more celebrated than most *Mastermind* champions:

The tension of appearing on the king of all television quiz shows was enormous. I had really swotted up on my subject. I went in feeling quite confident and quite happy. Having taught the subject for twelve years I reckoned I knew enough to tide me through any questions that could be thrown at me. But as soon as that music started, everything seemed to disappear. Then Magnus fired the first question at me, about the cynical art critic in 1874 who coined the term 'Impressionist' – and I got it wrong. How anybody could possibly forget the name of Le Roy now seems unbelievable, but I managed it. From then on it just got worse and worse. Halfway through I was asked for the name of the dwarf in Cézanne's painting submitted to the Salon in 1870, I was in such a state that I felt like saying, 'Who's Cézanne?' It was literally as bad as that. I just said 'Pass'.

The 'pass spiral' is an almost automatic reaction. You're worrying about the previous question so much that you can't even think of what you've just been asked, so you say 'Pass'. Then you think, 'Damn, I knew that answer'. It just seems to get a grip on you, and you keep on doing it. I just sat there like a bump on a log. At the end of the first round I only had 5 points. I was absolutely shell-shocked.

It didn't sink in at the time. You literally just don't believe it. I had watched people on the programme from my armchair at home, thinking, 'Why on earth are those people doing this programme? They don't know anything!' I considered that I knew most of my subject, but turned out to be one of those people!

Arfor certainly doesn't lack a sense of humour. His wife invited his pub-quiz friends and neighbours (and the local evening paper photographer) to their home to watch his humiliation when the programme was transmitted on the Sunday evening; the house was filled with helium balloons marked PASS. On the following morning (and for many mornings thereafter) he good-naturedly braved the inevitable ribbing at school. The staff nicknamed him 'Eddie the Eagle'. The school corridors buzzed with the sound of the *Mastermind* theme being hummed; in class his questions would be answered with 'Pass' and a snigger.

In the end he had had enough. In the summer of 1991 he took early retirement (at the age of fifty-three), but he soon became bored and took a job as a bus-driver in Stockport. He now works as a chauffeur based at Manchester Airport, driving business executives and air crews all over the country. He continues with his artistic activities in his spare time, including painting murals on the walls of a local Spanish restaurant; he also teaches Welsh conversation at the Stockport Adult Education Centre.

Arfor came to enjoy the somewhat equivocal glory of being the lowest living scorer on *Mastermind*. When I met him again at a programme recording in 1996, I asked him if he was planning to return for another go now that 'recidivists' were being allowed back. 'Certainly not!' he replied. 'I'm not coming back until somebody beats my low-scoring record!'

Well, I have bad news for Arfor. He is not, and never was, the lowest scorer on *Mastermind*. Others had scored fewer points in earlier years – and later in the same series, Wing-Commander Tony Alder (retired) would score only 11. Long before then, however, three Masterminders had even failed to reach double figures.

The first, back in 1973, was a fudge chef from Edinburgh, Armando Margiotta, who was a bit of an expert on opera; he had won £1,000 on *Double Your Money* and felt very confident about tackling the same subject on *Mastermind*. Alas, he came a terrible cropper in Heat 5 and scored only 3 on 'Opera', plus 6 on general knowledge, to record a lowest-ever 9. Armando died in 1982, but he always said he had enjoyed himself on the programme: indeed, when the Mastermind Club was founded in 1978 he became one of the first committee members, representing Scotland.

An equally modest score was recorded in Heat 9 by a housewife from Tittensor, Stoke-on-Trent, Sally Copeland (who died in 1983). She had a degree in classics and chose 'Classical Mythology' as her specialised subject, in those far-off days when specialised subjects tended to be all-embracing. She scored only 4 on that and only 5 in her general knowledge round, for another total of 9.

In 1984 the same fate befell a community worker from Kenilworth in Warwickshire, who was taking 'The Medici and the City of Florence 1200–1537' as his specialised subject. He has asked me not to print his name in case it provokes further media interest; but he, too, failed to reach double figures, scoring only 3, followed by 6, for another total of 9.

In fact, nearly all the lowest scores were in the 1970s. Another two Masterminders only scored 10: Martha Irvine, a Sheriff Court clerk in Glasgow who took 'The History of Costume from 1600' in 1977; and Neil MacGillivray, from Falkirk, a scientific assistant with ICI, who took 'Israel and the European Zionist Movement' in 1978. Both survived their ordeal unscathed, I am happy to say: Martha Irvine, who is now retired from the Civil Service, has recently published a volume of poetry (*Green Moon Riding*, 1993), while Neil MacGillivray is now working as an analytical training officer with Zeneca in Grangemouth.

The 1970s also brought a brace of 11s. One was Paul Wood (1979), from Newbury, a local government officer in the hospital service, who took 'The Reign of George III' and scored only 3 on that for an overall total of 11. The other was Margaret (Maggie) Garratt (1976), who would later become the first secretary of the Mastermind Club. She, too, scored only 3 on her specialised subject for an overall total of 11; in her case the subject was 'Dietetics' and she was the hospital dietician at University College Hospital, London. I can just imagine the ribbing she must have endured at work next day! Her questions had been set by her former lecturer, Dr A. S. Trusswell (now Boden Professor of Human Nutrition at the University of Sydney); but Maggie had forgotten much of the theoretical and chemistry side – she knew all about nutrition, not so much about the theory of dietetics. It was a classic case of the questions not matching a contender's current knowledge, and reinforced the advice of the *Mastermind* team not to take one's 'professional' subject – simply because the questioning might not always fit the parameters of the contender's particular interest in the subject. Another 11 was scored in 1980 by Tony Veitch, from Bangor, a civil servant at Stormont, taking 'The Life and Works of A. E. Housman'.

In the 1979 series, another contender matched the 3 scored by Paul Wood and Maggie Garratt: Lai-Ngau Pauson, a Chinese-American freelance editor in Glasgow ('The History of Printing to 1860'). This was to be matched in 1980 by Nigel Viney, a publisher from Haddenham, Kent ('The Life of Sir Winston Churchill'), and in 1989 by Rosemary Jane Richards, from Wallasey on Merseyside, a factory machinist with Remploy, taking 'The Life and Reign of Henry VIII'; she seemed to panic and had a disastrous round of 3, but in the general knowledge round she redeemed herself and added 14 for a total of 17. Rosemary, alas, was killed in a traffic accident two years later. Her score was to be equalled again in 1993 by Pauline Beighton, a former teacher from Cowley; Pauline took as her specialised subject the travel writer Dervla Murphy, who had published more than a dozen books – and was asked questions on the 'wrong' ones! She too redeemed herself, however, by notching up the highest general knowledge score in her heat for an overall total of 17.

Other contenders were let down by their general knowledge. In the 1975 series it was felt to be a bit of a coup to attract a member of the House of Lords: Viscount Tenby (David), the first member of the House of Lords to take part in *Mastermind*. He took 'The American Civil War' as his specialised subject and scored 16, but collapsed in his general knowledge round and only scored another 3, thus earning the palm of notching the lowest recorded general knowledge score. Even this dubious honour was to be snatched from him the following year, when John Langford, a careers officer with the former Inner London Education Authority, scored only 2.

In the 1980s we had to think much harder about the relative difficulty of individual contenders' answers; we began to 'tailor' some of the general knowledge questions, to aim at their strengths rather than trusting entirely to the luck of the draw. Certainly, the scores in the 1980s showed less disparity; there were fewer disasters recorded on the scoreboard – until Arfor Wyn Hughes made his spectacular appearance in 1990. He did not become the champion, as he had secretly hoped; but he deserves some sort of accolade as one of the most sporting losers we ever had on the programme.

At the other end of the scale, the record for the highest score rose steadily – and sometimes dramatically – over the years.

Everything in the first year of a programme is a record of sorts, I suppose. In the 1972 Final, for instance, Nancy Wilkinson, the first champion, scored a total of 37; but that first Final had only three finalists and they each got rounds of two and a half minutes (specialised subject) and three minutes (general knowledge), so the scores should not be compared with later occasions when the rounds were markedly shorter.

On the other hand, in a semi-final in 1979, Captain Joe West, a North Sea helicopter pilot operating out of Shetland, had an extraordinary round of 22 for his specialised subject ('The Life of Horatio Nelson'), which was thereafter always quoted as a record. Reluctantly, I have to say that this was before we had started timing the questions and the answers as strictly as we came to do, and I think that this exceptional score might have been the result of an aberration on our part. Nonetheless, he acquitted himself very well in every round, and came second equal in the Final (the winner was Philip Jenkins); when he returned to the programme in 1996, by which time he was a helicopter consultant living in Wimborne, Dorset, he again reached the semi-finals.

It was with the 1975 series that the records race started in earnest. It began with Dr Francis Lambert, the Glasgow University lecturer who scored 35 in his first round and 37 in the semi-finals to earn himself a place in the *Guinness Book of Records*. His record 37 was equalled by Sir David Hunt in the Jubilee Final two years later; it then stood for another seven years, until the Final of the 1984 series, when Margaret Harris raced to the title on board HMS *Hermes* at Portsmouth with 38.

Another *annus mirabilis* for records was 1986. In that year, Jennifer Keaveney equalled Margaret Harris's record 38 in her heat. Then she broke it with a thumping 40 in the semi-finals, and matched it with another 40 in the Final.

I did not believe that this record could ever be broken. It was equalled, certainly, in the first heat in the 1989 series by Mary-Elizabeth Raw, the 1989 champion; but 40, I reckoned, was right at the limit of any contender's capacity. But I was wrong. Yet another *annus mirabilis* was to dawn in 1995, with the remarkable Kevin Ashman.

1995: Kevin Ashman

In 1995 former Masterminders were allowed to reapply for a second attempt at the title, provided that they weren't past champions, hadn't been on the programme in the previous five years, and had three new specialised subjects to offer. After rigorous auditioning fifteen 'recidivists' were accepted. One of them was a civil servant from Winchester, Kevin Ashman. He had appeared in the 1987 series when he was working in the Ministry of Defence and had thrown down the gauntlet with an impressive 38 in his heat (including 20 in his general knowledge round); he looked a champion in the making, but faltered in the semi-finals – he scored 'only' 34 and lost on passes to another civil servant, Margaret Spiller, who worked in the Lord Chancellor's Department. For Margaret Spiller, effervescent and ever-smiling, it was another record of a sort: she became the only person ever to beat Kevin Ashman on *Mastermind*.

Kevin's time was still to come. In 1987 there was no indication that Masterminders would ever be allowed a second chance. But he had discovered something he could do well and where he could actually win; quizzes were his element and, having discovered this talent, he went on to try to make the most of it. He entered for practically every quiz which came up and became very systematic in his reading: everything was aimed specifically at winning whichever particular quiz he entered.

In 1988 he went in for William G. Stewart's new Channel 4 quiz, *Fifteen to One*; in fact he appeared in four early series – six appearances in all, including two Grand Finals, in the second and third series. He won the third series in 1989 (the prize was a large silver salver).

In 1989 he went to Australia as one of nine British contestants in the World Championships of *Sale of the Century*, where he was runner-up to Peter Richardson (1977 *Mastermind* semi-finalist) in the British section of the championships.

In 1990 he appeared on *Sale of the Century* on Sky TV, a new British version of the Australian show, and won the top prize, a car (the irony is that he can't drive).

In 1992 he appeared on *Brain of Britain*. He won the first round, but in the semi-finals he lost by a point to Mike Billson (the *Mastermind* runner-up of 1987) who went on to win the title (Mike had previously been a *Brain of Britain* finalist in 1989).

In 1993 he was a member of the champion team ('Ye Olde White Bear of Hampstead') on ITV's *Quiz Night*; it involved victories in three league games, a quarter-final, a semi-final and the Final itself. Also in 1993 he won *Trivial Pursuit* on Sky TV. The prize was a holiday to the Canaries, but Kevin had to take the money instead because they had run out of holidays.

In 1994 he was captain of the champion team in the *Great British Quiz*; the team was 'The Allsorts', which played in the South London Quiz League from The Rose and Crown in Southwark. His team-mates on that occasion were Bob Collier (twice a semi-finalist on *Brain of Britain*) and Paul Webbewood (*Mastermind* finalist in 1990). The prize was a holiday in Australia.

By 1995, then, Kevin was an experienced and successful quizzling. Even so, when he applied for *Mastermind* again he only achieved the reserves list – until another contestant dropped out before a recording. Kevin was called in at short notice, and this time he was to make no mistake.

His heat was recorded in the mock-medieval ambience of the Great Hall of Warwick Castle, one of the finest medieval castles in England. It is actually a complex of buildings which has evolved over the centuries from a stronghold in the turbulent Middle Ages to the softer luxury of a nineteenth-century stately residence, and is now a twentieth-century tourist attraction. The Great Hall at the heart of the castle was constructed in the fourteenth century but owes much of its present appearance to the nineteenth-century restoration, which presented a romantic Victorian interpretation of the medieval style, with suits of armour and heraldic shields lining the walls. This was the resonant setting for Kevin's second tilt at the title.

His specialised subject was 'Dr Martin Luther King Jr and the Civil Rights Movement'. He was taking on a retired school librarian from Chesterfield, Helena Rogers ('John of Gaunt'); a discrepancy controller in a parcels depot in Derbyshire, John Mellor ('The Battle for Arnhem'); and a rocket-motors research scientist from Stourport-on-Severn, Suzanne Salsbury ('The History and Repertoire of the Clarinet'). In the first round, Helena scored 16, John Mellor upped it to 17, but Kevin swept in with a huge 20; Suzanne, unnerved perhaps, scored 12.

From then on it was no contest. The other three all achieved respectable overall totals in the twenties; but Kevin Ashman, last in the lists, answering with great pace and economy, added a majestic 21 for a total of 41, breaking the high-scoring record held jointly by two previous champions, Jennifer Keaveney (1986) and Mary-Elizabeth Raw (1989). He had received twenty-two questions and got twenty-one of them right. 'You can't do much better than that, can you?' he said afterwards.

The semi-finals turned out to be little more than a canter. The arena for Kevin's tourney was the Swan Theatre in Stratford-upon-Avon. The Swan had risen from the ashes of the first Shakespeare Memorial Theatre which stood on the site from 1879 until it was razed by fire in 1926; sixty years later the burnt-out shell of the original auditorium was transformed into a beautiful galleried playhouse with its echoes of Elizabethan and Jacobean theatres.

This time he was offering as his specialised subject 'The History of the Western Film'. He was up against another recidivist, Greenwich University law lecturer Michael Taylor (1988), who had won his heat with 'The Life and Career of W. E. Gladstone' and was now offering 'Desiderius Erasmus'; Tony Rennick, a mature student at Boston College, Lincolnshire, who had won his heat with 'Steam Locomotives of the LNER' and was now offering 'The Life and Works of Woody Guthrie'; and Bill Stratton, a project manager with BT Satellite Communications, who had won his heat with 'The Apollo Manned Space Programme' and was now offering 'Venomous Snakes'.

In the first round, Kevin scored 18, but was given stiff opposition by Bill Stratton, who also scored 18, and Michael Taylor, who scored 17. But as so often happened, the general knowledge round proved decisive, and Kevin left all his rivals trailing with another powerful 20 to reach 38.

So the scene was set for what promised to be a memorable Final. It was staged in the General Assembly Hall of the Church of Scotland, in Edinburgh. Here, every year, commissioners appointed by the presbyteries – ministers, elders, deacons and deaconesses – meet for a week to debate the major church issues of the day; but the Hall has an ancillary use, as a theatrical arena, a splendid theatre-in-the-round for Edinburgh International Festival and other productions, like the historic and spectacular revival of *The Thrie Estaites* by Sir David Lindsay of the Mount. There was a tremendous sense of occasion, heightened by the fact that, for the first time, everyone was in evening dress.

The finalists all had rather differing attitudes to the occasion. Henry Boettinger was an American telecommunications consultant, originally from Baltimore, now living in Crackington Haven, near Bude, Cornwall. This was his second appearance on *Mastermind* (he had been a semi-finalist in 1988), and at the age of seventy-two he was now much the oldest of the finalists. What he has said about *Mastermind* is very heart-warming:

> For an American, repelled by the mindless state to which quiz shows in my country had degenerated, my first view of Mastermind in 1976 was a revelation. The design and production refuted all assumptions and canons which made such shows tawdry, shallow and cluttered with garish, distracting sets. Every aspect of Mastermind bespoke an effortless elegance and showed the presence of superior intelligence and manners in those responsible for it. Retention of the design for twenty-five years shows the truth of the old adage: 'When it is not necessary to change, then it is absolutely necessary not to change.'

In 1988 Henry had taken two American inventors as his specialised subjects – Alexander Graham Bell and Thomas Edison. In 1995 he was specialising in American statesmen – Franklin, Jefferson and (for the Final) Lincoln. Why? 'Because they are transatlantic characters who shared in the history of both our nations, and because I want the British to remember that at one time the American Dream was represented by three figures of really heroic stature.'

Robert Jones, from Romford, Essex, was a civil servant with the employment service. He had reached the Final with 'The Life of King George V' and 'The Byzantine Empire'; he was now offering 'Ancient Egypt: The New Kingdom'. His game-plan was basically simple : 'Don't say pass if you can possibly help it, don't cuss out loud if you get a question wrong and, above all, just enjoy it.' He wanted to win, obviously: 'I'd like to see the look on my Mum's face if I present her with the Glass Bowl – but if I don't win, well, as far as I can see, everyone who's been on *Mastermind* throughout the entire series is a winner. It's like that scene from *Chariots of Fire* where Nigel Havers says that he is running for the honour of Repton, Eton and Caius; myself, I would be running for the honour of Scargill Junior, Abbs Cross Technical High and Devonshire Hall, University of Leeds – and the employment service.'

Melvyn Kinsey, from Ravenfield near Rotherham, was an organising secretary with Park Gate Recreational Services for United

Kevin Ashman

Engineering Steels. He had reached the Final with 'US Presidential Elections' and 'World Series Baseball 1903–50'; he was now offering 'The Winter Olympic Games'. The secret of winning? 'Concentrate. Ignore everything else. Sit down, look at Magnus, prepare, listen. When I first sat in the Chair, it seemed only like five seconds before the bleeper went – time just seemed to fly.' Winning was important – but not overwhelmingly so: 'Just being here is a bonus – I have won just by being here.'

Kevin Ashman, who was offering 'The Zulu War' for the Final, made no secret of his desire to win: 'When I first came on *Mastermind*, eight years ago, it was the first quiz I had done on TV; since then I have done a number of TV quizzes, but I have also become very involved with pub quizzes, club quizzes at work, all kinds of things. It's become almost a way of life, it's gone well beyond being a hobby. Because I'm so involved with quizzes these days, and *Mastermind* is seen as the number-one show in terms of TV quizzes, yes, winning it is very important to me.'

And with that, battle commenced. Henry Boettinger, who had become a tremendously popular figure with viewers with his old-world American charm and courtesy, got the specialised subject round off to an electrifying start with a commanding 20. Then Robert Jones – 11; Melvyn Kinsey – 16. They were already out of it, it seemed. How would the formidable Kevin Ashman do? He did pretty well, but not as well as Henry Boettinger, and at the halfway stage was lying second with 19.

In the general knowledge round, neither Robert Jones nor Melvyn Kinsey could mount a serious challenge. Now it was the ultimate confrontation. Kevin settled himself comfortably in the Black Chair and stormed to a flawless 20, to set the target at 39. Could Henry match it? He started brilliantly, but halfway through his round his stride faltered, and he ended with 34.

So Kevin Ashman won – very decisively, in the end. I suspect that a lot of people were secretly hoping that Henry Boettinger would pull it off, but Kevin is an awesome competitor for anyone to face. To underline his prowess, he went on to win the Christmas *Masterbrain* contest between winners and runners-up of that year's *Mastermind* and *Brain of Britain*; it was a clean sweep for *Mastermind*, with Kevin and Henry coming first and second. The following year he appeared on *Brain of Britain* again and this time he won it, after equalling the programme's scoring record with 37 in the first round. This meant another *Masterbrain*, which he also won.

Only one other Masterminder had ever won both titles: Roger Pritchard had previously won *Brain of Britain* when he became *Mastermind* champion in 1976. What made Kevin's feat even more remarkable was that he became *Brain of Britain* champion while he was still the reigning *Mastermind* champion – the only person ever to hold both titles simultaneously.

11

More Champions: 1990–97

'Mastermind *is not so much a television programme – it is more a* *national institution. Year on year we marvel at the depth and range of* *knowledge displayed by the participants; year on year these brave* *individuals give us a salutary reminder of the depth of our own* *ignorance. Quite frankly, watching* Mastermind *is enough to send you* *to the Open University.'*

JONATHAN POWELL, then Controller BBC1,
presenting the Caithness Glass trophy to David Edwards in 1990

At the start of a decade we have no way of knowing how it might come to a close. The 1990s would bring *Mastermind* to the end of its course; but at the beginning the programme was still developing, still introducing new ideas, still moving with the times. In particular, as we have seen, from 1995 former Masterminders (except champions) were allowed to apply again.

The decade started for *Mastermind* with a long and sometimes acrimonious debate in the media about the standard of the questions and the standard of the contenders. After the searingly high scores of the two preceding series, the scoring in the first half of the 1990 series was comparatively very low, highlighted in the very first heat by the 12 scored by Arfor Wyn Hughes. In general, the overall scores were markedly lower than in previous years; some heats were won with 20 or 21, and the general knowledge rounds were uniformly low. It was not until Heat 11 that any contender scored more than 30, when Allan Draycott, a part-time lecturer in economics at the City of London College, won with 34 (and the eventual champion, David Edwards, came joint second with 27). By that time the low scores had started to provoke public comment, and an article in the *Independent* on the day before the transmission of Allan Draycott's heat on 24 March

1990 suggested that the 'best minds' had all been used up over the preceding eighteen years! Had the questions suddenly become much harder, or had the quality of the contenders plummeted?

Peter Massey, who had been with the programme for a very long time and was now starting his second stint as producer (1990–91), was quoted as saying, rather delphically, that it was due to a combination of things: 'Slightly more difficult general knowledge questions and a puzzling drop in the quality of competitors.' He no doubt intended his comments to damp down speculation, but instead they merely inflamed the story. For my own part I have no doubt whatsoever that in the first half of the series the questions *were* made deliberately more severe than before, as a reaction to the high scores of previous years, but that in response to the dire scores in early 1990 the policy was eased as the series progressed.

Another feature of the early 1990s was the appearance of our second wheelchair contestant: Dr Patricia Pay, a solicitor and land registrar from Dunsford near Exeter, who had been disabled in an accident in 1975. Ever since the accident she had been annoyed that the *Mastermind* set was 'wheelchair-inaccessible', and she harboured ambitions to be the first wheelchair contestant. She had applied soon after her accident, giving as her prime reason for wanting to take part the desire to show that it could be done from a wheelchair. She received no response, so she gave up in disgust. In 1985 she decided to try again, without mentioning the wheelchair. This time she was accepted for an interview in the Royal Clarence Hotel in Exeter (the oldest hotel in England), only to discover that the audition was up a flight of stairs. Eventually she managed to struggle through a very difficult doorway and arrived, backwards, to confront a surprised Peter Massey. But her general knowledge was not considered up to the required standard, and Peter Massey advised her to do some more studying and reapply the following year. It was the start of a regular series of five spring-time 'assignations' with Peter (although they met downstairs from then on).

When Mary-Elizabeth Raw won the title in 1989, it thwarted Patricia's ambition to be first contender in a wheelchair. By this time, however, Patricia was hooked. Finally Peter Massey rang to offer her a slot for the 1991 season if she were prepared to take her second choice subject, 'The Life and Work of Tolstoy'. It involved many absorbing and quite draining months of intensive study.

Calibre, an Aylesbury-based Talking Book charity for blind and severely disabled people, lent her *War and Peace* on forty-seven cassettes and *Anna Karenina* on twenty-eight, and she played them through twice in the car as she commuted to and from her work in Plymouth, forty miles away. She also worked hard on her shaky general knowledge, studying quiz books and committing to memory the chemical elements, kings and queens, gods and goddesses, capitals, currencies, presidents, prime ministers, poets laureate and so on – she would recite them while walking the dogs.

Her heat was recorded at the University of Exeter, where she had collected four degrees: a BA in French and Russian, an MA, a Ph.D. in French, and an LLM for European Legal Studies. Her score of 29 (including 13 on general knowledge) was sufficient to take her through to the semi-finals, in which she offered 'The Life and Works of Nabokov'. On this occasion, however, in an even lower-scoring contest, she could amass only 22 and was knocked out. But she had made her point: as chairman of the Spinal Injuries Association, she had shown her independence by pushing herself into position on set, and she and Mary-Elizabeth Raw had done a great deal to raise public awareness and challenge public misconceptions about people with disabilities.

1990: David Edwards

Welsh-born David Edwards, the son of a Royal Navy rating and a railway booking clerk, was a physics teacher and Head of Science at Cheadle High School. But he was not everybody's idea of a science boffin. At University College, Swansea, where he took a degree in metallurgy, he had played the guitar with a folk group in various parts of the country (didn't they all, in the 1970s?) and become enamoured of 'rapper', the traditional sword-dance of the Northeast, before taking a postgraduate certificate in education and settling down to the more sober life of a teacher.

David entered the quiz world through winning a competition in a local newspaper. This led to a national final for the title of Mensa Superbrain 1985, which he won. In 1988 he took part in *Brain of Britain* and reached the semi-finals, where he was narrowly beaten by the 1985 *Mastermind* champion, Ian Meadows.

He applied for *Mastermind* more on a whim than through burning ambition. The received wisdom was that it took years of applications, or else a bizarre occupation or unusual specialised subjects, to have a chance of getting on to *Mastermind*; he was pleasantly surprised to be auditioned and accepted on his first application. However, his first choices for specialised subjects ('English Folk Customs', and the 'Geography and History of the Vale of Glamorgan') were rejected as being boring, and David was forced back on to his other areas of expertise – science and scientists.

David's heat was recorded in the Great Hall of the University of Aston in Birmingham, which had been established as one of Britain's first technological universities in 1966. In the specialised subjects round he did well, scoring 18 on 'The Life and Work of Michael Faraday' to share joint lead with Alan Draycott, who was taking 'British Politics Since 1900'. But in the general knowledge round, he almost blew it; he passed on the name of the former dictator of Portugal (Salazar), and found his mind straying back to it for the next four or five questions, like a tongue drawn to a sore tooth. His despairing solution to this drift of concentration was to force himself to focus on the knot of my tie! I have scrutinised the video of the recording with painstaking care and could find nothing untoward or unusual about the way I wore my tie, but for David it apparently loomed as large as a lifebelt.

Nevertheless the outcome was that he scored only 9 on general knowledge, and was caught on 27 by Mary Rattle, a housewife in Stafford who had been an executive officer in the Civil Service, taking 'The Life and Shropshire Novels of Mary Webb', while Allan Draycott streaked away to win with 34. However, because of the generally low level of scoring, both David and Mary qualified for places in the *repêchage* semi-final.

This time he made no mistake. In the fifth semi-final he took a 1-point lead over Mary Rattle with 17 on 'The Life and Work of Benjamin Thompson, Count Rumford' in the specialised subject round and, going last in the general knowledge round, he spread-eagled the opposition with another 17 to finish on 34, nine points ahead of Mary.

For the Final, David had been planning to revert to 'The Life of Michael Faraday' as his specialised subject; but he was told that it would be difficult to prepare another set of questions on him, and that he would have to settle on someone else – what about the

**David Edwards (in chair), with MM and Jonathan
Powell, then Controller BBC1**

Scottish physicist, James Clerk Maxwell? I have to confess that I had
a hand in this suggestion myself, because James Clerk Maxwell, one
of the greatest theoretical physicists the world has ever known, had
been a pupil at my old school, The Edinburgh Academy, in the
1840s, and I thought it was about time that he was given due recognition on *Mastermind*. It only gave David Edwards four weeks to
swot up on him, however.

I have already described in Chapter 5 the unforgettable Final in the banqueting hall of the City Chambers in Glasgow when Chantal Thompson, the trainee solicitor from Bristol, almost snatched victory with her breathtaking 22 for general knowledge. David Edwards had done his homework on James Clerk Maxwell and had been lying second at the halfway stage with 18; he was two behind Paul Webbewood, a civil servant at the Department of Health, who had scored a massive 20 with 'The History of the British Labour Party from 1900'. When the crunch came it was Paul Webbewood whose nerve cracked, scoring only 13 for general knowledge, while David Edwards added 19 to get home with 37.

Chantal Thompson had the last laugh, perhaps, in the annual *Masterbrain* competition between the *Mastermind* winners and the *Brain of Britain* winners: it was Chantal who won and David Edwards who came second.

1991: Stephen Allen

For the nineteenth series the programme reverted to its former length of seventeen programmes, after five years of being extended to twenty-two programmes.

The nineteenth champion was an actor, Stephen Tomlin, whose TV and film career had included roles in *Coronation Street*, *Harry's Game* and *The Beiderbecke Affair*. But he applied for *Mastermind* under his own name of Stephen Allen and not his stage name, because he felt that *Mastermind* was a personal challenge not directly connected with his profession.

Stephen Allen was born in 1951 in Saltash, Cornwall, the son of a butcher and a telephonist. When he was six the family slipped across the Tamar into Devon when his father got a job in Tavistock. At Tavistock Comprehensive School, where he found the history and English teachers particularly inspiring, he had a great thirst for reading and learning. The school library was an Aladdin's Cave for a boy whose only home reading was a pre-war set of Arthur Mee's *Children's Encyclopedia*; he would spend his lunch-breaks engrossed in novels, poetry, reference books and magazines like *Look & Learn*. Many years later, when he was casting around for specialised subjects to offer for *Mastermind*, he came across a back-number of *Look &*

Learn from 1966 at a friend's house in Lancaster; on the back page was the illustrated life of a famous figure – Sir Francis Drake. Drake, of course, came from Tavistock; his grand bronze statue dominated the road past Stephen's school, which itself stood only a short way from his birthplace at Crowndale Farm. And with that, Stephen's specialised subject for the *Mastermind* Final was decided.

Stephen trained as a teacher at the Central School of Speech and Drama, and in 1976 moved to Lancaster to become an actor/teacher with the Duke's Theatre in Education. Moving into mainstream theatre in the early 1980s he performed with Cumbria's professional touring theatre company, Pocket Theatre, based at the Brewery Arts Centre in Kendal. A high point there was the world première of Charles Dickens' *Hard Times*, adapted by Steven Jeffries for only four actors, each one playing five characters; it proved enormously popular and toured all over the country. In 1983 he was co-founder, with other Lancaster-based actors, of Target Casting – an actors' co-operative personal management company.

Pub quizzes were always part of his social life as a touring actor, a way of making friends and acquaintances outside his immediate circle of professional colleagues. In 1990 he had captained a team from the Moorlands Hotel in Lancaster to the quarter-finals of Granada TV's pub quiz knockout, *Quiz Night*. He applied for the 1991 series of *Mastermind* because he was at a loose end, recovering from an operation on a finger he had injured in a stage accident, and felt the need for a new challenge. He had been watching *Mastermind* as regularly as he could over the years and thought it was time to have a go himself.

His first heat began a trifle inauspiciously. It was recorded in the ornate Academy Room of Stonyhurst College, the celebrated Jesuit foundation in Lancashire and one of the pre-eminent Catholic schools in Britain. He was taking as his specialised subject 'The Life and Reign of Henry VII', and despite scoring 16 was lying fourth at the halfway stage behind David Burnham, a local government officer in Preston ('The Heroic Age of Antarctic Exploration 1827–1922'); Linden Adams, the Acting Head of English at Stanley High School in Southport ('The Life and Works of Barbara Pym'); and Andrew Francis, a senior lecturer in geography and planning at Liverpool Polytechnic ('The Life and Career of Erwin Rommel'). In the general knowledge round, Stephen started awkwardly, when he was

Stephen Allen, with MM

unable to recall the currency of Spain: 'P . . . p . . . p . . . pass,' was all he could say, much to my bemusement. Curiously enough, thinking that he had blown his chances completely, Stephen now relaxed; he picked up speed and fairly spat the correct answers back at me. It was enough for him to snatch the lead and earn him a place in the semi-final; but the other three all qualified for the *repêchage* semi-final and he was to encounter one of them again in the Final.

Stephen's semi-final, recorded in the McEwan Hall of Edinburgh University, caused him much less trouble. He was now offering 'Dartmoor and its Environs' and held a comfortable lead at the half-way stage over Dr Richard Francis, a lecturer in French at Nottingham University ('The City of Paris'); Ian Sadler, a computer analyst from Wombourne, Staffs ('The Life and Works of J. S. Bach'); and Stephanie Brooke, an administrative assistant with Barrow-in-Furness Council for the Disabled ('Shakespeare's History Plays'). In the general knowledge round, however, Stephen had another aberration when he was asked a theatrical question (something he had dreaded, like a doctor being asked about medicines or illness). The question was 'In which pantomime does Widow Twankey appear?' He told me afterwards that his mind went a complete blank. 'O Lord,' he thought, 'as an actor I should know this – but I don't. Help! I'll never work again!' He passed. The audience laughed, and that helped him to relax again and coast to victory.

The Final was recorded in the Old College Dining Hall of the Royal Military Academy at Sandhurst, which was celebrating its 250th anniversary. In those days, finalists could revert to their original subject if they so wished (this rule was changed in the following series); Stephen was the only one of the four finalists to offer a new specialised subject – 'The Life and Voyages of Sir Francis Drake'. His rivals for the title were Andrew Francis again ('Erwin Rommel'); Kate Ford, a branch librarian at Borden, Hampshire ('The Life and Work of Frank Lloyd Wright'); and Trevor Brown, a retired official with the Yorkshire Bank in Halifax ('The Films of John Ford'). Stephen established a commanding lead in the first round with a resounding 20, consolidated it with a sound 15 in the general knowledge round – and the title was his.

After his victory Stephen devised and marketed a simple *ad hoc* tour of arts centres and social clubs around the country, presenting *An Evening With Mastermind*. It consisted of a short humorous talk on the programme and his involvement with it, followed by questions from the audience and, in the second half, a fun team table-quiz which he set and presented. But after the initial public attention died down he found that winning *Mastermind* had made a real qualitative difference which only became apparent later; he had found a greater self-confidence and a greater sense of well-being, because anything, after *Mastermind*, seemed possible!

1992: Steve Williams

There had been, in previous years, a certain unrest among finalists because some of them could revert to their first-round subject, while others were pressed to find a third subject for various reasons – usually because their original subject was not considered suitable for another set of questions. In the 1988 Final, for instance, Barry McCartney ('The British Home Front in the Second World War') had been pressed into offering a third subject ('The Mutiny on the *Bounty* and the History of Pitcairn Island to 1970'), while Roy Bailey, who had taken 'The Life and Times of John Hampden', was required to broaden his subject considerably to cover 'The English Civil War 1642–49'; meanwhile the other three finalists, including the winner, David Beamish, had been allowed to revert to their first subject – despite strong pressure in David's case, he told me. Roy Bailey had written a letter of mild complaint about it, and there was a general feeling in the new production team (David Mitchell and Penelope Cowell Doe) that it would be much fairer to make a new subject in the Final obligatory for all.

The champion in 1992 – the twentieth – was Steve Williams, from Solihull, a quiet and unassuming computer analyst/programmer with a penchant for home-made curries. The new ruling might have been tailor-made for him, because he displayed an extraordinary versatility of interests. He won his heat with 'Surrealist Art Between the Wars', he won his semi-final with 'The Life and Reign of Peter the Great', and the Final with 'Pre-Socratic Philosophy'!

Perhaps it had something to do with his cosmopolitan upbringing. His father was a retired Captain in the Army Pay Corps, and an administrator in further education; his mother was a nurse who came from rural County Tipperary. Steve had attended primary schools in Malaya, Kidderminster and Solihull; he went on to Solihull School for seven years, and left with 'A' levels in physics, chemistry and biology. He then read zoology at the University of Liverpool but dropped out after five terms. In 1972 he was accepted by the Civil Service as a computer programmer. He worked for the Home Office and for the Department of the Environment before a lengthy period of unemployment in the late 1980s. In 1989 he joined Kenrick & Jefferson Ltd, a printing firm in West Bromwich.

Steve was not a quiz tyro when he appeared on *Mastermind*. In

1987 he had joined his brother Frank in 'The Irregulars', a team in a general-knowledge quiz league based in the South Birmingham area; in the years which followed he had come out either top or runner-up in the individual competition. This encouraged him to enter television quiz programmes: *Fifteen to One* (1988), *Countdown* (1988 semi-finalist) and *Catchword* (1988), *Cross Wits* on Tyne Tees TV (1989) and *One False Move* on BSB (1990). All this gave him sufficient confidence to apply for the 1992 series of *Mastermind*, although he did so with some trepidation, for ever since the 1970s he had considered it to be the ultimate quiz programme.

Steve is also the only contender in the history of *Mastermind* (as far as I can recall) to have given up voluntarily a point he had been awarded. At the end of the first round in his semi-final (where his specialised subject had been 'The Life and Reign of Peter the Great') he indicated that he felt he had been awarded a point he should not have been given. In answer to the question, 'In which fortress did Peter's son, Alexis, die as a prisoner in 1718?', he had replied 'Peterhof', which I in my ignorance had interpreted as an acceptable version of the 'Peter and Paul Fortress'. It had given him a total of 19 points. Steve now suggested that, in all fairness, his score should be reduced to 18. There's honesty for you.

It's not as if he could afford to throw points away. It was another vintage year for contenders – and a vintage 'family' year, too. We had Jennifer Keaveney's father, former civil servant Bernard Downing, who just failed to make the *repêchage* semi-final. We had David Dewar, a history teacher at Old Swinford Hospital School in Stourbridge, whose father, the Rev. Dr Michael Dewar, had taken part in the first series in 1972; like his father, he reached the semi-finals.

Nevertheless there was something inexorable about Steve's advance to the title. His heat was recorded in the medieval College Hall of the King's School in Worcester, which was celebrating the 450th anniversary of its refounding after the Reformation by Henry VIII. The hall was originally the refectory of the pre-Reformation priory, and on the east wall there is a fine Norman sculpture, badly damaged by the King's Commissioners in the reign of Edward VI, depicting 'Christ in Majesty'.

Steve took the lead with his specialised subject, scoring 16 on 'Surrealist Art Between the Wars', and then extended it in the general knowledge round to win with 33; the runner-up, Drusilla

Steve Williams, with MM

Armitage, from Earl Shilton in Leicestershire, a retired bank manager with Lloyds International, qualified for the *repêchage* semi-final.

His semi-final, recorded at Aberdeen University, quickly became a two-horse race. Steve, going first, apparently scored a massive 19 with 'The Life and Reign of Peter the Great', to hold a 1-point lead over Dr Ken Emond, from Camberwell, a Scots-born civil servant in the Department of Transport, who scored 18 on 'The Life and Miss

Marple Stories of Agatha Christie'. It was then that Steve volunteered the information that he had been awarded one point too many; it left him level on points with Ken Emond, and neither had had any passes. In the general knowledge round, however, Steve scored a steady 15, which Ken was unable to match, and Steve ended up a comfortable winner.

And so to the Final, which was recorded in the impressive setting of the Great Hall of the University of Birmingham, founded in 1900 and the prototype of red-brick universities.

Steve was up against formidable opposition. Peter Todd, a carpenter from County Durham, had taken 'The Life of St Cuthbert' in his heat and won the *repêchage* semi-final with 'The History of the Derby', finishing on a handsome 35; he was now offering 'The Life and Reign of King Alfred'. Glen Binnie, an environmental health officer with Falkirk District Council, was an experienced quizzer who had come second in the Final of *Brain of Britain* in 1989 and then won *Brain of Brains* when he was required to stand in for that year's winner; he had now come through with 'The German Army 1933–45' and 'The Life and Novels of Gore Vidal', and was taking 'The American Civil War' in the Final. Film-buff Richard Ford, a greetings-card company director and marketing consultant in London, had won through with 'The Life and Films of Fellini' and 'The Animated Cartoons of the Warner Brothers'; he was now offering 'The Life and Films of Kurosawa'.

It was a fast, furious and high-scoring first round of specialised questions. At the halfway stage Steve, bearded and impassive, had scored 19 to hold a 1-point lead over Glen and 2 points over Richard, with Peter trailing on 15. In the general knowledge round, Peter added a solid 16 to set the target with 31. Richard also added 16, to raise the target to 33. Glen ran into problems in the second half of his round and was out of the running. Steve needed 15 points to win outright. He had had no passes in his first round, while Richard had amassed 4 over the two rounds. Steve now changed his tactics: he passed, very quickly, to save maximum time. He had added 14 (with 5 passes) to equal Richard's 33 when the bleeper went during his last question. The question was: 'Which American cartoonist created a ghoulish family which bears his name, inspiring a 1960s television series and a recent feature film?' Without hesitation Steve replied, 'Charles Addams' – and with that he had won on the tape.

Winning *Mastermind* didn't really change Steve's life; his managing director bought him a bottle of champagne, and that was that. He had a go at *Brain of Britain*, where he shared a heat with Paul Overall (1993 semi-finalist), but neither won. He is still a member of 'The Irregulars', along with Paul Overall, which has won the league in the last couple of seasons. He appeared in teams on *The Great British Quiz* (which were trounced by a crack team from the Merseyside Quiz League), and on *Quiz Night*, in a team consisting of himself, his brother Frank, and his father – at seventy-seven the oldest contestant in the series. They narrowly failed to get through to the knock-out stage.

But that has made no difference to Steve Williams. He enjoyed the *Mastermind* experience very much, even though the change of rules on specialised subjects meant a lot of hard labour:

> *I had to work very hard on all of them – I spent most evenings revising them in Birmingham Library. I have no illusions as to how lucky I was to win my series; I think anyone (except perhaps Kevin Ashman!) needs a great deal of luck to win any of the more taxing quiz programmes. Even so, I got a lot of personal satisfaction from being able to 'perform' under the intense conditions of the programme and from managing to revise successfully at my advanced age [he was an old man of 39!].*
>
> *My best memories, however, are of the outstanding sportsmanship shown by all my opponents in all three rounds. They must have known that I was no better than them except on that particular day, but they showed outstanding generosity and largeness of spirit which, in their circumstances, I could not have matched.*

And that, I thought, is typical of the champion who sportingly gave up a point which he felt he had not fairly earned.

1993: Gavin Fuller

There's nothing quite like an anniversary to bring out the best (and the worst) in people. This was our twenty-first-birthday series, and it fully lived up to expectations. We had a fiercely high-scoring heat at historic Rugby School, when all four contenders went forward to the semi-finals and two of them met again in the Final. We recorded a heat in the Barons' Hall of Arundel Castle, the ancestral home of the Dukes of Norfolk, which provided the lowest score for a specialised subject on record (3, by Cowley housewife Pauline Beighton). We had a disastrous semi-final in the eighteenth-century Assembly Rooms in Bath — a programme which provoked a huge and sometimes unseemly flurry of media interest when Glenys Davies was publicly accused by another semi-finalist of flagrant gamesmanship.

And we also had the youngest-ever winner of the championship — 24-year-old Gavin Fuller, a part-time archivist at HMS *Warrior* at Portsmouth.

The series began with a bang — a tremendous cliff-hanger of a programme which saw the future champion squeeze through by the narrowest of margins. It was recorded in the Pritchard Jones Hall of the University College of North Wales in Bangor. The hall was named after an Anglesey man of humble origins who rose to become managing director of Dickins & Jones and a vice-president of the college — just the sort of career which makes a *Mastermind* champion!

Gavin was up against two 'outsiders' from the south-west of England: Peter (Freddy) Feint, from Dartmouth, a former civil servant and now a wine shop manager in Bristol, taking 'The Life and Career of Admiral Lord Jellicoe'; and David Penfold, from Berwick St John, near Shaftesbury in Dorset, a self-employed financial economist, taking 'The Life and Reign of Tiberius'. Neither did himself justice, and both were soon out of the running.

The third rival was to prove a real threat, however: George Long, from Manchester, a young medical assistance co-ordinator for Assistance International in Chandler's Ford, near Southampton, taking 'Clarice Cliff and English Art Deco Ceramics 1928–36'. George was practically a quiz professional. He had graduated from Lancaster University with a degree in German and French. After a brief spell working as a commodity broker in the City, he had spent nine years in retailing, first with Habitat and then with Next. By now he had caught the quiz bug: in 1989 he had taken part in *Sale of the Century* on Sky One, which won him a Citroën AX. He was invited back the following year to take part in a Champion of Champions tourney, which he won after a further eight appearances and gained, *inter alia*, another car. In fact he won approximately £23,000 worth of prizes, which was at that time the highest amount ever amassed on a British television programme in a straight run. In 1990 he started working for the Reg Grundy Organisation in London as a question setter/adjudicator on programmes like *Going for Gold*, *Jeopardy* and *Press Your Luck*. He then went on to work as an office manager for Burns & Porter, Europe's largest competition organisers. George Long had form, as the professionals say.

After the specialised subjects round, Gavin, who was taking '*Dr Who*', was leading George by 2 points on 16; he had 2 passes, while George had 3. In the second round, George went at it with a will and added 15, to set the target at 29; however, he had had another 2 passes, one of them *after* the bleeper, making 5 in all – but after the unfortunate Dawn Tozer episode in 1989 I wasn't going to intervene. Gavin, going last, added 13, also with 2 passes (making 4 in all), and on the passes rule Gavin was declared the winner. It had been a very narrow shave indeed.

As the series progressed, the other main contenders for the title declared themselves. The key heat was undoubtedly the seventh, recorded in Rugby School, where Dr Thomas Arnold, father of the poet Matthew Arnold, had revolutionised the course of public-school education in Britain and where William Webb Ellis, 'with a fine disregard for the recognised rules of football first picked up the ball in his arms and ran with it', thus originating the game of rugby football.

The four contenders were: Barrie Douce, from Derby, a third-year physics student at the University of Bristol, taking 'The Life and Career of Malcolm X'; Paul Overall, from Birmingham, a production manager with Cadbury's, taking 'The Canals of England and Wales'; Maurice Roberts, from Malvern, a former English and economics teacher and retired Principal of Ewell Sixth Form College in Surrey, taking 'The Life and Works of Joseph Conrad'; and David Tombs, from Worcester, a mathematician and civil servant working as a scientist with the Defence Research Agency, taking 'The Great Northern Railway'. At the halfway stage Barrie and David were neck-and-neck on 18, with the other two hard on their heels. In the general knowledge round, Barrie jumped into the lead with an 18 which David could not match (he scored 16), and Paul and Maurice were tied for third place on 30. So Barrie went forward to the second semi-final; but the three others lived to fight another day in the *repêchage* semi-final.

Then came the semi-finals. Gavin Fuller was in the first semi-final, in St Paul's Concert Hall at the University of Huddersfield, and this time had an easy ride, taking 'The Medieval Castle in the British Isles 1050–1500' and winning very comfortably with 33. Barrie Douce, who was now offering 'The Manhattan Project' in the second semi-final, scored another 18 and ended with 32, but was given another close call, this time by Frank Kirkham, a retired Russian and French teacher at Farnworth Grammar School ('The Fall of the Western Roman Empire AD 375–476'), who came in only a point behind. In the fourth semi-final, recorded in Bath, David Tombs offered 'The Solar System' and beat both Paul Overall and Maurice Roberts again, this time with 33. But it was the third semi-final which produced perhaps the most spectacularly ill-fated programme of them all.

The Assembly Rooms in the Georgian City of Bath are an elegant reflection of the Age of Reason and Enlightenment. The recording of the programme there was anything but that, however, and became an absolute nightmare for everyone concerned.

The four semi-finalists were:

John Burke, from Rochester in Kent, a printer with The Printers at Chatham. He had won Heat 11 with 'The Architecture and History of the City of London Churches'; he was now taking 'German Armoured Fighting Vehicles 1939–45' and scored – apparently – 15.

Glenys Davies, from Liverpool, a historical novelist (writing as June Wyndham Davies) living in Wooburn Green in Buckinghamshire. She had won Heat 12 with 'The Siege of Paris 1870–71'; she was now taking 'The Californian Gold Rush' and scored – apparently – 14 (with 3 passes).

Stuart Johnson, from Northwood in Middlesex, a factories inspector with the Health and Safety Executive (and now husband of Kathryn Jones [1978]). He had won Heat 6 with 'Railway Signalling in Britain 1830–1947'; he was now taking 'The Life and Work of Isambard Kingdom Brunel' and scored 17.

John Colverson, from Marlow in Buckinghamshire, a financial
services consultant. He had won Heat 5 with 'The Life and Works
of Gerard Manley Hopkins'; he was now taking 'Model Railways
in Great Britain 1920–90' and scored 14.

At the halfway stage, the scores were given as:

3rd =	*Glenys Davies (14)*	
3rd =	*John Colverson (14)*	
2nd	*John Burke (15)*	
1st	*Stuart Johnson (17)*	

There was no recording break between the rounds. We went straight
on to the general knowledge round, and it was Glenys Davies, as the
joint lowest scorer at the halfway stage, who came to the Chair first.
Before I had time to embark on the first question, she asked quietly,
'Am I too late to challenge one of the questions on which I passed?'
It was a very courteous request; I realised that this was the first
opportunity she had had to raise a query: there had been no time at
the end of her round, when I gave the answers to her pass questions,
and I had no reason to decline to discuss it.

Her eighth question in her specialised round had been: 'What was
the name of the first Gold Rush steamship to dock in San Francisco
in 1849?', and she had passed on that. She got through twenty questions, and was given a score of 14, with 3 passes; as usual, I read out
the pass questions, and had given the answer to the steamship question as 'The *California*'. Glenys, who had done a great deal of
research for her novel on the Gold Rush (*Fool's Gold*), acknowledged
that the *California* had been the first *mail* ship, but claimed that there
had been countless unknown steamships which went there in 1848
and 1849. The upshot was that we agreed to do a retrospective
retake: we dropped the disputed question and substituted another:
'Of which religious movement was the prominent pioneer and Gold
Rush publicist, Sam Brannan, an elder?' Glenys got it right ('the
Mormons'), and her first-round score was adjusted to 15 (with 2
passes).

Unfortunately, this retake was followed by a desperately long
technical breakdown; and during that delay, John Burke took the
opportunity to question the adjudication of one of *his* questions, too.

It was agreed that an error had been made in his round as well, so it was decided to give him another point, too, to raise his score to 16 (with no passes).

When the technical breakdown was eventually repaired, I restarted the proceedings by recording a new ending to the first round, giving the adjusted scores:

4th	*John Colverson (14)*
3rd	*Glenys Davies (15)*
2nd	*John Burke (16)*
1st	*Stuart Johnson (17)*

In the adjusted second round John Colverson went first and added 10, for a total of 24. When it was the turn of Glenys Davies, the scoring device could not cope with the corrected score, and Glenys had to do no fewer than six walks to the Chair (plus retakes of the first questions) before her round got under way; despite this she added 16 to set the target with 31. We had to do a restart with John Burke, too; eventually he added 10, for a total of 26. Stuart Johnson, who had been calm and impassive throughout the lengthy delays, added 12, for a total of 29.

The final scores were:

4th	*John Colverson (24)*
3rd	*John Burke (26)*
2nd	*Stuart Johnson (29)*
1st	*Glenys Davies (31)*

We all heaved a deep sigh of relief when the recording was at last completed; at least it was all in the can, and we knew that, as usual, it would look smooth and seamless after skilful editing. But then the media storm broke.

After the recording that evening, John Colverson's son, Nigel, who was in the audience and had become incensed by the delays, angrily denounced Glenys Davies to the production team as a cheat. In some irritation at the Colversons' complaints, I apparently growled at them, 'It's only a bloody game' – I can't remember doing so, but it sounds par for the course. Nigel repeated the allegations in a letter to the BBC, and when a reply wasn't forthcoming immediately he released the letter to the local press. It was too good a story for the nationals to miss: both *The Times* and the *Daily Telegraph* carried long accounts of his allegations of gamesmanship and his claims that it was Glenys who had been responsible for the half-hour delay in order to upset her fellow-contestants. The BBC was even accused of having engineered the result 'in order to get a woman into the Final'. John Colverson himself, in his only letter to the newspapers, disclaimed any suggestion that the delay had made a difference to his own chances of winning (he came fourth), but claimed instead that the other contenders were visibly distressed and that Stuart Johnson, in particular, was the main sufferer and should have been the winner.

The newspapers leapt on to the story. 'You Cheated My Father, Magnus Told' was the headline in the *Daily Express*. The *Sun* did even better: 'Tears of Mastermind Brainbox Branded a Cheat' it carolled about Glenys, who was quoted extensively as she 'sobbed' a lengthy denial of these 'poisonous lies'.

In the interests of accuracy I have listened to the unedited sound tape of the recording with all its comings and goings. It is hardly surprising that tempers can occasionally get a bit frayed: any recording is a tense affair, but this one was positively diabolical. However, the tape makes it perfectly clear that both Glenys Davies and John Burke had entirely proper reasons for challenging my rulings on the two disputed questions. The cause of the rumpus was the appalling and repeated technical breakdowns during the recording, not the actions of individual contenders.

Throughout it all, and afterwards, Stuart Johnson preserved a dignified silence. He told me that at the time he had been a little surprised when Glenys raised her objection to a question in the first round, but that she seemed to have a valid point which was worth making. He remembers sitting on the set fascinated by the one-sided exchanges he could hear between me and the control room in the van outside, and that he felt interested rather than frustrated; and no, he didn't think that the incident affected his performance. John Burke wrote to the relevant newspapers to protest at the distortions in their stories, but his letters were not published. It was typical of the sportsmanship displayed by the overwhelming majority of Masterminders.

And so, at last, we were ready for the twenty-first Final. And what

Gavin Fuller (right), with MM and Sir David Hunt

a glittering occasion it was. It was recorded at the Commonwealth Institute in London, which was celebrating its centenary. It was a tremendously dramatic setting – a spectacular blue, glass-walled building on the corner of Holland Park, opened by the Queen in 1962. Inside the building, flights of stairs lead from a floating central platform to three levels of main exhibition galleries showcasing the individual Commonwealth countries. Gavin told me afterwards that he had felt absolutely terrified: 'It was like being in the Coliseum in Rome, with Nero throwing you to the lions.'

The opening titles presented a collage of previous winners accompanied by some anniversary statistics, such as: about 100,000 people have applied to take part; more than 1,000 contenders have been asked 50,000 questions; specialised subjects have ranged from 'The History of Nuclear Power' to '*The Archers*'; and *Mastermind* has taken place in 150 locations, including on board a ship, in a cathedral, an aircraft hangar and a castle.

In the audience was a very select group of people who understood better than most the tension of the occasion – seventeen of the previous twenty *Mastermind* champions were present to celebrate the programme's twenty-first birthday.

One by one the four finalists were introduced and took their seats on stage: Gavin Fuller, David Tombs, Glenys Davies and Barrie Douce. They all had their new subjects to wrestle with, of course: Gavin with 'The Crusades 1095–1154'; David with 'The Modern Olympic Games'; Glenys with 'The Life and Reign of Napoleon III'; and Barrie with 'The French Indo-China War 1945–54'.

David, who had come to be regarded as the favourite for the title, took an early lead with 19, followed by Gavin (17), Barrie (16) and Glenys (14). Glenys, no doubt affected by the media storm which had broken over her head, was visibly nervous but nevertheless added 16 to reach 30. Barrie added 15, to squeeze past at 31. Gavin misunderstood his first question and floundered so badly we had to start again (he got it wrong!), but after that he focused better and added 15 to raise the target to 32 on his last question. But would that be enough? As David Tombs stood up to go to the Black Chair, Gavin said to him, 'It's all yours, go for it.' But it was not to be. David started well, but then his challenge began to disintegrate. Becoming more and more agitated he added only 9 to reach 28, and came last. It was agonising to watch.

So Gavin Fuller won the title. But to my eternal shame I have to admit that I made a bad mistake, unprompted, in Barrie's specialised round on 'The French Indo-China War'. Question 5 was: 'Which leader reputedly described the Indo-China War as a conflict between an elephant and a grasshopper?' In a misguided attempt to be help-ful, on the spur of the moment I added a horribly wrong epithet – 'Which *Chinese* leader reputedly described . . .' Barrie replied 'Mao', but the answer was 'Ho Chi Minh'. All I had managed to do was to confuse him, because Ho Chi Minh was not Chinese, of course – he was Vietnamese. Barrie merely raised his eyebrows, but did not object. Viewers phoned the BBC in outrage on the evening of the broadcast, and the media picked it up. In fact it did not affect the outcome, because he would have lost on passes, anyway – and Barrie Douce himself refused to complain. Sportingly he declared that Gavin was the rightful winner and had beaten him fairly and squarely.

It was only appropriate that the Caithness Glass trophy should be presented by Sir David Hunt, eighty years old by then, *Mastermind* champion in 1977, Champion of Champions in 1982, and a long-time Chairman of the Board of Governors of the Commonwealth Institute.

1994: George Davidson

In 1994 we notched up the 400th edition of *Mastermind*, with a gala performance in Coventry Cathedral. It was the last of several other spectacular locations that year, however. The first two heats were recorded in the Fleet Air Arm Museum at Yeovilton in Somerset – a heroic setting, surrounded by veteran aircraft of all kinds, with Concorde 002 (the prototype test plane) in pride of place. In the audience was an impressive array of Fleet Air Arm officers' uniforms; in the hot seat was the third of the Thompson dynasty on *Mastermind* – Army officer Major Peter Thompson, twin brother of Chantal (1990 finalist) and son of Richard (1977); he took 'The Monmouth Rebellion', but failed to progress to the semi-finals.

Another intriguing, albeit rather challenging, location was Oakham Castle, in Rutland, for two of the semi-finals: a medieval castle which is now a Magistrates' Court, complete with Victorian benches. It was a much smaller location than usual; luckily there were little gaps here and there where cameras could be tucked away behind pillars, out of sight of the other cameras.

Another location was memorable for entirely different, and entirely personal, reasons – Rochdale Town Hall, to celebrate the 150th anniversary of the Co-op. It concerned my late father, Sigursteinn Magnusson, and the reason why I was brought to Scotland from Iceland as a baby to make my life and career in Britain and not in Iceland. My father worked for the Icelandic Co-operative movement, and in 1930 he had been promoted to European Export Manager, based in Edinburgh – hence the family move. In May 1945 he attended the 75th Annual Co-operative Congress in Nottingham (the 'Victory Congress') to present greetings from the Icelandic Co-operative movement; on that occasion he had made a pilgrimage to Rochdale where he visited the original 'Pioneers Shop' (now a museum) at Toad Lane, which opened for business in 1844. I, too, made a pilgrimage to Toad Lane, and was thrilled to find my father's signature in the visitors' book. After the *Mastermind* recordings the chief executive of the Co-operative Union, Lloyd Wilkinson, presented me with a bound volume of that historic Co-operative Congress of 1945; in it was my father's speech, headed 'Iceland's Message'. It was an inspired gift which I cherish to this day.

★

The 1994 champion was Dr George Davidson, the senior lecturer in inorganic chemistry at the University of Nottingham. A Northumberland man by birth, the son of an agricultural and fertiliser salesman, he had earned a scholarship to my old college, Jesus College, Oxford, where he took a first in chemistry in 1964 and a Ph.D. on 'The Investigation of Molecular Structure by Vibrational Spectroscopy' in 1967. He went straight to his first job at Nottingham University, where he has become very much a member of the local community, as a town councillor on Bingham Town Council (he was Mayor when he won *Mastermind*) and, since 1995, a Liberal Democrat borough councillor on Rushcliffe Borough Council.

At Oxford he had been captain of the Jesus College team which reached the quarter-finals of *University Challenge* in the 1965–66 series. He enjoyed the experience of quizzes, and when *Mastermind* came along he applied for the 1976 series but failed his audition. After many further years of watching the programme, and having thought of some potential specialised subjects which he felt would enable him 'at least not to look too foolish', he applied on the spur of the moment for the 1994 series. Despite what he felt was another poor audition, this time he was accepted.

His heat was recorded in another intriguing location – the Countess of Huntingdon's Hall, in Worcester. And what a story lies behind its founder, the indomitable Countess herself. She built the chapel in 1773 for the dissenting sect known as 'The Countess of Huntingdon's Connection'. Inspired by the populist religious fervour of those times the Countess sought to bring to salvation her own class, which was scornful of the spiritual humility of the Methodists. The Connection attracted crowds of worshippers throughout the nineteenth century, and the chapel had to be extensively remodelled to accommodate them all. After falling into a sad state of decay in the 1960s the hall was restored to its late Georgian glory and reopened in 1987 as an arts centre, concert hall and music school.

George's opposition in his heat consisted of a management accountant (George Lewis); a retired chemist (Terry McDonald); and a retired telephone engineer who had at long last achieved his ambition to appear on *Mastermind* after seventeen applications and three auditions (Gordon Troughton). Was it worth the effort? Certainly! Gordon took 'Classical Ballet Since 1870' and scored a creditable 27. He came second to George Davidson, who had scored a massive 19 with his specialised subject, 'The Coinage of England 1066–1662', and went on to run out a comfortable winner with 33.

The 1994 series featured three tie-breaks. The first happened in the other programme recorded in the Countess of Huntingdon's Hall. It involved Christopher Argyle, an author, researcher and proof-reader, who had taken 'Japan at War 1937–45' and scored 31 (with 2 passes); and Joe Brookstone, from Northfield in Birmingham, a retired British Rail passenger sales instructor, who had scored pre-cisely the same with 'The Life and Career of Fred Karno'. For Joe, Fred Karno was not only a specialised subject but a very special one, too. Both of his maternal grandparents had been members of Karno's London Suburbia Company; indeed, when his newly-married grandfather turned down the chance of playing the Inebriated Swell in the 'Mumming Birds' on an American tour, the replacement was a youngster called Charlie Chaplin . . . Joe had clearly inherited the family taste for the limelight; he had appeared in the inaugural series of *Fifteen to One* in 1987, followed by *Crosswits* (1991), *Countdown* (1992), and *First Letter First* (1993). *Mastermind* had seemed a natural progression, and he had been accepted for the 1994 series on his fifth application.

Joe Brookstone lost the tie-break 2–4. But he qualified for a place in the *repêchage* semi-final.

The first two semi-finals, each of which also had to be resolved by a tie-break, were recorded in Haddo House Hall, in Aberdeenshire, a thriving arts centre in the grounds of Haddo House itself. Now owned by the National Trust for Scotland, it is the ancestral home of the Gordons of Haddo and the Marquesses of Aberdeen and Temair. June, the 4th Marchioness of Aberdeen, is the driving force behind the cultural activities at Haddo House Hall.

The first tie-break was between two doughty opponents. One was Geoff Thomas, from Manchester, a retired college lecturer in foreign languages at Mid-Cheshire College and an inveterate quizling. He had won his heat with 35 points on 'The Life and Career of K. S. Ranjitsinhji'; he was now offering 'The History of the Football World Cup 1930–90' and scored a resounding 19, plus 15, for a total of 34. The other was civil servant John Wilson, from Edge Hill in Liverpool, a computer programmer with the Home Office. He had won his heat with 31 on 'The History of the Rugby League in

Great Britain'; he was now offering 'The Life and Music of Paul Simon' and scored an even more resounding 20, plus 14, also for a total of 34. The outcome of the tie-break was a 4–3 win for John Wilson.

It was only during the ten-minute break between recordings that I realised we had not prepared a second set of tie-break questions. It was a million-to-one against, I reckoned – but perhaps, just to be on the safe side . . . Penelope Cowell Doe and I hastily put together a pack from the travelling box of spare questions. We barely had time to ensure that none of the questions reflected the specialised subjects of the second batch of semi-finalists before it was time to go back into the Hall for the second semi-final.

This was George Davidson's semi-final – and sure enough, it happened again. This time George, who had offered 'The History of Chemistry 1500–1870' and scored 19 plus 14 for a total of 33, tied with retired lecturer John Coggrove who had achieved the same overall score (20 plus 13) with 'The Life and Works of James Joyce'. Out came the tie-break questions, which were perhaps a little easier than usual because of the haste with which they had been put together; George Davidson won 5–4.

And so George was set for his bid for *Mastermind* glory in the splendour and dignity of Coventry Cathedral, which had been built in a spirit of renewal and reconciliation after its medieval counterpart had been destroyed by bombs in the winter of 1940. It was one of the most superb settings for any *Mastermind* programme I can recall, and a fitting location for the 400th programme: a place of challenging beauty with the celebrated stained-glass window by John Piper (which, incidentally, had been the subject of the second question I asked on *Mastermind*).

George was sitting in the fourth seat. Against him were three opponents who had all scored heavily in their earlier rounds. The first was Stephen Wood, from Brixton, a freelance English tutor for foreign students; he had come through with 'The Buddhist Sage Nichiren' and 'American Blues Harmonica Players 1935–65', and was now offering 'The 1798 Irish Rebellion'.

Next came John Wilson, who had won the first semi-final against Geoff Thomas on a tie-break and was now offering 'Beers and Breweries in Great Britain' (the questions had been set by a 1988 finalist, real-ale enthusiast Roy Bailey).

George Davidson, with MM and Bamber Gascoigne

The third was Graham Roe, a systems development librarian at Sheffield University. He had taken 'The Life and Works of Arnold Schoenberg' in his heat to earn a place in the fourth semi-final, which he had won resoundingly (36) with 'The Life and Works of Samuel Beckett'. He was now offering 'American Classical Music 1910–70'.

George was offering 'The Life and Works of John Dalton'. His three opponents scored 14, 14 and 19 respectively, but George swept into the halfway lead with a commanding 21. By then, only Graham Roe had any chance of catching him; but in the general knowledge round he suffered an unaccountable mental blank on his 'local knowledge' question – he was asked in which English county Peveril Castle was (it's in Derbyshire, quite close to Sheffield), but he answered 'Kent'! He reached 15, however, for a total of 34; but George now had the bit between his teeth and galloped home with a 16 to give him a winning total of 37.

The guest of honour who presented the trophy was the undisputed monarch of all quiz-masters, Bamber Gascoigne. As it happened, he was an unusually appropriate choice, because three of the four finalists had been on *University Challenge* in their time. It's relatively small, the serious quiz world.

1995: Kevin Ashman

See Chapter 10 (pp. 157–63).

1996: Richard Sturch

Our very first clerical champion came in 1996: the Rev. Dr Richard Sturch – 'Sturch the Church', as I somewhat irreverently called him. Richard had been a lecturer in philosophy and theology at Ripon Hall Theological College, at the University of Nigeria and at the London Bible College before returning to pastoral work, and was now Rector of St Nicholas's Church, Islip, with Charlton-on-Otmoor, Oddington, Noke and Woodeaton. He had applied for *Mastermind* fifteen years earlier with the vague notion that the intellectual status of the clergy ought to be more widely recognised; he was not to know that, in 1996, three other clergymen had had the same idea and that they would all meet in a memorable joust in Norwich Cathedral.

In very secular contrast the first heat, recorded in the Drapers' Hall in London, was enlivened by the appearance of former punk Alan Whitaker, from Penzance, who had qualified in computer studies and energy studies but had been a labourer and bartender and was currently unemployed. He took 'The Sex Pistols and Punk Rock', which provoked the BBC to bleep out the word 'bollocks' in the title of their hit album. Alan won easily and went forward to the semi-finals.

Norwich Cathedral was not the only spectacular location. For me the most thrilling was Blackpool Tower Circus for two of the semi-finals, because I was allowed to don a ringmaster's scarlet uniform for some publicity pictures. But only for the publicity pictures, alas; it would have been fun cracking the whip over the contenders – literally, for a change.

Another great pleasure for me that year was meeting so many former Masterminders who had been accepted for another tilt at the title. This change of rules had been introduced the previous year in response to repeated requests from members of the Mastermind Club to be allowed another go, as in some other quiz programmes. This was interpreted in some sceptical quarters as a sign that *Mastermind* was beginning to scrape the barrel for talent – an absurd and unjustifiable aspersion on the vast numbers of people in the land who all have it in them to achieve success in quiz games.

It meant welcoming back many aspirants who had become familiar friends over the years through the Mastermind Club: people like Eleanor Macnair, a semi-finalist in 1973, who had had a fascinating career as a scientific officer with the Admiralty; Amanda Hill, a postal officer in Croydon who had been a finalist in 1976; Joe West, the former North Sea helicopter pilot who had been a finalist in 1979; Isabelle Heward (1983) from Scunthorpe, a former teacher who now described herself as a job-seeker; Leslie Pye, the blind contender who had made such an impact on his first appearance in 1986; Margaret Thomas, a former teacher of religious knowledge, drama and history, now a housewife in Brereton, near Rugeley in Staffordshire, who had appeared on *Mastermind* in 1990 and was now taking 'Famous British Poisoners 1850–1950'; and Christine Moorcroft (1988), a publisher from Liverpool, formerly a schoolteacher and lecturer and now a writer of educational books and a qualified schools inspector; she took a refreshingly different specialised subject, 'Perfume', and although she didn't progress any further she clearly enjoyed the occasion greatly. She was then in the process of taking over as Editor of *PASS*.

Norwich Cathedral was celebrating the 900th anniversary of the laying of the foundation stone by Herbert de Losinga in 1096. This was the programme which featured, for the first time, a quartet of clergymen; it had been specifically planned for transmission on Easter Sunday, but BBC schedulers being what they are, the programme actually went out several weeks later. Ah, well!

The four ecclesiastics were a fascinating bunch. The Rev. Ian Walker was Rural Dean of South Holderness in the East Riding of Yorkshire, with responsibility for twenty-seven parishes; a great jazz enthusiast, he was taking 'The Life and Music of Benny Goodman'. The Rev. Henry Mayor was Rector of two inner-city parishes in Manchester; an active conservationist, he was taking 'The Characteristics and Uses of British Native Trees'. The Rev. James Wheatley, from Newcastle upon Tyne, had trained as an engineer but was now assistant priest at St Cecilia's, Parson Cross, a parish in Sheffield;

appropriately for the location, he was taking 'The Lady Julian of Norwich and the *Revelations of Divine Love*'.

It was a contest of rather mixed fortunes. Richard Sturch challenged successfully on one question in his specialised subject, 'The Life and Literature of Charles Williams' (the writer and theologian): 'Where in Holborn did Williams work as a clerk before joining the Oxford University Press?' Richard replied, 'The New Connection Bookroom', but I said it was the Methodist Bookroom. Richard insisted it was another name for the same place, and we took his word for it – he was a man of the cloth, after all! That helped him to a lead at the halfway stage with 18. Henry Mayor, on the other hand, got a rather rough deal, I thought; he was taking 'The Characteristics and Uses of British Trees' and got landed with (and passed on) two, arguably three, questions about their *diseases*, which seemed a bit peripheral to his subject. It left him trailing the field with 12. In the end Richard was the undisputed winner with 32.

Thereafter he went forward to one of the semi-finals being recorded in Blackpool Tower Circus. It was a remarkable location in every way. The waiting area for the contenders was the high-ceilinged old Elephant Room, while the backstage corridors seemed to have been designed for circus dwarves. The central arena had the capacity to be flooded, and I was very tempted to suggest that we should revert to Philip Lindley's original idea for the set of *Mastermind*: he had wanted the Black Chair to be on an island surrounded by water.

One of the guests in the audience was the horse-racing novelist Dick Francis, who had flown in specially from Germany for the occasion, because his books were to be the specialised subject of one of the semi-finalists, the political risk consultant Boris Starling. Dick's presence no doubt inspired Boris to an impressive 19 on his subject; but he was matched by Richard Sturch, taking 'The Emperor Frederick III', and in the general knowledge round, Richard pulled ahead to win with 34. For Boris, however, it scarcely mattered; he spent the rest of the evening at the feet of his hero, Dick Francis, and loved every minute of it.

In the other semi-final at Blackpool, Richard Heller, an American-born journalist and author, powered his way to victory with 33, taking 'British Political History 1918–40' after winning his heat with 'The Presidency of Harry Truman'. The other two semi-finals, which were

Richard Sturch

recorded in the Opera House in Jersey, brought two recidivist Masterminders to the Final – Gwen Kingsley, a semi-finalist in 1983, and Elsie Sadek (1987).

And so the stage was set – literally – for the Final. It was recorded in the Bristol Old Vic, which was celebrating its fiftieth anniversary as a theatre company. We were in the main auditorium of the splendid Theatre Royal, which dates back to 1768 and is the oldest continuously working theatre in the country. And what a beautifully dramatic setting it provided for what turned out to be a very dramatic Final.

Richard Sturch went first. He told me that he had been thinking of wearing a frock-coat in the hope of daunting his opponents – but decided that it would probably have daunted himself rather than them. He took 'The Operas of Gilbert and Sullivan', and scored an uncompromising 19 (with 1 pass). Gwen Kingsley followed; a trained librarian, she is now a professional genealogist (in 1983, when she was pipped on passes from reaching the Final, she had been a Crystal Works guide and an assistant museum curator). In her earlier 1996 rounds she had won with 'The Life and Literature of Lewis Carroll', and 'The Life and Works of Donatello'; she was now taking 'The Life and Work of Florence Nightingale' and she too scored 19, but with no passes. Richard Heller, cricket fan and cricketing author, took 'The Career of Garfield Sobers', to score 18. The fourth finalist, Elsie Sadek, from Blackpool, I had privately marked as the dark horse candidate. She was a former English and music teacher at Millfield High School, Thornton, and had come thrusting through to the Final with 'The Ottoman Empire to 1700' and 'The Life and Reign of Charles II'; she was now taking 'The Life and Music of Mendelssohn', and scored 16, to find herself trailing.

It seemed to knock the confidence out of her. Going first in the general knowledge round she managed only 11 for a total of 27. Richard Heller, who had also promised much, did little better (with 12) to finish on 30. The field was wide open. Richard Sturch now came to the Black Chair and produced one of the most extraordinary rounds I have ever seen. His face was a study. He was struggling with himself throughout, and agonised grimaces alternated with huge beams of delight, followed by dejection. By the end of the round he had added 13 and was quite sure he had blown his chances.

Gwen Kingsley now had only 32 to beat. She had 19 already – surely she could manage another 14 on her general knowledge? She was, after all, a seasoned quiz campaigner: she had won a car on Anglia's *Sale of the Century* and another on *Jeopardy*. Her prize money from other quizzes had topped £5,000. She had also appeared five times on *Fifteen to One*, reaching the Grand Final twice. Once again the ultimate prize was to elude her, however. She struggled even more than Richard Sturch had done, and could add only 11 to end with 30, joint second with Richard Heller.

So Richard Sturch had fulfilled his ambition to 'vindicate the intellectual status of clergymen'. Had he enjoyed it?

> *It was enjoyable only in the way a fairground helter-skelter or Ferris wheel is: a feeling of mild terror combined with the knowledge that it is wholly unjustified, that no actual disaster is going to take place. I found that my hands were literally shaking as the time to record neared, although once it started there was too much else to concentrate on.*

It's not only the winners who feel they have been on a roller-coaster. Count me in!

1997: Anne Ashurst

The twenty-fifth series – our Jubilee year – was endowed with a special aura of significance by the knowledge that it was to be our last. The winner was Anne Ashurst, a former journalist and now a successful writer in the Mills & Boon stable (her pen-name is Sara Craven). Her victory brought the final tally of *Mastermind* champions to seventeen men and eight women. It also meant that the first and the last champions were women.

The 1997 series was the shortest ever: only thirteen programmes, with thirty-six contenders. There were nine heats, three semi-finals comprising nine outright heat winners and the three highest-scoring losers, and a Final comprising the three semi-final winners and the highest-scoring loser.

Long before we heard that 1997 was to be the final series we had been hatching plans to make the twenty-fifth series a memorable one. I had long hankered to take the programme to the Northern Isles of Scotland (we had already been to Jersey and the Isle of Man, so why not Orkney?), and St Magnus Cathedral in Kirkwall had the obvious attraction of making it an all-time ego-trip. When it was announced that the twenty-fifth was to be the last series the BBC promised to give us a 'memorable and fitting' send-off – and this made St Magnus a feasible location, despite the very considerable expense of transporting a full Outside Broadcast rig across the Pentland Firth.

There were a few loose ends to tie up which had been bothering me for years. One such was the case of Sheila Altree (1985), who was disqualified after appearing that year against the rules. Now that Masterminders were being allowed to take part for a second time, why not offer Sheila an opportunity to do so legitimately? I was delighted when she agreed to apply. In the event she acquitted herself well: she came second in Heat 9 with 'The Stories of H. P. Lovecraft' to reach the semi-finals as a highest-scoring loser (31), but came third with 'The Discworld Novels of Terry Pratchett'.

I was also keen to bring the wheel full circle in other ways. It would have been pleasing if the very first contestant in 1972, Alan Whitehead, had taken part in the first heat twenty-five years later, but alas I failed to find any trace of him. However, I managed to trace Ivan Limmer, who had won that first heat. He leapt at the chance of another audition, and was accepted for the first heat of 1997.

Ivan had won the first heat in 1972 with 19 points. This time, in what turned out to be one of the lowest-scoring heats in the series, the contenders all failed to do themselves justice; Ivan took 'The Russian Revolutions of 1917' and scored only 17. But he didn't mind a bit – he had appreciated the chance of having another crack at the title, for old times' sake.

Another notable recidivist was Tony Dart, a semi-finalist in 1981 and now the President of the Mastermind Club. His heat, like Ivan's, was recorded at Blenheim Palace. He took 'The Life and Career of Sir Thomas Sopwith' and reached the semi-finals with a score of 30, defeating a young man from the Woolwich, Colin Cadby, who came second with 29. Colin qualified for the semi-finals, too, as a highest-scoring loser. In the first semi-final, which was recorded at Britannia Naval College in Dartmouth, Colin got his revenge, and beat Tony comfortably (33 to 29). So Colin Cadby, from Hove in East Sussex, became our first finalist.

The second finalist was Clare Ockwell, from Bognor Regis, who insisted on describing herself as a 'full-time housewife and mother'. A recovered anorectic herself (despite her listed hobbies of 'cookery and cake decorating'), she had won Heat 1 taking 'Anorexia Nervosa' as her specialised subject and scoring a total of 26. The second semi-final was recorded in the Old Laundry Theatre, Bowness-on-Windermere. Clare took 'The Duncton Chronicles' of William Horwood and scored a sweeping 19, followed by 15 in the general knowledge round for a winning total of 34.

The third semi-final, also recorded in the Old Laundry Theatre, was won by Andrea Weston, a housewife and amateur singer from Knowle in Solihull. She had won Heat 6 with 'English Church Music 1505–1625', and she now won her semi-final with 'The City of Prague', gaining a total of 31 points.

So we had three finalists. There was one more to come – the highest-scoring loser. This turned out to be Anne Ashurst, who had defeated Sheila Altree by one point in Heat 9, offering 'Frances Howard, Countess of Somerset'. In the second semi-final, taking 'The Regency Novels of Georgette Heyer', she had scored 33 but had been pipped by one point by Clare Ockwell. Her score was the highest losing total, however, so Anne, too, qualified for the Final.

And so to the Final itself. Before we left for the journey north, producer David Mitchell received a generous letter from John Birt, Director-General of the BBC:

> *During its twenty-five series, the programme has given huge enjoyment to millions of television viewers. It has been a marvellous combination of entertainment and erudition, expertly hosted by Magnus and supported with great professionalism by the programme team.*
>
> *Please pass on to them my thanks and good wishes for a most successful Final. I am sure the occasion will be a fitting farewell to a national institution.*

And so it turned out. The people of Kirkwall welcomed us with open arms and helped to make it a truly memorable occasion.

Orkney was the farthest north the programme had ever been. The

Anne Ashurst, with MM

cathedral, 860 years old, was not an easy location. The cameras had to be backed hard up against the massive pillars. Space was very tight at the crossing of the aisle and the nave, where we had our set – so tight, indeed, that we had to cut up the set in order to fit it in, but since it was the last programme it didn't matter.

In the audience for the Final were forty-nine Masterminders who had made pilgrimage to Kirkwall to be with us, including eight previous champions ranging from Nancy Wilkinson, the 1972 champion, to the Rev. Dr Richard Sturch, the reigning 1996 champion. Also in the audience were Denis Mann, who had engraved all the twenty-five championship Caithness Glass trophies, and Neil Richardson, who composed the *Mastermind* theme music ('which has kept me in whisky for twenty-five years').

The atmosphere in the handsome old cathedral was . . . what can I say? 'Electric' is a terrible cliché, but there was certainly a tremendous sense of expectation, an awareness of taking part in another historic event in the long story of the cathedral of St Magnus. In the recording we had a few technical problems (so what's new?), but the programme itself was one which brought *Mastermind* to an end on a soaring note.

As the four finalists took the chair in turn, the scores moved up and up. At the half-way stage they were closely bunched: Colin Cadby ('The Novels of Thomas Hardy') and Clare Ockwell ('Genesis, the Rock Band') were joint third on 15, Andrea Weston ('The Life and Works of Julian Barnes') was on 17, and Anne Ashurst ('Barbara Villiers, Duchess of Cleveland') was just in the lead with 18. In the general knowledge round, Andrea made her bid with 14 points to reach 31; but Anne Ashurst, going last, swept past her with 16 points for a winning total of 34.

I had one private ploy left to play. I wanted to make the very *last* question on *Mastermind* echo the very *first* question I asked in 1972. We rehearsed the ploy secretly, over and over again, and decided that if the outcome of the Final did not depend on it (and that was crucial), I would get a cue in my earpiece when there were only eight seconds left in the last general knowledge round. It worked! With Anne Ashurst in the lead, I got the eight-second cue, and as soon as she concluded her penultimate answer I fished out the appropriate card and launched into the very last question:

> *'Sixty years ago, during the Spanish Civil War, which town in the Basque country was destroyed by German bombers, an event which was commemorated in a painting by Picasso?'*
> 'Guernica.'
> *'Correct!'*

At least *we* got it right, too, this time: the bombers were German, not Spanish. There's research for you!

And with that, twenty-five happy years of *Mastermind* came to an end: an unbroken run of 447 programmes, with 1,231 contenders, 64,500 questions and 450 million viewers. I departed my beloved St Magnus Cathedral with a host of happy memories – and a very tangible memento in the shape of the Black Chair itself, which had been with us, stool and chair, from the very beginning. I had started. Now I had finished.

12

The Mastermind Club

'It's a remarkable fraternity (and sorority), the Mastermind Club: when we started Mastermind *all those years ago, we had no idea what we were starting. What has emerged is not just a 'cult', as the newspapers used to call it, but a very real friendship based on shared ordeal – rather like ex-servicemen!'*

MAGNUS MAGNUSSON, *PASS*, April 1979

The Mastermind Club was founded in 1978, six years after the programme itself began, and it is quite simply unique, as *Mastermind* itself was. It is the only social club ever to be directly associated with a TV quiz programme. It is a rigorously exclusive club, open only to those who have experienced the ordeal of the Black Chair (although honorary memberships have been granted to members of the production team and a few special supporters). It was founded by Masterminders, serves to reinforce and perpetuate the *Mastermind* experience they all share, and is run by them to this day – not by or for the BBC.

The person who started the club was Charles Key. A contender in the 1973 series, he had won his heat with 'The City of Paris', but lost in the semi-finals with 'The Sherlock Holmes Stories'. He was a genial, urbane man with a full white beard, a strong voice and a wide range of knowledge and skills. He had been a rally driver and an aviator. He had travelled all over the world. He was a fluent French speaker and a great rambler. He played several musical instruments, and had run a dance band as a young man. After the Second World War he had taken a BSc degree in mathematics and science. He knew everything there was to know about cricket, and played billiards and snooker well. He was, in the words of an affectionate friend, 'rather a nice old buffer'.

The idea for a Mastermind Club came to him, he wrote, while he was 'ambling along the M4 during the London rush hour':

> *I fell to musing upon other dangerous pursuits like parachute-jumping or sitting in the Black Chair of* Mastermind. *Parachutists, I remembered, had a 'Caterpillar' Club, which had a special tie and which they were entitled to join if they had saved their lives by parachute . . . But why was there no 'Mastermind' Club, with its own special tie and periodic reunions?*

Late in 1977 he attended the recording of two *Mastermind* semi-finals at the University of Surrey in Guildford in order to discuss his idea with Bill Wright. Both Bill and I responded with unqualified enthusiasm. The BBC quickly gave its formal consent – it was, after all, the first occasion on which a virtual 'supporters' club' had been mooted for a BBC quiz programme; it also, to be honest, sounded as if it could well turn out to be a useful publicity ploy for *Mastermind* itself.

In January 1978 Charles wrote to all the 288 contenders who had appeared during the six years *Mastermind* had been on the air, suggesting a get-together to discuss the idea:

> *Our worthy and genial producer, Bill Wright, has invited me to make some soundings of the support which would be forthcoming for a 'Mastermind' Club, membership of which would be open to anyone who had faced the cameras from the awesome black chair . . . such an Association would be an ideal vehicle for furthering charitable ventures, perhaps for the mentally handicapped – even though the outer world may sometimes question the sanity of those who enter for programmes like* Mastermind.

Of the 288 existing Masterminders, 165 sent replies: 160 were strongly in favour. The response was encouraging enough for Charles to call an 'interest meeting' at twelve noon on Saturday, 8 April 1978, at the Bloomsbury Centre Hotel (now the Bloomsbury Crest Hotel) in Coram Street, London. Eighty enthusiasts attended from all over the country. Mary Craig came as an observer on behalf of the programme. A resolution was passed unanimously:

That a club to be called the 'Mastermind Club' be, and hereby, formed, the membership of which is to be limited to those who have appeared as contestants on the BBC TV programme Mastermind *and those actively engaged in its production.*

The general aims and structure of the proposed Club were aired. A good deal of discussion took place about insignia and apparel for the Club, and about the prospects for annual reunions. There was talk, too, about Charles's idea of the Club having a charitable as well as a social function.

Charles Key, naturally enough, was elected Founder-President; John Palmer-Barnes (1976), a baker from Dudley, was elected Vice-President, with Maggie Garratt (1976), a hospital dietician from Trowbridge, as Secretary. An informal committee was formed to represent the eight regions into which *Mastermind* recordings were divided. It comprised Lance Haward (1976, London and the Home Counties); Patricia Owen (1973 champion, also London and the Home Counties); Sue Jenkins (1977, South-east Region); Dr Gerald MacKenzie (1974, South-west Region); Margery Elliott (1973, Midlands); Robert Hesketh (1977, the North); Dr Michael Dewar (1972, Northern Ireland); and Armando Margiotta (1973, Scotland).

This group was charged with designing a logo, drafting a constitution, identifying suitable Club charitable works and organising a first Masterminders' reunion. The annual subscription was set at £2. The 'interest meeting' adjourned for lunch in high good humour at 1.30pm.

The committee held three meetings in Charles's rambling, book-lined house in Streatham. On 2 September 1978 the fledgling Club held a rather grand inaugural luncheon at the Café Royal in London's Regent Street. As R. H. Greenfield put it, writing in the *Daily Telegraph* the following day, 'the Mastermind Club is open to all those who have taken part in the ordeal and survived with their sanity intact'. Bill Wright attended, along with his wife Sheila and Mary Craig, and brought the Black Chair with him. Fifty-nine potential members were present, along with twenty-five guests.

There were speeches, of course. Cliff Morgan, Head of Outside Broadcasts at the BBC, in proposing the health of the Mastermind Club, announced that *Mastermind* was now attracting audiences of more than 10 million in the UK, and had spread to Australia, New

Zealand, South Africa and Nigeria. Charles, as President, responded. 'Our visitors' were toasted by the Vice-President, John Palmer-Barnes, and Bill Wright replied.

One of Bill Wright's most endearing quirks was his difficulty in remembering people's names. He could remember details of hundreds of camera shots – but not the names of the people in them. He worried about it so much that he even took a course in Pelmanism in an attempt to overcome what he found an embarrassing social handicap. At the Café Royal lunch he looked in despair at the sea of half-familiar faces at the tables around him; he started scribbling notes for his speech on the back of his menu, identifying members of the Club by the specialised subjects they had offered on the programme: for instance, 'Venomous Reptiles' (John McKean, 1977) sitting next to 'Henry VI' (Angela Alves, 1977), and 'Children's Literature' (Sue Jenkins, 1977) next to 'The History of Linguistics' (Tom Dawkes, 1977).

I, too, had been due to speak ('the last word'), but alas! – I had been felled by a bug I caught on a filming trip to Greece and could not attend.

The formal meeting of the Club was held after lunch, which made for a rather long and expansive affair. The Club was constituted, and a draft constitution adopted, subject to 'minor drafting amendments'. (In the event, the 'minor drafting amendments' were to exercise the committee, and several AGMs, for years, and it was not until 1991 that the Club constitution was finally adopted.) In my absence I was elected Honorary Life Member of the Club, along with Bill Wright and Mary Craig. Charles was confirmed in office as President for two years, and also took on the post of Treasurer ('in view of his large experience'), despite an objection from Lance Haward (a solicitor and assistant town clerk of Barnet, who would become the Club's second President) that, under the constitution, the two offices were required to be separate.

A formal committee was elected on a regional basis, drawn largely from the original working group. The committee was to meet bi-monthly, mostly at Charles Key's home, although other members might act as host in turn. The intention was that the representatives would arrange regional get-togethers for various parts of the country; the early attempts were abortive, but now there are four such regional groupings, meeting monthly in wine bars or pubs in London, Manchester, Birmingham and Newcastle upon Tyne.

And so the Club was well and truly launched. Fifty-seven members stayed on for a group photograph, with Bill Wright sitting in the Black Chair.

Insignia and Club motto

It had been decided that the Club's logo should be the Black Chair, and Charles Key made a drawing of it which is still featured as the official emblem of the Club. Production of ties and silk scarves bearing the Club insignia was in hand; but there was a great deal of argument about the design for the ties, and the scarves took a long time to produce. In the end only one batch of scarves was made, and they are now collectors' items. The Club merchandise now includes a badge, cuff-links and pendants, along with sweatshirts and T-shirts. For the 1997 annual function, in celebration of the twenty-fifth series of the programme, a special T-shirt was designed bearing the words 'I've started, so I'll finish' on the front and 'It's only a bloody game' on the back.

Various ideas for a Club motto were mooted in the early months:

I shall not pass this way again *[attributed to Stephen Grellet, 1773–1855]*

Ils ne passeront pas *(They shall not pass)*

In cathedra, ex cathedra respondeamus *(In the chair we give infallible answers)*

Instanter, instantius et instantissime *(Immediately, more so and most urgently) [from the Tridentine service for the enthronement of a new Pope]*

Nemo solus sapit *(No one is wise alone)*

Nil scio nec nescio *(I know nothing, except that I know nothing) [Plautus, quoting Socrates]*

Not even the fool when he holdeth his peace is accounted wise *[adapted from Proverbs 17: 28]*

Periculum in mora *(There is danger in delay)*

Qui non proficit, deficit *(He who does not advance goes backward)*

Semper paratus *(Always ready)*
Veni, dixi, vici *(I came, I spoke, I won)*

The Club never actually adopted a formal motto. But in later years the phrase which I would use in order to calm contestants' nerves ('It's only a bloody game!') achieved the status of unofficial Club motto; it was felicitously translated into idiomatic Latin by Gerald MacKenzie as *Ludus non nisi sanguineus*, and applied to a sweatshirt for my own special use.

PASS: *the origins*

Soon after the foundation of the Club the suggestion arose that there should be a Club newsletter, to be called *PASS* (of course!) and distributed to all members. An appeal was made for an editor. Although he had never intended to become heavily involved with the Club, Martin Leadbetter (1977) was one of the four volunteers. Martin was Fingerprint Expert and Deputy Bureau Head at the Hertfordshire Constabulary HQ; he was also co-editor of *Fingerprint Whorld* (1975–90), the official journal of the international Fingerprint Society. With this experience he was selected by the Club committee as the person best qualified to undertake what was almost bound to be a thankless task. There was neither money to finance the project nor any secretarial back-up, but Martin blithely took it on as an unpaid short-term appointment just to help to get it off the ground.

The first issue of *PASS* came out in April 1979. It was intended to be bi-monthly, but over the years it has become quarterly. It was an unassuming little publication, just ten duplicated pages stapled together. The front cover was designed by another fingerprint expert, John Berry, co-editor with Martin of *Fingerprint Whorld*; it portrayed the Seven Pillars of Wisdom. It aroused a bit of controversy (*everything* seemed to arouse controversy in those days), and was described variously (in letters to the Editor) as 'a ladder inside a hamburger' and 'some of the temples Elgin knocked about a bit'. The design was later computerised by Gerald MacKenzie's son Alasdair and was used until the May 1993 issue. After this the Seven Pillars were replaced by a drawing of the Black Chair.

Early issues of *PASS* carried a number of quizzes set by members for one another. These soon coalesced into plans for an annual Club quiz competition which would have a Grand Final at the annual function.

Martin eventually relinquished *PASS* in the middle of 1981 to devote more time to his consuming interest, which was composing music (he is a published composer of some repute). The torch was taken up by a succession of Editors, each of whom would bring new ideas and attitudes to the task.

The Club: the 1980s

The fledgling Mastermind Club held its first annual function and AGM in London in September 1979. The BBC provided a buffet lunch at Television Centre, a new Vice-President (John George, 1978) was elected and it was agreed that the post of Treasurer should be separate from that of President, especially since the financial affairs of the Club were not being run very satisfactorily. Bob Hesketh (1977), a taxi-driver from Warrington who was now running a business of his own, was appointed Treasurer.

Despite its euphoric beginnings, however, the Club was already showing signs of stress. Charles Key was now suffering from lung cancer and was unable to attend committee meetings; he died in August 1980. Bill Wright was also struggling against terminal illness and died in September of the same year.

The second AGM and annual function was arranged for 6 September 1980, in Bath, but it never took place. It was planned to start at 10am, and there would be a slap-up luncheon in the Grand Pump Room. Alas! Only sixteen members (and seven guests) had booked to take part, well short of the official quorum of forty, and the event was cancelled at the last minute. Ten members who had not heard the news in time turned up, however, and spent a disconsolate day in Bath. It was agreed that the formal quorum was too large for such a small club (it was soon reduced to twenty-five), and that only a residential weekend function could attract sufficient members from all over the country.

An attempt was made to salvage the 1980 AGM by planning to hold it in Bath on 1 November. No feast was to be arranged and there would be no cost. It was to coincide with the Final of the Club quiz competition, but there was insufficient interest and both events were cancelled.

The Club was now in dire straits. There was no meeting of the committee between September 1980 and July 1981. The administration, such as it was, was creaking ominously: new members complained that they had not received their membership cards or even acknowledgements of receipt of their subscriptions; old members were not renewing their subscriptions but were still receiving copies of *PASS*. Indeed, an editorial in *PASS* (February 1981) mourned: 'Well, there doesn't seem to be much happening within the Club these days. Can this be due to apathy, I wonder?' It seemed symptomatic of the general inertia that this issue of *PASS* was itself the most meagre issue since the first one – only ten pages.

There were also fears that, with the death of Bill Wright, *Mastermind* itself might not survive. If *Mastermind*, the sole *raison d'être* of the Club, had ended in the early 1980s, I do not think the Club would have carried on. Today, however, even with the demise of *Mastermind* a reality rather than a fear, the Club is in such tremendous heart that there is every confidence for a long and thriving future, programme or no programme.

In June 1981, however, it was crisis time. Despite all the initial good intentions the Club was now rudderless, drifting without purpose or direction. John George, as Acting President, eventually convened a special committee meeting to try to get things back on an even keel. Sheila Ramsden (1977) volunteered to take over as Editor of *PASS*. Bob Hesketh, as Treasurer, reported on the parlous state of the accounts, which had never been audited, and the committee decided to recommend an increase in the annual subscription from £2 to £5.

Maggie Garratt, the Secretary, could not attend because of family commitments, and in fact never attended another committee meeting. In her place, Margery Elliott took over as Acting Secretary; she conducted an arduous overhaul of all the membership records and correspondence, got the membership list in order and persuaded dozens of lapsed members to renew their subscriptions.

Everything now depended on the 1981 annual function and AGM, which was held at Television Centre in September and attended by forty members. Could the new committee with its handful of committed, hard-working officers resuscitate membership enthusiasm sufficiently to make the Club viable? When the planned issue of *PASS* with the full agenda for the AGM failed to materialise in time it looked unlikely.

But things turned out much better than had been feared. A new President was elected – Lance Haward – and a new Vice-President, Gerald MacKenzie, to replace John George, who had been in desperately poor health. Lance was upbeat in his presidential address: membership figures were 'healthy'; the spirit of the Club, he felt, was equally healthy. There was a much clearer idea of the way ahead, he claimed, and *PASS* would be given more attention to make it both interesting and punctual. The Final of the Club quiz had to be abandoned once again, but Lance gave assurances that it was going to become a lively and popular event.

And so the Club seemed to be over the worst. The committee was functioning again, thanks to the indefatigable efforts of Margery Elliott, who had been confirmed as Secretary. It was all very positive. But just as everyone was thinking that all was running smoothly, the Club suffered another blow: Bob Hesketh, the Treasurer, simply dropped out of sight. He had done absolutely nothing about the finances of the Club. He had neither acknowledged nor paid in the subscription cheques which had been posted to him in several batches; he had not paid any expenses which had been agreed by the committee. He was unavailable on the telephone and did not answer letters; he was sitting on the books, and not returning them. There was no skulduggery involved – he simply ceased to operate. In the end a writ was served on him and within days the missing books and expired cheques were returned unceremoniously in a carrier bag. That was the last anyone in the Club heard from him.

Margery Elliott took over as Acting Treasurer until a new Treasurer was appointed: John Withrington (1981), who worked for a bank (the NatWest), helped by Tony Dart (1981), who had an accountancy background, as Assistant Treasurer. John Withrington, however, was transferred by his bank to Paris after a year and had to step down.

The subscription had meanwhile been raised from £5 to £7 at the 1983 AGM (mainly to cover the rising costs of *PASS*). Tony Dart was now appointed Treasurer – and that was probably the most significant appointment in the story of the Club. Tony, who later became deputy Rector of the University of Westminster, was Treasurer of the Club from the middle of 1983 until he was elected President in 1990. He is acclaimed by all as the person who really put the Club on its feet. As he was to recall in an article in *PASS* in May 1988, it was then a tiny private club which was getting rapidly tinier. The assets of the Club totalled only £96 (in his first year as Treasurer, Tony had to lend the Club £100 to keep it going). It was being run by a bunch of well-meaning amateurs who were slowly driving it into the ground. They confused paid-up membership with the number of *PASS* magazines issued: they had been sending *PASS* to people who had signed up but had never been heard from again. The annual functions were also losing a lot of money: a Club which took in £2,000 a year in subscriptions was trying to run functions costing £5,000 or £6,000, with no reserves to cover mishaps.

Nearly everyone who took part in *Mastermind* joined the Club immediately, but most of them left after only a year: the Club had nothing to offer them, apart from the opportunity to buy a very exclusive tie. Sometimes they did not receive their copy of *PASS* and there was nothing to make them renew their subscription – especially since they weren't ejected if they didn't. Tony introduced incentives for wanting to remain in the Club: better functions were arranged which actually *made* money instead of losing it, and he introduced standing order payments for subscriptions, putting the onus of positive cancellation on the member.

In 1984 Lance Haward was succeeded as President by Gerald MacKenzie, and for the next six years the Club enjoyed an unparalleled period of stability. The finances were in order, and improving. The real membership figures were rising. In 1986 a new Secretary was appointed to succeed Margery Elliott: the late John Widdowson (1977), former headmaster of Keil School in Dumbarton. Apart from teaching, his great passion in life was crossword puzzles. He composed crossword puzzles for the *Listener* under the pseudonym 'Bart' (his middle name was *Bart*holomew, and he was a teacher in Dum*bart*on), and contributed puzzles to various other journals. John introduced the use of a spreadsheet to reorganise the membership list, and was on the production sub-committee of *PASS* for several years.

The highlight of Gerald MacKenzie's presidency (1984–90) was undoubtedly the 1988 annual function, which was held in Jesus College, Cambridge – his old college. The Club dinner was a wonderfully elegant occasion, complete with a magnificent swan carved from ice and filled with fruit and flowers in the style of Tom Sharpe's *Porterhouse Blue*. Gerald was in his element. The BBC came and filmed the occasion, as did an NBC team from the USA. Nancy Wilkinson, the first champion, was a guest at the dinner, and Fred Housego attended at the BBC's invitation. It was the first time that an annual function had an attendance of more than 100 members and guests.

At the 1990 AGM in Edinburgh, Tony Dart was elected President in succession to Gerald. Membership was now a record 319. The Club's cash balance, as a result of Tony Dart's stewardship, stood at an extremely healthy £3,167. The annual functions, which were held alternately in London and in 'the provinces', were firmly in place as the high point in many members' social calendars – and certainly in mine. As the Club entered the 1990s, it was unrecognisable from the ailing infant it had been at the start of the decade.

The Magnum

The common interest which had brought all the members together was taking part in quizzes. It was therefore only natural that the Club should run its own in-house quiz. The trophy was 'the Magnum' – a Toby jug in the likeness of 'the Interrogator' fashioned, from photographs and sketches, by Gwyn Price, the Birmingham potter. The competition involved two preliminary written rounds (published in *PASS*), the leaders of which qualified for a 'live' Final at the annual functions for which I was cast as question-master – a busman's holiday role which I have come to enjoy immensely.

The Club quiz is essentially a one-man effort, with all the questions set by Gerald MacKenzie, assisted latterly by Phillida Grantham, who now sets Round 1 of the written preliminaries. For Gerald it is a labour of love spread over several months (helped by his daughter Victoria), supplying questions for the second written round as well as for the Final itself, which alone requires 150 usable questions.

We have had a lot of fun with the Magnum, Gerald and I, and will continue to do so for a long time, I hope. I particularly treasure the Saturday afternoon sessions before the Final when we would argue furiously about some of his more wilfully eccentric questions. Question-setting for the Magnum is much more difficult than most people realise – even more difficult than setting questions for *Mastermind*, where we always had a bank of specialised question-setters to fall back on.

The Club quiz had got off to an inauspicious start, however: there was no Final at all in 1980, and the Final of the second competition, in 1981, also had to be abandoned. But the Magnum trophy was awarded, by default, to the highest scorer in the preliminary rounds, Kathryn Jones; it was handed over a few weeks later in a ceremony in the foyer of Broadcasting House by the late Dr John Sykes (1976).

It was not until the 1982 annual function, which was held in Birmingham, that the first Final took place. I was abroad, filming for *Chronicle*, and was unable to attend, but I sent a recorded message to be relayed to the assembled company. In my absence Gerald MacKenzie acted as question-master. As was to be expected with a new venture there were numerous teething troubles. The staging was so flimsy that at one stage it collapsed, depositing Gerald on the floor with all his books and ledgers; furthermore, he had to do all the marking and scoring on his own, and as a result it was all rather slow and laborious. The competition was also late in starting, and a reporter from the *Birmingham Post* who came to cover it gave up in despair and left long before the end. Those who stayed the course saw Kathryn Jones win the title for the second year running.

From then on, 'the Magnum' settled into a regular and much appreciated part of the Club calendar and, for many, the high point of the annual functions. We had our own little problems, of course. When the event was held in York in 1984, for instance, there was panic over the questions, because Gerald had posted them to me at the Viking Hotel for a quick preview – but they had been delivered to a *different* Magnus Magnusson who was staying in the same hotel. It could only have happened in a hotel dedicated to the Vikings!

A problem of a different nature arose when, horror of horrors, the Magnum itself got broken. It happened in 1987 when Kathryn Jones (by then Murton), as the holder of the Magnum for the third time, had had a smart protective carrying case made for the trophy. Due to a slight miscalculation in the placing of the padding in the case, however, the box was too tight and when the lid was closed a large crescent piece of my forehead was broken off. It was impossible to find a professional ceramics restorer in the time available, so it was repaired by her then husband, Peter Murton, who used diluted paint in toning colours to camouflage the missing fragments. Time has now caused the glue to darken, and the break is much more obvious than it was at the time: the Magnum, like its original, has acquired a certain patina of antiquity.

What makes the quiz so enjoyable, for me at any rate, is the nature of the after-dinner Club audience. Most of them are hardened quizlings who take a lively (and occasionally unruly) interest in the questions. I usually throw unanswered questions to the audience (a bit like feeding the lions to keep them quiet), and there is always *someone* who knows the answer. Nothing pleases them more than catching Gerald or myself out in a disputed answer. In the early days I think I had a rather cavalier attitude to it all ('It's only the Magnum, after all'); in my first stint as question-master, in 1983, for instance, I blithely accepted an answer from Phyllis Hartnoll (1973), the eventual winner, to the effect that an aneroid barometer was one which used mercury (*everyone* knows that it uses no liquid, don't they?)! Poor Gerald was reduced to waving the card with the correct answer at the howling mob to prove that it wasn't his fault!

Gerald MacKenzie described his amiable quiz philosophy in an article in *PASS* in January 1993:

> *My philosophy is quite simple. Games have two raisons d'être: preparation for 'life' or survival, and recreation and relaxation – in a word, enjoyment. To paraphrase Disraeli, I believe that a quiz should be so constructed that the participants, both contestants and audience, should 'approach it with confident hope, and never relinquish it with anything worse than a feeling of amiable despair'!*

For a list of Magnum winners, see Appendix III.

The Mugnum

The obverse of the Magnum is the 'Mugnum' competition, which is held at the annual functions for the princely prize of a mug. The

Mugnum is an off-the-cuff quiz, with one question set by each member who attends. Conceived by Lance Haward in 1982, it was all rather *ad hoc* in the early years. The idea was for each member to bring a question on a postcard with the answer in a sealed envelope; these were to be handed to the organiser, who would pin up the questions on a Mugnum noticeboard. The possibilities for confusion were legion: the organiser might be late arriving, or members would pin their own questions up willy-nilly. Latecomers had their questions pinned up late, so other members had to keep going back to the noticeboard to check if there were any new questions. There was often an unseemly scrum at the noticeboard, but everyone enjoyed it. Nothing could demonstrate more vividly the competitive appetite of Masterminders for quizzes in the face of any adversity!

The questions are *supposed* to be of *Mastermind* general knowledge standard, with only one possible correct answer; but despite constant pleas from the organisers for easier (or at least more accessible) questions, Masterminders take a gleeful delight in setting deliberately obscure questions. There is now a special prize for the member who sets the question which attracts the largest number of correct answers.

One bonus, of course, is the witty, the quirky and the unexpected question. Sue Jenkins (1977), the Mugnum organiser from 1985 to 1993, says:

> *I always found it fascinating to see the extraordinary mixture of questions which Masterminders could produce . . . for instance, I learned that railways trucks are all named after fish or other marine animals, and I never pass a railway siding without spotting it now. At times we are in danger of getting too clever for our own good, I suppose, and there's a bit of showing-off involved (I'm sure that I've been guilty of that myself!) – but above all it's a bit of harmless fun.*

Now run by Phillida Grantham, the Club Secretary, the Mugnum is much more streamlined and systematic. Members have to send in their question in advance with their booking form for the annual function, together with the answer in a sealed envelope. The questions are then collated on to a question sheet, and members arriving for the annual function are handed a printed copy at lunchtime on the Saturday. The participants are required to write their answers on the answer sheet and return it by the deadline of 11pm, after the Magnum Final. The system isn't entirely 'Masterminder-proof', however; some members forget to include the answer to their own question and have to be telephoned; some seem incapable of cutting along a dotted line on a form, and others forget to put their name on the answer sheet. The 1990 Mugnum winner, Ella Thompson (1984), even forgot the answer to her own question (it was the name of the first woman AA patrol rider [Georgina King]).

Lance Haward, the father of the Mugnum, feels that it is the ideal quiz competition, free from all the vagaries of fortune: 'The person who wins it, on the spur of the moment and without recourse to any reference books, has to cope with an extraordinary batch of obscure and esoteric questions compiled from totally arbitrary sources.' Except, of course, that there are plenty of bookshops and libraries open on the Saturday of the annual function weekend. Some members are sneaky enough to bring with them a trunkful of reference books, and a fair amount of devious activity also goes on over dinner as members trade answers with one another.

The Mugnum carries little of the prestige of the Magnum or the *Mastermind* championship itself, but it is held in great affection: it is essentially a competition for the rank-and-file rather than the stars. Indeed, it has only been won on three occasions by a *Mastermind* champion. For a list of Mugnum winners, see Appendix IV.

PASS: *continuation*

PASS has always been one of the most important factors in giving the Club cohesion and reinforcing its identity. Like the Club itself, it had its ups and downs in the 1980s. From 1981–88 the Editor was Sheila Ramsden from Sheffield (1977); Sheila was then working as a nurse at Lodge Moor Hospital and a part-time cleaner at Hallwood Hospital where her husband was caretaker. The logistics of the operation were always fraught, however, especially with the precarious state of the Club's finances. Sheila had the magazine duplicated by the psychiatric patients at Middlewood Hospital as part of their occupational therapy. The typing was done by the late tutor/librarian June Maggs from Wales (1976), whose quirky asides enlivened the issues but tended to disconcert those few members who contributed occasional articles.

Material for each issue was haphazard, and the constant labour of editing, stapling and binding and distributing the copies took its inevitable toll.

After the Spring issue of 1988 Sheila gave up the long struggle and retired from the editorship after seven arduous years. In the most difficult circumstances, and with no experience of editing whatsoever, she had helped to keep the Club together with the lifeline of *PASS*. But what *PASS* had perhaps lacked during those years had been a coherent editorial policy on the real *purpose* of the magazine, which was to provide a forum for members to share ideas on issues of importance to the Club and to themselves.

After a brief interregnum, Margery Elliott, who had been Club Secretary from 1981–86, stepped into the breach again as Editor for the next five years. New technology was now enabling production and distribution to be improved out of all recognition as Craig Scott (1981) – 'a superannuated hippie from California' as he calls himself – lent his desk-top publishing skills as production manager. Distribution became the responsibility of Phillida Grantham; it is now done commercially.

Looking back on her five years as Editor, Margery says:

> *My main aim was to produce an interesting and accurate magazine. I sought to maintain a balance between all the quiz material (which had become the staple fare of* PASS*) and contributions by members on a variety of interesting topics . . .* PASS *is, after all, what keeps members in touch with one another, particularly if they cannot attend the annual functions. It is practically all they get for their subscriptions, and so it is the Editor's job to make it as good value as possible.*

When Margery retired from the editorship she was succeeded by Patricia Cowley (1991), a consultant publisher's editor who had been a production editor for Mills & Boon. With her expertise and experience Patricia seemed the obvious successor. She agreed to take on *PASS*, simply registering the fact that there was some talk of using a computer; but it did not really penetrate until she tried to get to grips with a computer herself for the first time. Her first issue was November 1993 and her last was March 1995, and it was not a happy time. She enjoyed the editorial work, but the computer became a nightmare. Her learning process consisted of a single long session with Craig Scott, but that was not enough for a technological tyro. She needed far more assistance, and after struggling for a year to master the principles of the operation she concluded that it wasn't going to work.

Craig himself took over temporarily as Editor, and was succeeded in the spring of 1996 by Christine Moorcroft from Liverpool (1988 and 1996). Christine is a writer of educational books and a school inspector, a former schoolteacher, lecturer and publisher. She brought a new discipline to the business of commissioning contributions (free!) and producing the magazine on time, as well as new thinking to the business of how to make the magazine both readable and relevant to the essential interests of the Club and its members. She has introduced colour on the front and back covers, and widened the magazine's appeal by commissioning articles from people who work on other quiz programmes.

The Club: the 1990s – and onwards

Under Tony Dart's steady chairmanship, the Club has continued to prosper. Phillida Grantham, who succeeded John Widdowson as Secretary in 1991, has brought to the post endless patience and tact, and a cool and meticulous organising ability. She also makes all the arrangements for the annual functions – an extremely delicate and demanding task in itself.

Since 1989 the finances have been under the care of a new Treasurer, Paul Henderson (1987), an astrophysicist by training and a member of the crossword-setting team of the *Independent*, now working as a scientific research officer with the Home Office. The annual functions continue to flourish (and to make money). At the time of the announcement of the demise of *Mastermind* the Club's assets had risen to nearly £10,000; the subscription is £7 a year, unchanged since the AGM of 1984.

The membership was standing at an all-time high of 455. A new Membership Secretary had been appointed in 1992: Peter Chitty (1987), a telephonist in Brighton, who had been in the 250th programme taking as his specialised subject 'The History of the British Secret Service 1909–40' (spy books having been a lifelong interest).

Peter had seen me on television enthusing about the Mastermind Club, 'and wanted above all to be able to join such a prestigious assembly'. So seriously does he take his job as Membership Secretary that he taught himself how to use the Club's laptop to computerise the membership list – but still retains the index-card system as a back-up, just in case!

Although the programme is no more, the Mastermind Club goes on: the living repository of the memories of an extraordinary programme which became a broadcasting legend long before it finished.

13

The Team Spirit

'For twenty years this well-loved programme has entertained, stimulated, excited and instructed us. I would like to take this opportunity of thanking and congratulating everyone concerned with the programme, not only those whose faces we see on camera – all of those whose hard work, enthusiasm and dedication have contributed to this marvellous record.'

P. D. JAMES, a Governor of the BBC, at the presentation of the twentieth *Mastermind* trophy to Steve Williams, 1992

I devoted the first chapter of this book to the 'onlie begetter' of *Mastermind*, Bill Wright. It is only proper that the final chapter should be devoted to those who succeeded him, the producers, directors and researchers down the years: the teams who nurtured the *Mastermind* ethos and ideal he had conceived.

Practically every letter I received from Masterminders in response to my initial plea in *PASS* for help with my research for this book made glowing reference to 'the team'; a major theme running through their correspondence was the pleasure they still felt at the memories of taking part – in particular, the friendliness and warmth with which they were treated by every member of the production team. Just to take one example of many: Joe Brookstone, who reached the semi-finals in 1994, concluded his letter about his experiences on the programme as follows:

So ended my participation in Mastermind. *It was a wonderful experience, and I shall always appreciate the efforts of all – yourself, Penny Cowell Doe, the technical and floor staff – for helping to put everyone at ease; nothing appeared to be too much trouble. I must also mention the intense goodwill and camaraderie of the contenders.*

I think this added an extra dimension to the *Mastermind* experience. All the men and women who came on to the programme had a vision for themselves, and we gave them a chance to live out that vision. Even if they lost in the first round it was a significant achievement for them simply to have got there; once there, they were treated as people of an importance which matched their own private sense of themselves. They never felt that they were simply camera fodder for a programme. The thank-you letters which reached us after each recording were appreciated in a very special way, because they proved that the experience had really worked for them, as it had done for us. Penelope Cowell Doe (producer, 1992–95) says:

> *We hated it when someone went home feeling disappointed or hard done by or undermined in any way. We were trying to make good programmes which would thrill the viewer, but not at the expense of our contestants. They were not the professionals: they couldn't do retakes to save their blushes, as we ourselves could. They were putting themselves on the line, for us, for the programme, as well as for themselves. We wanted them to enjoy the experience, whether they won or not, whether they were run-of-the-mill programmes or not, and we did all we could to contribute to that feeling; when we knew that they hadn't achieved that feeling, it was a deep disappointment to all of us.*

For me, one of the most pleasing aspects of the programme was the quite remarkable team spirit which it generated. Every member of the team felt a tremendous sense of commitment to the programme and to one another. I remember fondly the pre-programme occasions just as much as the programmes themselves. I recall in particular the eve of the 1994 series. We were to record the first two programmes in the Fleet Air Arm Museum at Yeovilton in Somerset. It so happened that our floor manager, John Gilpin, and his wife Isobel had recently bought a converted barn in Dorset in the village of Stourpaine, ten miles from Shaftesbury. Here they entertained the team to dinner. It was a wonderfully happy occasion for all of us, reinforcing the camaraderie of the team at the start of a new series as nothing else could have done.

I also recall with pleasure a stirring sing-song when we were recording programmes in Glasgow; the team came out to my home in the village of Balmore, just to the north of Glasgow, and my children, all of whom are much more musically accomplished than their father, played music all evening and we sang until midnight.

The most memorable from my point of view, however, was a totally spontaneous party in St Andrews late in 1989; on the day we gathered for the programme-making the newspapers had announced that I had been awarded an honorary knighthood (KBE) for services to the heritage of Scotland. I believe that my colleagues at the time – John Gilpin, producer Peter Massey, director Andrea Conway, assistant producer Penelope Cowell Doe, production assistant Damaris Pitcher, engineering manager John Wilson and his crew – were all as genuinely delighted as I was, and showed it. At the next day's rehearsals the scene crew had a lot of fun, treating me with exaggerated reverence and converting the Black Chair into a temporary throne.

So step forward and take your bow, all my trusty friends and colleagues.

John Gilpin, the floor manager, was practically built in with the bricks of *Mastermind*; he superintended the sharp end of more *Mastermind* programmes than anyone else. A tall man of unruffled calm, whatever the crisis, he was the assistant stage manager at the pilot programmes in September 1971. In the first years of *Mastermind*, the stage managers (floor managers, as they are called nowadays) were provided by the regional Outside Broadcast units wherever the programmes were being recorded, so John only did the occasional 'big occasion' *Mastermind* in the London area, such as the Jubilee Final at Guildhall in 1977. In 1982, however, it was decided to retain a floor manager as a regular member of the production team. John Gilpin was selected and, as a result, supervised every recording from 1982 until taking early retirement from the BBC at the end of the 1993. *Mastermind* would have been unthinkable without John, however, and he was pressed to continue with us in a freelance capacity.

John had studied telecommunication engineering at Leicester Technical College before he joined the BBC in London in 1958, at the age of twenty-one, as a radio engineer trainee. It was in his blood. He was the son of a mechanical engineer who ran a small factory making bronze bearing-bushes for various vehicles (including tanks and planes during the war). His grandfather, according to family legend, was the first person in Britain to have a telephone in his house! He was a Post Office engineer, and, when Alexander Graham Bell came over from the USA to demonstrate his new invention, John's father was given the task of installing the machine; to ensure that he knew how it worked he dismantled it, made a couple for himself and tried them out at home.

The task of the floor manager is to be constantly present and constantly unobtrusive. The floor manager is the living link between producer and participant. An important part of the role is to try to put the participants, and the audience, at their ease. His idea of a successful *Mastermind* was when the participants, win or lose, went away feeling that they had had a wonderful experience which might one day make a chapter in their memoirs.

If he ever writes his own memoirs, John will no doubt reminisce about the apogee of his role as *Mastermind*'s floor manager, in the 1989 series. In the old days we used to change people around in the ten minutes between programme recordings, to make it look as if we had different audiences for the programmes; I would have to change my suit and tie for the same reason. The climactic moment came when we were recording the 300th and 301st programmes at the Museum of Army Transport in Beverley, in Yorkshire. On that occasion the Army took over the seating arrangements – and how! Colonel David Ronald issued a 'Rules of Engagement' memo to his staff ('everyone who moves is sitting on a red chair'); between the recordings, huge blocks of audience were shunted around the hall with military precision. It was like Trooping the Colour, and John Gilpin has never forgotten it. After that, we quietly dropped the pretence that the programmes were being recorded on separate occasions.

Peter Massey was the second-longest serving team member, as director, producer (twice), editor of the Quiz Unit and executive producer. He, too, had been involved in the pilot programmes in 1971, as the director. He was then director for five series (1974–78), producer for six series (1985–88 and 1990–91), and executive producer for one series (1992). Peter, a Manxman by birth, was educated at Stockport Grammar School and then took a degree in music and arts at Manchester University with a view to becoming a teacher.

A career in the BBC had, however, been taking shape for a long time by then. Stockport Grammar School had a strong dramatic tradition. The school's prowess in drama came to the notice of the BBC in Manchester. The redoubtable Nan Macdonald, who was then head of *Children's Hour* in the north, auditioned for a youngster to take part in a radio production called *London Calling Switzerland*. Peter won the part, that of a Swiss boy called Hansi. That launched a schoolboy (and, later, student) radio career with the BBC in Manchester, in which he clocked up some 300 broadcasts as both an actor and a programme presenter. He also co-presented a teenage monthly magazine programme, *Out of School*, with a young Judith Chalmers.

Nan Macdonald's successor at *Children's Hour*, Trevor Hill, encouraged Peter to think of broadcasting, rather than teaching, as a career, and drew his attention to a vacancy as a studio manager with the BBC in Manchester. Peter got the job and started work immediately in a studio, creating live sound effects for programmes. He became a dab hand at door-slams, stationary walking on various surfaces, horses' hooves (plus a resounding whinny) and a celebrated guillotine-in-operation effect, using the core of a music stand, a sliding block of wood and a cabbage.

He stayed in Manchester in radio until 1962, by which time he had graduated to being a sound mixer and was being loaned out (as a vision mixer and sometimes a floor manager) to the early television programmes which were being produced in the old Dickinson Road studio (a converted church), such as the early Val Doonican and Harry Worth shows, Harry Corbett and Sooty, and Barney Colehan's *Make Way for Music* programmes.

Peter had now caught the television bug, and early in 1962 he obtained an attachment as an Outside Broadcasts stage manager in London. Four years later he was promoted to production assistant (what is now called assistant producer) in OB Events, working for Bill Wright, who encouraged Peter to learn how to direct programmes. He was also loaned out to major OB occasions like the 1966 World Cup, the 1968 and 1972 Olympics, and various state occasions in Britain, including the Papal Mass in Liverpool's Catholic Cathedral and the television coverage of the raising of the *Mary Rose*.

After directing the *Mastermind* pilots, Peter continued doing *Television Top of the Form*. He came back to *Mastermind* for the third season (1974), and stayed with the programme until he retired from the BBC immediately after the 1992 Final.

Mary Craig was the third of the long-service (and long-suffering) stalwarts of the programme. For fifteen years, from 1975 to 1989, Mary was the backbone and mainstay of *Mastermind*, as researcher, then chief researcher and finally as assistant producer. Before that, she had been in at the birth of the programme idea in 1971 and had given it its arresting title. For most of her years on *Mastermind* she was the 'Dark Lady' who sat beside me at my desk, keeping the score, keeping the time and keeping me right.

Mary was born in Alexandria, in Scotland, and has never lost her distinctive Scottish accent. Her father was a county councillor and the Scottish organiser of the Dyers, Bleachers and Textile-Workers Union (the area was famous for its textile industry until the late 1950s). After school at Vale of Leven Academy she took a secretarial/business course at Lennox College in Dumbarton, and in 1961 she applied for a job as a trainee production secretary with the BBC in London. Her first job was working as secretary to the BBC's head of catering, where the most difficult part of the job was operating what seemed to her a mini telephone exchange on her desk (her family had never been able to afford a telephone at home).

She hankered to join Current Affairs, however, because she had always been very politically motivated. Soon she was posted to Television News at Alexandra Palace as a news transmission assistant, where she worked with some of the biggest names in broadcasting of the time, among them Michael Aspel, Richard Baker, Robert Dougall, Gerald Priestland, John Tidmarsh and John Timpson. In 1965 she applied for a post with Outside Broadcasts, which was doing *everything* in those days, from theatre excerpts to the Greyhound Derby. One of the people on the appointments board was Bill Wright, who at the time was one of the OB producers immersed in organising coverage of Sir Winston Churchill's funeral. Mary's experience in current-affairs live broadcasting stood her in good stead, and Bill snapped her up as his production assistant.

When Bill turned to quizzes and took over *Television Top of the Form*, Mary went with him. She attended the pilot programmes of *Mastermind* in 1971 but was too burdened with other quiz programmes to take on *Mastermind* as well, and had to miss out on its first three series. When *Television Top of the Form* came to an end in the summer of 1975, Mary worked full-time on *Mastermind* as senior researcher. She brought to the job a wealth of experience on quiz programmes and a rigorous attitude to question research. When Bill died near the end of the 1980 series she took over for the rest of the series as acting producer. In the following year she became assistant to the new producer, Roger Mackay.

Throughout the 1980s, Mary was an indispensable member of the team. With Boswell Taylor she established a common standard for the specialised questions, and conducted every one of my briefing sessions before the programme recordings. She enjoyed or suffered all the triumphs and crises. And then, as the decade was to close, she ended her long association with the programme.

It was caused by a combination of factors. In the first place, she had been feeling that she had been doing it for long enough. Secondly, she felt that the BBC itself was also changing. The attitude towards staff was becoming less concerned and caring. There was growing pressure to compromise; standards were being sacrificed to financial imperatives. Mary Craig was having to fight a lonely corner to retain these standards on *Mastermind* and felt that she was being sidelined as an old-fashioned anachronism. Life became a constant hassle. Michael Grade, Controller BBC1 at the time, exerted considerable pressure to have *Mastermind* turned into a daily programme, recorded in a studio in multiples of four at a time like a sausage machine, and that had to be fought off (I myself made it clear that I would not be prepared to continue on the programme on those terms). The compromise was to raise the output of programmes in the 1986 series from seventeen to twenty-two; it was not until the 1991 series that it was reduced to seventeen again.

Mary was feeling more and more beleaguered and realised that she was no longer enjoying the job. The extra programmes were causing a great deal of additional work, with insufficient resources; Mary was being worn down, and wanted more time to pursue her own interests. She had been thinking of leaving for several months; but the actual decision to go was made on the night of the recording of the 1989 Final. She resigned the next day and left in August, having completed the auditions and commissioned the specialised subjects for the 1990 series.

After leaving *Mastermind* Mary went freelance and spent a couple .

of years working with an independent production company. She developed some programme ideas of her own, including a quiz for Channel 4 called *Polymath*, which (unlike *Mastermind*) was designed to test different parts of the brain. There were no specialised subjects (although science and technology featured prominently) and it was based on visual activity through interactive television. Mary wrote all the question material herself. It achieved two pilots, only to be rejected in the end because of the cost – the technology involved became more and more expensive. Since then she has worked as a consultant on other people's programme ideas. In 1992 the BBC used her for nearly a year as a host to VIP groups visiting Television Centre; as she says wryly, 'It was my favourite job – I got to dress up and talk a lot!'

Underlying the stability and continuity of the 1980s provided by these three stalwarts there was a great deal of change at director level (and, to a lesser degree, at producer level). The first director of *Mastermind* (1972–73) had been **Martin L. Bell** – tense, energetic, idealistic, endlessly questing and questioning, he gave the programme much of its original visual style and identity. Martin moved to other programmes, as directors always do, and eventually left the BBC in 1978 to set up his own independent business (now called Bell Television Associates) as a freelance producer.

Peter Massey succeeded him in the director's chair. When Peter moved on to higher things in 1978 he was succeeded for three years by **Antonia (Toni) Charlton**, who saw the programme through the trauma of Bill's death in 1980, most of the *International Masterminds* (1979–83) and the Champions Tournament in 1982. I can recall many highlights of the programmes we did together: particularly the moment when a lady contender who had taken Valium to calm her nerves also indulged in a glass or two of pre-programme sherry. The effect on her was both electrifying and stultifying. At the halfway stage Toni muttered into my earpiece, 'Are we worried about this lady?' I waved my glass of water at the camera and said, *sotto voce*, 'Yes, but there's nothing we can do about it.' We weren't sure whether she would get through the second half at all – but she did. It made us all rather careful about the hospitality on offer to contestants from then on! Since *Mastermind*, Toni has had a varied career in BBC News and Current Affairs; she is now chief assistant, Drama Group.

Toni's move in 1982, on secondment to Television Current Affairs, meant having another new director. Her successor was **Laurence Vulliamy** (1983–85), a former vision mixer with a great eye for a picture. He recalls with particular pleasure the opening shot for the 1984 Final on board HMS *Hermes*. He had put a camera on board the main lift which took the planes from the deck down to the big hold in which we were recording the programme, and had to wait for the time when the exterior light over Portsmouth was the exact shade of dusky blue he wanted before the camera dived into the bowels of the ship. It took nerve to hold back until precisely the right moment; there would not be another chance. It worked, triumphantly. After his three-year stint on *Mastermind*, Laurence was promoted to producer and then he, too, went freelance, working as series producer on *Gardeners' World*, director of *Question Time* and co-ordinating producer for ITN's royal specials.

His producer during that period had been **Roger Mackay** (1980–84), who had taken the helm after Bill Wright's death. Roger brought a refreshing insouciance to the business which we had not known before (his abiding passion was horse-racing, and the *Sporting Life* was never far from reach). He had been weaned on the World Service, and came to us from Planning. He had never produced a television programme in his life, but he was a good motivator and delegator and put the programme back on the rails after Bill's death.

When Roger returned to Planning we welcomed Peter Massey back, this time as producer. The continuity of the Bill Wright legacy was re-established. And in place of Laurence Vulliamy, **David Mitchell** was appointed director (1986–88).

In summary like this it all sounds a bit hectic, but it wasn't. Change there was, but it was unhurried change. Directors served their time on *Mastermind* as a stepping stone to promoted posts; others followed, each bringing a fresh look at the programme's production values and adding a little here and a little there as technology and taste allowed. None of them wanted to change *Mastermind* for its own sake, or to use it as a personal proving ground at the programme's expense; all of them respected the *Mastermind* traditions and sought to enhance them, not to traduce them.

Just as Bill Wright's death in 1980 had caused a change in the programme's course, so the end of the decade provided another major watershed in our affairs. Nineteen eighty-nine saw the departure of

Mary Craig. It also saw a new director – **Andrea Conway** (1989–92) – to replace David Mitchell, who had been promoted to producer in place of Peter Massey. Andrea is one of those bubbly characters who seem to enjoy life more than anyone has a right to; effervescent and constantly cheerful, a born extrovert, she could have made a career as a TV star as easily as a director or, as she has now become, a producer.

And so the 1990s dawned. The dominant factor for *Mastermind* was the arrival for the 1990 series of **Penelope Cowell** (Penelope Cowell Doe as she became after her marriage) as successor to Mary Craig. Penny, as everyone called her, was born in Clitheroe, in Lancashire, the daughter of two schoolteachers. She studied English and Librarianship at the University College of Aberystwyth, and after two years' work on the *Annual Bibliography of English Language and Literature* she returned to Aberystwyth to take a Master's degree in Librarianship. She had thoughts of looking for an academic job in the library world, but academic appointments were becoming increasingly difficult to find and she applied for a post in the BBC's Film and Videotape Library in 1982.

With that her future career was determined. She worked first as a film researcher, then as a researcher for *Breakfast Time* and *Newsnight* in Lime Grove in Shepherd's Bush; she moved on to a department called the Interactive Television Unit, a multimedia department which had grown out of the ambitious 'Doomsday Project' – an attempt to create a modern computerised Domesday Book. There she became, in effect, an assistant producer, working on scripts and directing some film. When the job of assistant producer on *Mastermind* was advertised in the summer of 1989, Penelope won it against stiff opposition.

David Mitchell had meanwhile moved on to the History and Archaeology Unit, and Peter Massey had returned as producer. Penelope inherited a fully-planned series: the contenders for the 1990 series had already been chosen by David Mitchell, as had the locations, and the specialised subjects had already been agreed with Boswell Taylor. But no one had planned the outcome of her very first programme at the University of Lancaster – it featured 'Disastermind' himself, Arfor Wyn Hughes.

After two years as assistant producer, Penelope was promoted to producer (1992–95) in succession to Peter Massey. In her first year she took on the additional responsibility of finding the specialist question-setters when Boswell Taylor retired. In 1994 she was joined by David Mitchell for his second stint as director; there was a nice irony here, for it had been David as producer in 1989 who had selected Penelope to be his assistant producer.

Penelope's last two years as producer, with David as director (1994–95), worked extremely well. Penelope concentrated on the intellectual context and content of the programme rather more than previous producers had done, while David could give full rein to his great skills as a programme visualiser. David was also prepared to try out new locations, despite apparent obstacles; for instance, he chose to go to Gibside Chapel, the National Trust property in Northumberland, in 1995 – a tiny little chapel with a curious three-tiered pulpit in the centre and a railed enclosure in which we put the Black Chair. Other locations in that year included Salisbury Cathedral with its celebrated soaring spire, Warwick Castle, the elegant Georgian Theatre Royal in Bury St Edmunds (another National Trust property, because 1995 was the NT's centenary year), and the National Westminster Hall in London. David needed a producer who would say yes to these unconventional locations, and Penelope needed a director with David's skills and his close understanding of the programme.

In the summer of 1995 Penelope resigned from the programme and from the BBC. The programme base had moved from London to Manchester and she found the commuting extremely difficult; she certainly did not feel that she could make a long-term commitment to Manchester. Soon she began working on the *Mastermind* CD-ROM, an offshoot of *Mastermind* run by BBC Worldwide, which was launched in November 1996. She had to work on 5,500 *Mastermind* questions, which I recorded in a marathon session lasting five days; it gave both of us an unexpected insight into how *Mastermind* question-setting had evolved over the years.

Penelope was aided and abetted throughout by **Dee Wallis**, who had been senior researcher on *Mastermind* since 1983 under Mary Craig and would herself become assistant producer in 1996. Like Penelope, Dee had qualified as a librarian, but her early passion was for the theatre. After college she spent a Bohemian year with a theatre group called Hairspring ('small but dynamic'), doing pub theatre in Leeds with a mime show called *Psst*, followed by a second show called *Psst Again*. After that the idea of becoming a professional librarian lost its appeal; her real interest was in research, and she was appointed to a post in the BBC Reference Library. From there, at the second attempt, she joined *Mastermind*. For the rest of the run of *Mastermind* she brought a fiercely meticulous care to the business of checking every comma, every nuance, every implication of every question and every answer. She was assisted by many excellent researchers over the years, who would occasionally emerge blinking from their lairs to attend a recording: Irene Levin, Bridget Ardley, Elizabeth Salmon, Brenda Haugh, Katie Fields, Sean McGeown, Saira Dunnakey . . . Together they helped to give me unbounded confidence (well, *nearly* unbounded!) in the questions I had to fire at the Black Chair. Boswell Taylor's opinion of Dee, after working with her for many years, is good enough for me: 'Dee Wallis is a wonderful researcher. She is a jewel. She should be kept by the BBC for ever – such persistence, and such an eye for detail.'

When Penelope left the BBC, Dee succeeded her as assistant producer while David Mitchell took over as producer/director for what would turn out to be the last two years of *Mastermind*. At school in Coventry he had intended to become an architect, and was accepted for a university place with that still in mind. However, he decided he wanted to work in television or films. He still doesn't quite know why, but as an eleven-year-old, when he was in the Boy Scouts, he had appeared in a feature film called *Privilege*, directed by Peter Watkins (of *Culloden* fame). There was a sequence in Birmingham City football ground when the boys marched around in Boy Scout uniform in what was supposed to be a pseudo-Nazi rally. David loved the ambience of it – the excitement of filming, the lights, the technicians swarming all over the place; it was great fun, and the memory had always stuck with him. As a result he wanted to do something in films or television, but his teachers tried to dissuade him – grammar school pupils didn't do that sort of thing.

On the spur of the moment, however, David opted for a course in film and photography at art school in Nottingham instead of taking up his university place. Afterwards he joined *Pebble Mill at One* in Birmingham as a temporary assistant film editor. There he became interested in the production process and started doing some film research for the programme as well. From there he went to BBC Bristol where he gained valuable experience at an early stage in his career; he was a film editor on *Wildlife on One*, and worked on several music and arts programmes like *Omnibus* and *Arena*.

By now he was now hankering after a job in production proper. He spent seven months working with Outside Broadcasts in the Sports Department in London, which gave him an introduction to the electronic, rather than the film, side of television. On his return to Bristol as an assistant producer he worked for four or five years on a fledgling OB programme called *The Antiques Roadshow* with Arthur Negus, where he cut his teeth directing as well as producing.

In 1986 he landed the job of directing *Mastermind* in succession to Laurence Vulliamy. He did it for three years and was then promoted to producer for the 1989 series while Peter Massey went on three months' sabbatical leave, returning as editor of the General Programmes Unit (which included *Mastermind*). After only one series (1989), however, David joined the History and Archaeology unit (after leaving art college the call of academia was still strong – he had taken an Open University degree in history in his spare time). He was there for three years, working on *Timewatch* after a popular history series called *Byways* with Francis Pryor, the archaeologist at Flag Fen, and an archive series on the Second World War which I scripted and narrated, called *Another War, Another Peace*. Network production at BBC Elstree then closed down, so David went free-lance; but he was soon back as director of *Mastermind* when Penelope Cowell Doe invited him to take it on again. Then in 1995 he took over as producer/director.

Programme roles are constantly evolving. At one time it would not have been possible for the producer to be the director as well, because the producer had a lot to do with the staging of the event and making sure that everyone knew what they had to do, while the director was directing the cameras. The producer had responsibility for the editorial content, while the director had responsibility for the stylistic content. When Penelope took over from Mary Craig, and then became producer, she kept a lot of the former assistant producer's role and continued to do that; she concentrated on commissioning the specialised question sets and supervising that process and left the directing side alone. When David took over again as producer/director, he was in more of an executive producer's role, and asked Dee

Wallis (who had been the senior researcher) to take over much more programme responsibility. The house-style of questions was basically Dee's style; and she was so familiar with the way everything went that it seemed logical for her to become assistant producer, supervising the other researchers and putting me through the briefing sessions on location.

David took care to give additional attention to another important aspect of the programme: the audiences. The people who came to watch the recordings added an extra dimension to the experience: being an Outside Broadcast made the programme an *event*, a happening, in a way that few studio programmes could. David shared my concern for the audience. He wanted to record every programme as if it were live:

> Our audiences have to be allowed to feel part of the TV drama of the event; they quite enjoy seeing mistakes and re-takes because they feel they have been let in on the secret, and it gives them a conspiratorial glow when they watch it at home – they know what the back of the tapestry looks like. Producers sometimes tend to forget that; for us it's a job, but for most people it is their only contact with what they pay their TV licence for, and it's very important for them.

There is no space to detail all the people who worked on and for the programme, but I remember them all with gratitude: the lighting engineers – Bill Jones, John Wiggins, Jim Baker, Peter Greenyer, Dennis Butcher, Geoff Higgs and John Wilson; the designers – Philip Lindley, Andy Dimond, Kate Spence and Richard Dupré; the sound engineers, ending with John Nottage; the production assistants – Carol Shackley, Maureen Smith, Julia Anderson, Dinah Long, Doreen Munden, Anne Foster, Cathy Layton, Lisa Perkins (now married to David Mitchell), Damaris Pitcher and Julie Corcoran. Many Masterminders will remember the production assistants better than anyone else on the team, for it was they who looked after their travel arrangements and their creature comforts on location.

And then, last but by no means least, the scene crews, the riggers, the people responsible for creating the stage for the television dramas of the evening, and then making it all vanish in a trice, leaving not a rack behind. I shall mention only one by name, but he stands for all the unnamed colleagues who worked on and for the programme:

Mike Jennings, 'the water-carrier', as I called him. A veteran of Outside Broadcasts (he used to be a 'show-working supervisor'), he made it his special business in the latter years to ensure that my water-carafe was always topped up.

Everyone to his or her own task. This team spirit, involving every single member of the operation, was always one of the great secrets of the success of *Mastermind*, the programme which made a little bit of unlikely television history.

Coda

In March 1987 Charles Plouviez wrote a parody ('On the 15th Anniversary of *Mastermind*') in the style of Alexander Pope for a competition in the *New Statesman*. Let it stand for the 25th, too:

> *With steps reluctant, eye cast down in Care,*
> *The Shiv'ring Champion mounts the horrid Chair.*
> *Fluorescent tubes their lambent Beams decrease,*
> *And all the sounds of sibilant whisp'ring cease*
> *As, like the Judge who rules o'er gloomy Dis,*
> *Grave* Magnus Magnusson *applies the Quiz.*
>
> Thomas *from Tunbridge Wells responds on cue*
> *'The Life and Works of James Bell Pettigrew',*
> *And spends two Minutes cudgelling his Wits*
> *To please ten million Teli-watching Twits.*
>
> Magnus, *the Question puts, the Points awards,*
> *Then stoups to read* Tom's *Fortune in the Cards,*
> *While* Tom, *his tongue unloos'd like* Balaam's Ass,
> *Will sometimes answer give – and sometimes Pass.*
>
> *A little learning is a tedious thing,*
> *But tedium mounts as passing Minutes bring*
> *Old* General Knowledge *riding on the Field*
> *Where futile facts are copiously reveal'd.*
> *'I've started, so I'll finish!'* Magnus *cries,*
> *And stands rebuk'd, for all know that he lies.*

Appendices

I
The Champions

1972	**Nancy Wilkinson**
1973	**Patricia Owen**
1974	**Elizabeth Horrocks**
1975	**John Hart**
1976	**Roger Pritchard**
1977	**Sir David Hunt**
1978	**Rosemary James**
1979	**Philip Jenkins**
1980	**Fred Housego**
1981	**Leslie Grout**
1982★	**Sir David Hunt**
1983	**Christopher Hughes**
1984	**Margaret Harris**
1985	**Ian Meadows**
1986	**Jennifer Keaveney**
1987	**Jeremy Bradbrooke**
1988	**David Beamish**
1989	**Mary-Elizabeth Raw**
1990	**David Edwards**

★ Champion of Champions tournament

1991	**Stephen Allen**
1992	**Steve Williams**
1993	**Gavin Fuller**
1994	**George Davidson**
1995	**Kevin Ashman**
1996	**Richard Sturch**
1997	**Anne Ashurst**

II
Specialised Question-setters

This list is by no means definitive, but provides a broad sample of the people who have set specialised questions for the programme, and their subjects.

CYRIL ALDRED, on Egyptology

RUPERT ALLASON, on Police History (and also, as NIGEL WEST, on the British Secret Service)

JOHN ALLISON, on Puccini

ZAKI BADAWI, on the prophet Muhammad

JOHN D. BAREHAM, on Medieval History

LORD BLAKE, on Benjamin Disraeli

ANTONY BRETT-JAMES, on Military History

STEPHEN BRIGGS, on the Discworld Novels of Terry Pratchett

RICHARD BUCKLE, on Ballet

HUMPHREY BURTON, on William Walton

DAVID BUTLER, on British Politics

BRUCE CAMPBELL, on Birds

HARRY CARPENTER, on World Boxing Championships

LORD DAVID CECIL, on Max Beerbohm

BERNARD CRICK, on George Orwell

PROFESSOR DAVID DAICHES, on Robert Burns and Scottish Literature

HUNTER DAVIES, on the Lake District and also on the Beatles

GORDON DONALDSON, on Scottish History

MARGARET DRABBLE, on her own novels

DAVID DUFF, on Royalty

MARTIN ESSLIN, on Samuel Beckett

DIGBY FAIRWEATHER, on Jazz
FELIX FRANCIS, on the novels of his father, Dick Francis
GEORGE MACDONALD FRASER, on the Border Reivers
DAVID FRITH, on Cricket
PAUL GAMBACCINI, on Pop Music
DENIS GIFFORD, on Cartoons
SIR MARTIN GILBERT, on Politics and Politicians
VIVIAN GREEN, on Richard III
REAR-ADMIRAL TEDDY GUERITZ, on Naval History
RICHARD HOLMES, on Military History
KEVIN HOWLETT, on Rock Music
CHRISTOPHER HUGHES (1983 champion), on Railways
TOM HUTCHINSON, on Cinema
H. R. F. KEATING, on Agatha Christie
MICHAEL KENNEDY, on Music and Musicians
WOLFGANG LIEBESCHUETZ, on Classical Greek History
ELIZABETH LONGFORD, on the Duke of Wellington
HUMPHREY LYTTELTON, on Jazz
DAVID MILLER, on Anarchism
PATRICK MOORE, on Astronomy
DESMOND MORRIS, on Mammals
DON MOSEY, on Yorkshire CCC
NORMAN PAINTING ('Phil Archer'), on *The Archers*
ALAN PALMER, on Modern British and European History
BARBARA REYNOLDS, on Dante and also on Dorothy L. Sayers
HAROLD ROSENTHAL, on Opera
SIR STEVEN RUNCIMAN, on Byzantine History and Art and also on
    the Crusades
STANLEY SADIE, on Music and Musicians
JON SAVAGE, on the Sex Pistols
DUDLEY SMITH, on Medieval Welsh History
JULIAN SYMONS, on Detective-story Writers
BOSWELL TAYLOR, on English Literature
HARRY THOMPSON, on Tintin
BARRY TOOK, on Radio Comedy
NIGEL TRANTER, on Scottish History
DAVID WILSON, on Science
CHRISTOPHER WOOD, on Dante Gabriel Rossetti
BRIGADIER PETER YOUNG, on the English Civil War

III
Magnum Winners

1981   Kathryn Jones*
1982   Kathryn Jones
1983   Phyllis Hartnoll
1984   Peter Richardson
1985   Peter Richardson
1986   Kathryn Murton (formerly Jones)
1987   Leslie Grout (1981 champion)
1988   Peter Richardson
1989   Peter Richardson
1990   Ivor Cooksey
1991   Kevin Ashman
1992   Kevin Ashman
1993   Kevin Ashman
1994   Kevin Ashman
1995   Kathryn Johnson (formerly Murton)
1996   Kevin Ashman (1995 champion)
1997   Kathryn Johnson

* As leader from the written rounds

IV
Mugnum Winners

1982   David Flower
1983   Sue Jenkins
1984   John Sykes
1985   Keith Bogle
1986   Sue Jenkins
1987   Keith Bogle
1988   David Blackman
1989   Kevin Ashman
1990   Ella Thompson
1991   Patricia Owen (1973 champion)

1992	Ray Ward	
1993	Steve Williams (1992 champion)	
1994	Kevin Ashman	
1995	Sonia Anderson	
1996	Kevin Ashman (1995 champion)	
1997	Trevor Montague	

V
List of Masterminders

This is a definitive list of everyone who appeared on *Mastermind* between 1972 and 1997. Names marked with an asterisk indicate those who are currently members of the Mastermind Club. Those whose names are in italics are known to be dead, but there are doubtless many others, alas.

SURNAME	FIRST NAME	YEAR
★ Abbott	Godfrey F.	81 (SF)
★ Acious	Viv	96
Adams	Anne	83
Adams	*Linden*	*91 (SF) (d. 1997)*
Adams	Roger	95 (SF)
Addyman	Martin	93
★ Ahmed	Shafi	97
★ Ajayi	Akinade	97
★ Akinkunmi	Dr Akintunde	97 (SF)
Alcorn	Roy	78
Alder	*Wing Cdr Anthony*	*90 (d. 1997)*
Aldous	Richard	86
Alexander	James	90
Allen	Derek G.	74
Allen	Stephen	Champion 91
Allum	Jonathan	78
★ Altree	Sheila	80 (as Sheila Denyer), 85 (disqualified), 97 (SF)
★ Alves	Angela M.	77 (SF)
Anderson	Cicely	91
★ Anderson	Michael J.	86
Anderson	Neville W.	72
★ Anderson	Sonia	95
Andrew	Martin R. G.	91

Andrews	Graham	77
★ Andrews	Mary E.	94
Angel	Dr Joseph H.	84
Appleby	Daniel	73 (SF)
Arbuthnott	Peter	81
Archer	E.	73
Argyle	Christopher J.	94 (SF)
★ Armitage	Drusilla	92 (SF)
Arnold	Arthur	81
Ashdown	Dulcie M.	74
★ Ashman	Kevin	87 (SF), Champion 95
★ Ashurst	Anne	Champion 97
★ Askew [Sillwood]	Margaret	75 (SF)
Aslett	Hilary	83
★ Atkinson	Liz	92 (SF)
★ Atkinson	Philip	90 (SF)
★ Attree	Fr Anthony G. F.	87
Austin	Erica	80
Bacon	M.	73
Bacos	Peter	91
★ Bailey	Roy H.	88 (Finalist)
★ Baker	Alison	88
Baldwin	Judith	92 (SF)
Banerjee	Ashis	91
Banfield	John N.	89
Bannerman	Charles	73
Barker	Janet	81 (SF)
Barlow	Peter	81
Barnard	Dr Robert	90
Barnes	Rev. Edwin	89
Barnes	Gordon	86
★ Barr	Kenneth H.	91 (SF)
Barrett	Barbara	83
Barton	Hutton	81
★ Barton	Ian	81 (Finalist), 95 (SF)
★ Batchelor	Sarah	88
★ Beamish	David R.	Champion 88
★ Bean	Thomas J.	89 (Finalist)
Beatty	Richard	81 (SF)
Beaumont	Bill A.	80
Beaumont of Whitley	Timothy (Lord)	77 (SF)
Beggs	*George T.*	*83 (d. 1991)*
★ Beighton	Pauline F.	93
★ Bell	Alison M.	90
★ Bell	Graham	94

★ Bell	Tony	97 (SF)
★ Bellingham	William	87
Bennett	Christina R.	74
Bent	Bill	78 (SF)
Bentley	Paul	92
★ Bertin	Albert	86 (SF)
Bettington	Clive	85 (Finalist)
★ Betts	John	95
Bibby	Brian	90 (Finalist)
★ Billson	Michael	87 (Finalist)
Billson	*Tom*	*88 (d. 1989)*
★ Binnie	Glen	92 (Finalist)
Bird	Dennis L.	75
Bird	*Peter B.*	*87 (d. 1990)*
★ Birkill	Dr Rosemary	78
Bitton	*James*	*81 (Finalist) (d. 1987)*
Black	Douglas G.	78
Black	Vicki	86
★ Blackburn	Alan D.	75 (SF)
★ Blackman	David J.	85
Blaha	Thomas	79
Blake	Keith	78
★ Blakesley	Maureen P.	81
Blenkin	J.	72
Bloch	Michael	78
★ Boettinger	Henry	88 (SF), 95 (Finalist)
★ Bogle	Keith W.	78
Bolitho	Paul	78
★ Bolt	Peter	97
Bolton	David J.	91
Bonfiglio	Colonel Vic	86
Booth	Christoper	78
Booth	Jennie	94
Booth	S.	73
Borer	Deirdre	86
Boss	Dr Jeffrey	73 (Finalist)
★ Bosworth	Winifred P.	85
★ Bovington	Brian	92
Bowers	John	86 (SF)
Bowers	Stephen	84
Bown	Rosemary	73 (SF)
Bradbrooke	Dr Jeremy	Champion 87
Bradley	Iain	86
★ Bradley	Ian	96
Bradley	Martin	79 (SF)

Bradley	Paul	90
Brain	Inspector Timothy	89
* Bramall	Sir Ashley	76
* Bramall	Gery (Lady)	87
* Branston	Sally	89
Brewster	Dennis B.	93
* Bridgman	Dr Joan	87
Brighton	Paul D. J.	83 (SF)
* Brindle	Steven P.	91
Britton	Sylvia	80
* Broadbent	Edmund J.	95
Broadbent	Tony	79 (SF)
Brooke	Stephanie	91 (SF)
Brooks	Judith	86
* Brookstone	Joe	94 (SF)
Brooman	Janet	90
Brough	Patrick J.	78
* Brown	Lt Cdr Barrie M., RN	86
* Brown	Gavin	96
* Brown	Michael	94
* Brown	Trevor	91 (Finalist)
Bruce	James A. B.	72 (SF)
Bruford	Dr Alan	76 (SF)
Bryan-Brown	Frederick D.	74 (SF)
Budd	Capt Christopher	79
* Budd	Sally	96
Buffham	Pauline	83
Bull	George R.	75
* Bullock	Richard	85
Bunting	Adam	88 (SF)
Burgess	Leading Steward Stephen F., RN	90 (SF)
Burke	Angela	84
* Burke	Jean	87 (SF)
* Burke	John	85 (SF)
Burke	John	93 (SF)
* Burkhill	Ruth	96
Burnell	Judi	88
Burnham	Alan	92
* Burnham	David	91 (SF)
Burns	*David*	*75 (SF) (d. 1989)*
Burton	Kenneth J.	75
Burton	Mary W.	84
Bushell	Dorothy F.	75
* Butler	Maureen	84

Butler	Ruth	77
Butterworth	Neil	85
★ Button	Henry G.	76
Byers	Dennis	77
Byers	John M.	76
Cabourn-Smith	Martin	75 (SF)
Cadby	Colin	97 (Finalist)
★ Cadden	Edward	88
Caig	Alan	80
Cains	Dr Peter W.	86
Cairns	R.	73
★ Cameron	Hamish	90 (SF)
Campbell	*Dr Archie J.*	*73 (SF) (d. 1991)*
Campbell	Iain	79 (SF)
Campbell	John	80 (SF)
Campbell	Katrina	97
Campbell-Suttie	David	86
★ Campion	Paul	83 (SF)
★ Capell	Colin E.	94
★ Capper	Rupert (Bob)	74 (SF), 95
Carden	Richard A.	75
Carlisle	Dr Hilary	88
Carr	Antony D.	75 (SF)
★ Carroll	David	89
Carter	Rev. Christopher	84
Carter	Judith A.	81
★ Cash	Alicia	97
Cashman	Con	79
Cassar	Wayne	89
Castree	Peter	90
Catling	Dr Sarah J.	79
Cawley	William	92
Chalmers	William	77 (SF)
Chapman	Peter	86
★ Charles	Malcolm	95 (SF)
★ Chase	Dr Liz	95
★ Chatterjee	Dr Himadri K.	92
Chesshire	Godfrey	84
Chester	*Dr John*	*87 (SF) (d. 1997)*
Chilton	Rev. R. Michael L.	86
★ Chitty	Peter W. J.	87
Chitty	Tom	83
★ Chivers	Michael	94 (SF)
★ Christie	Dr Ian G.	85
Clark	Ian G.	74 (SF)

★ Clark	Jack	90
★ Clark	Michael	90 (SF)
Clark	Sue	77
★ Clayton	Graham	89
★ Clayton–Gore	Phillip	86
★ Close	Robert	94
★ Coast-Smith	Dr Richard	80
★ Coates	James F.	75
★ Codner	Cdr Michael	95
Coggrove	John	94 (SF)
Cohen	Neville	84 (SF)
★ Colby	Alan	91
Coleby	John	73 (Finalist)
Coleman	Charles	72
★ Colesell	Sharon A.	85 (SF)
★ Collard	Miriam	96 (SF)
Colman	John	73 (SF)
★ Colverson	John R.	93 (SF)
Combe	*George A.*	*87 (d. 1994)*
★ Compton	Elizabeth B.	79
Cook	D.	72
★ Cooke	Christopher W. R.	80 (SF)
Cooke	Graham Q.	87, 96
Cooklin	Brian	83
★ Cooksey	Ivor D. C.	86 (SF)
Coombs	David M.	90
Coombs	Jolyon	78 (SF)
Cooper	Amanda J.	80
★ Cooper	Ken	72
Copeland	*Sally*	*73 (d. 1983)*
★ Copland	Iain M.	78
Corfe	Tom	74
Court	Dr Glyn	75
Courtney-Wildman	Barbara	73
★ Cowan	David	94 (SF)
Cowan	Robert	96
Cowell	Adrian	80
Cowen	Anne	92
★ Cowley	Patricia	91
Crampsey	Robert	72 (SF)
Craven	James	81 (SF)
Crawford	John	81
Crerar	Donald	86 (SF)
★ Cresdee	Martin	95
Cresswell	Simon	85

Crichton	John	89
Crill	Cdr Cecil G.	75
Crippin	John	87 (Finalist)
Crisp	Michael	80
★ Crockford	Neil	75 (SF)
★ Cross	Stewart	87
Crosswell	Keith N.	74
Crowe	Janet	97
Crowhurst	Frank	87
Cruse	R. B.	73
★ Currie	Sgt Robert D.	93
★ Curtis	Andrew	95 (SF)
Dakin	*Martin*	*74 (SF) (d. 1980)*
★ Dale	Richard	75
Dalrymple–Smith	Capt Jonathan	77 (SF)
★ Dart	Anthony R.	81 (SF), 97 (SF)
★ Daugherty	Brian	90
Davenport	Brian	87
★ Davidson	George	Champion 94
★ Davies	Gena M.	75 (SF)
★ Davies	Glenys (novelist June Wyndham Davies)	93 (Finalist)
Davies	Katherine	81
Davis	James A.	79 (Finalist)
★ Davison	Michael	84
Dawkes	Tom	77 (SF)
★ Dearnley	Geoffrey	87
Delvin	Dr David G.	76 (SF)
Denyer	Sheila	[see Altree, Sheila]
de Vito	Catherine	83
★ Devlin	Robert	96 (SF)
★ Dewar	David G. W.	92 (SF)
Dewar	Rev. Dr Michael W.	72 (SF)
Dicken	Mary	84
Diggins	Roderick	91 (SF)
Dixon	Michael	78
Docherty	Patrick	83
★ Dodds	Keith	94
Doherty	Charles W.	74
★ Dolan	Howard A.	91 (SF)
Donnelly	William	89 (SF)
★ Doubleday [Woon]	Gillian R.	89 (Finalist)
★ Douce	Barrie	93 (Finalist)
Douch	Major Arthur	80
Douglas	Robert	83

⋆ Downing	Bernard	92
Drake-Brockman	Rev. David	72 (SF)
Draycott	Allan	90 (SF)
⋆ Drew	Reginald J.	73
⋆ Driver	Colin F.	84 (SF)
Drury	Alan	90
Duffin	Lisa	76 (SF)
Dunbar	Robert	76
Durden	Richard	85
Dutton	David	85
Dutton	Judith A. P.	88
Dyche	Flight Lt Michael W.	76
Dyer	Thomas A.	81
⋆ Dymond	John C. G.	93 (SF)
⋆ Dyson	Fred	92
Eames	Christopher	77 (Finalist)
⋆ Earnshaw	George E. F.	75
Eaves	Eileen	88 (SF)
Ebert	Mary Ann	81 (SF)
⋆ Edgar	Capt Colin M.	87
Edmond	John F.	83 (SF)
Edwards	Brian	92
⋆ Edwards	David G. M.	Champion 90
⋆ Edwards	Malcolm H.	93 (SF)
Egan	John	79 (SF)
⋆ Elis	Meg	95
Ellender	Richard	80
Elliott	Brian N.	85
⋆ Elliott	Margery	73 (SF)
Elliott	Paul	79
⋆ Emond	Dr Ken	92 (SF)
Ennis	Jane S.	86 (SF)
Ernstbrummer	Dr E.	72
⋆ Erridge	Patricia	83, 96
Evans	Clive W.	85 (SF)
Evans	Jan	85
Evans	Madeline	83
Evans	Olga	74
Everett	Richard J.	75
Fagan	Noel J.	75 (SF)
Fairbairn	Lt Cdr Euan	83
⋆ Falcon	Judith	97
⋆ Falconer	Giles	92
Falloon	Anne	78
Fane-Gladwin	James	91

★ Francis	Roger D.	94
★ Frankland	Mary P.	94
★ Frary [Hall]	Annabel	92
★ Fraser	Ronald T. L.	85 (SF)
Frazer	Hilary	87
Friezer	*Alan H.*	*91 (d. 1994)*
★ Fromow	Robert W.	90
Fry	Malcolm	85
★ Fuller	Gavin	Champion 93
Fulton	Elizabeth	77
Gable	Jo	85
Gainsford	Michael J.	77 (SF)
Gallagher	Vera	72
Gamble	*Eric*	*89 (d. 1997)*
Gardner	*Jane*	*84 (d. 1986)*
Garner	Stephen	97
Garratt	Margaret A.	76
★ Gartside	Philip R.	89
★ Gaunt	Deborah	85
★ Geary	Michael	77
George	John C. G.	78
Gerard	Arthur T.	75 (SF)
Gethin	Geoffrey	72
★ Gibson	Christopher J.	85 (SF)
Gibson	Douglas	73
Gibson	*Rev. John C.*	*75 (d. 1985)*
★ Gibson	Mary E.	89 (SF)
★ Gibson	Robert	93 (SF)
Giddings	Dr Michael	89
Gielgud	Adam	79
★ Gifford	Christopher W.	88
Gittens	John M.	93
Gleeson	Robert	78 (Finalist)
Glover	Jennifer	85
Glover	Michael	78 (SF)
★ Godden	Michael J.	93
Godfrey	Gerard	86 (SF)
Godfrey	Thomas	76
Gold	Dr Nicholas	78
Goldie	Donald J.	80
Goldman	Michael	72
Goldstein	Anna M.	76
	[writer Anna Milford]	
Gonet	Christopher	91
★ Goodale	Richard	97 (SF)

★ Huntley	Marjorie	87
Hurlstone	Caroline	79
Hurman	Anthony	80
Hutchings	John	84 (SF)
★ Hutton	Geoffrey	88 (SF)
★ Hyde	Gavin	90
Iliffe	Alan H.	76 (SF)
★ Ingham	Robert	97
★ Ingle	Robert J.	79
Inglis	Barbara	92
★ Ingram	John	88, 95
Ireson	Tony	86
Irvine	Martha I.	77
Irving	Kate	77
Irwin	Thomas H.	80
★ Izzett	Norman A.	84 (SF)
Jackson	Paul G.	79
James	Alwyn	76
James	Bill	84
★ James	Rosemary G.	Champion 78
Jan	Madeline M.	74
Jeffery-Machin	Rev. Canon Dr Ivor	75 (SF)
Jeffs	Adrian	88
Jenkins	Dr Philip	Champion 79
★ Jenkins	Sue M.	77 (Finalist)
Joby	Dr Richard S.	84 (Finalist)
John	Brian	88
Johnson	Dr Jennifer L.	75
★ Johnson	Kathryn	78 (as Kathryn Jones), 95
Johnson	Roy S.	74
★ Johnson	Stuart D.	93 (SF)
★ Johnston	George E.	75 (Finalist)
Jones	Barry	79 (SF)
Jones	Byron H.	84 (SF)
Jones	Caroline	94
Jones	D.	72
★ Jones	Gethin A.	92
★ Jones	Graeme	93
Jones [Johnson]	Kathryn	[see Johnson, Kathryn]
Jones	Margaret	93
Jones	Olivier K.	96
★ Jones	Richard A.	89 (Finalist)
★ Jones	Robert T.	95 (Finalist)
★ Kahn	Raymond L.	89
★ Kane	Terence	84

Latimer-Sayer	Denise	87
Lavery	Rosaleen	91
Lavin	Jocelyn	97
★ Law	Stephen C.	94
Lawrence	Aubrey	78 (SF)
Lawrence	*Mary*	*74 (d. 1982)*
Lawrence	Capt Patrick	81
★ Lawrey	Josephine	80
★ Leadbetter	Martin J.	77
Leatham Thomas	Beryl	72 (Finalist)
Leem-Bruggen	Vernon	76
Lees	*Dr David*	*78 (SF) (d. 1990)*
★ Leng	Susan	97
★ Leonard	Rachel	84 (SF)
Le Page	David S.	86
Levine	Josephine	90
★ Lewis	George	94
★ Lewis	John	93
Lewis	Dr Mostyn	72
Ley	Robert	77
Ligertwood	Joyce	72
★ Limmer	Ivan	72 (SF), 97
Linfoot	*George*	*73 (d. 1995)*
Linton	Olwyn	80
Lipton	Julian	86 (SF)
Lister	Ian	77
★ Little	Mira	87
★ Lloyd	John E.	77
★ Lloyd	John E. R.	90
★ Long	George	93
★ Loring	Cdr Julian	88
Lunan	Maisie	84
★ Lydiard-Cannings	Cynthia	95
Lynch	Frank	78 (SF)
Lynch	Dr Michael	87
★ Lyon	Major Stuart R.	96
MacCarron	Donald	87
★ Macdonald-Cooper	Michael A.	86 (SF)
MacFarlane	Iain	94
MacGillivray	Neil D.	78
★ MacGregor	Jim	72 (SF)
★ MacIldowie	Douglas	93
★ MacKenzie	Dr Gerald	74
★ MacLachlan	Avril	89
★ Macnair	Eleanor	73 (SF), 96

Moore	Roderick	86
Moore	Sandra B.	85
★ Morgan	Geoffrey R.	92
Morley-Fletcher	Hugo	74
Morrell	Nick	84
Morris	David	76
★ Morris	Linda A.	89
Morris	Peter	74
Morris	Roger J.	81
Morrissey	Felicity	78
Mortimer	*Samuel T.*	*80 (Finalist)*
Morton	M. C. Jane	79
★ Mottram	John E.	90
★ Muir	William	86
★ Munn	Michael W.	75
Munro	Cynthia	78
Murgatroyd	Alan	94 (SF)
Murray	Rev. Dr Derek	80
Murray	Gerard	81
Murray	James	75
Murray	James	81
Myers	Marion	81
Narayanswami	Sandya	76
★ Nesbitt	Jim	79
★ Newbury	Ruth	95
★ Newman	Michael H.	87
Nicholls	Frederick	72 (SF)
Nicholls	Margery B.	74 (SF)
Nicholls	Martin	76
★ Nicholson	Ann M.	93
Noble	Ian A.	74
North	Peter	89 (SF)
Norton	Jonathan	96
Oakley	Dr Nigel R.	86
Oates	Richard	89 (SF)
★ Ockwell	Clare	97 (Finalist)
★ O'Donnell	John	95 (SF)
O'Hara	Arnold	75
O'Keeffe	Margaret-Louise	86
Old	John	79 (SF)
Oliver	Derek	85 (SF)
Oliver	Rev. Rhilip M.	74
★ O'Meara	Barbara	89, 95
Orr	Robert	76
Ortiger	Stephen	84

Orton	Archie F.	73 (SF)
★ Osmont	Isabel	90 (SF)
Ostermeyer	Malcolm C.	74
★ O'Sullivan	Michael E.	87
Oswald	J.	72
★ Overall	Paul	93 (SF)
★ Owen	Patricia	Champion 73
Owen	Peter	79 (SF)
Palfrey	Michael	88
★ Palmer	James R.	90
Palmer-Barnes	John	76
★ Pantin	Andrew D.	90
Pantin	Henry	76 (SF)
★ Parish	Alan	91
Parnell	Malcolm	84 (SF)
★ Parrott	Jeremy	91
Parry	D. Tim	81
Paul	Michael	74
Pauson	Lai-Ngau	79
Pavasovic	Milan	81
Paxton	Linda	83
Paxton	Timothy J.	75
★ Pay	Dr Patricia	91 (SF)
Peachey	Elizabeth	73
Pearce [Saunders]	Carolyn A.	74 (SF)
Pearce	Jacqueline	92 (SF)
Pearson	Jacqueline	75 (Finalist)
★ Pearson	Stephen J.	96 (SF)
Peat	Margaret E.	83 (Finalist)
★ Peck	Patricia	97
Pegg	Frederick	83 (SF)
★ Pelly	Christopher	80 (SF)
★ Penfold	David A.	93
Perkins	Dave	89
★ Perkins	Kevin J.	88 (SF)
Peters	'Rev. Dr' Robert	83
Pheby	Dr Derek	84
Pickett	Dr G. Douglas	86
★ Pickles	Colin	85
Pierce	Sgt Keith	79
★ Pilkington	Colin	92
Pitman	Sandra	87
★ Pizzey	Howard	88
Ponder	Paul	73 (SF)
★ Poole	Helen	88

Pope	Bryan	88
★ Potter	Ann	96
Potter	Matthew	96 (SF)
Potts	Charles	77 (SF)
Potts	Hilary	89
★ Potts	Ian	87 (SF)
★ Powell	Michael	89
Preston	Albert	79
Preston	Graham	88
Pretty	John	81
Price	Christopher	83
★ Price	Ernest	91
★ Priestley	Stephen J.	87
Pritchard	Roger	Champion 76
Protheroe	Rev. Robin P.	74
Pugh	Diana	76
★ Pugsley	Mildred F.	88
★ Pullen	Patricia	97
Purves	G. Dougal	74 (SF)
Pye	Leslie	86, 96
Quick	Steve	97
★ Radcliffe	David J.	92 (SF)
★ Ramsay	Barry	86
★ Ramsden	Sheila	77
Randall	Gerald D. W.	74
Rath	Tina	91
Rattle	Mary	90 (SF)
★ Raw	Mary-Elizabeth	Champion 89
Rayner	William	79
Read	Brenda M.	81 (SF)
Redmond	Fiona	97 (SF)
★ Reid	Gillian A.	89
★ Reish	Andrew F.	78
Renard	Georges	87 (SF)
Rennick	Tony	95 (SF)
Rennie	Bill	72
Rennison	R. Nicholas	83 (SF)
Renshaw	*David C.*	*91 (d. 1992)*
Revie	R.	73
Reynolds	Geoffrey	77 (Finalist)
Reynolds [Halstead]	Susan H.	74 (Finalist)
★ Rhoderick-Jones	Brigadier Robin	91
★ Ribbon	Gareth S.	97
Rice	Mike A.	88 (SF)
Richards	*Rosemary J.*	*89 (d. 1991)*

* Richardson	Peter C.	77 (SF)
Richardson	Ralph	83
* Ricketts	Joyce	92 (SF)
* Roberts	Alan M.	88
Roberts	David	87
Roberts	Maurice	93 (SF)
Robertson	James	77
Robertson	Malcolm	89 (SF)
Robertson	*Struan C.*	*86 (d. 1988)*
* Robey	Timothy	97
Robinson	Jean	78
Roderick	Christine	91
* Roe	Graham	94 (Finalist)
* Rogers	Frank M.	90 (SF)
* Rogers	Helena	95
Roney	Ralph	83 (SF)
* Rook	John A.	88
Rose	John	81
Ross	Dave	90 (SF)
* Ross	John A.	91
* Ross	Patricia	94
* Ross	Dr Sidney D.	74
Rowe	Christopher	85 (SF)
Rowlands	Brian	85
Rush	Alan	77
Sabine	Basil	72
* Sadek	Elsie	87, 96 (Finalist)
* Sadler	Ian L.	91 (SF)
Salmond	Sheila	80
Salsbury	Suzanne	95
Salt	Philip	89
* Samson	Alan H.	85
Sandell	Roger	80 (SF)
* Sanderson	Ian	94 (SF)
Saunders	Edward	80 (SF)
Savage	Barbara	86
Savage [Waters]	Janet	76 (SF)
* Schelts	Jasmin	88
Schneebaum	Steven M.	75 (SF)
Schofield	Mary	83
Scholefield	Susan	83
* Schwartz	Michael	91
Scott	Anne	92
* Scott	Craig E.	81
* Scott	Keith	87 (SF), 95

Scott	Roy P.	79
Scruton	Arthur	89
Seacome	Diggory C.	83
Searle	Roy	92
Senior	Anne	84
Senn	Stephen J.	79
Setterich	Jeanette	85
★ Settle	Michael	97
★ Sewell	Ian K.	77
Seymour	T. Malcolm	87
Shaw	Christine M.	78 (SF)
★ Shaw	Elizabeth	80 (SF)
Shearer	Alan G.	83 (SF)
Sheldrick	George P.	76 (SF)
Shepherd	John B.	79 (SF)
Shiels	David A.	95
Shilston	Peter G.	81 (SF)
Shirtcliffe	Peter W.	89
★ Siddell	Christopher J.	93
Side	Victor B.	75
★ Simmons	Doreen S.	72
Simms	David	88
Simpson	Anthony P.	89 (SF)
Simpson	John	85
Simpson	Madeline	81
Simpson	Marianne	77 (SF)
Sims	Brian	90
★ Sinclair	Sandy	92
Sinclair-Gieben	Gay	76 (SF)
Singleton	*Frederick B.*	*86 (d. 1988)*
Skinner	Lydia M.	90
Skottowe	*Philip F.*	*75 (d. 1980)*
Slater	Catherine	77
★ Slater	Paul	93
Slaughter	Lt Cdr J. M.	73
★ Sleep	Graham I.	90
Slocombe	Nicholas	84
★ Smallman	Jennifer A.	75
★ Smith	David C.	90
Smith [Fr Llywelyn]	Dorian L.	73
Smith	Dr Jack	80
Smith	John	94
Smith	Kenneth C. P.	80
Smith	Michael	97 (SF)
Smith	Robert	76

★ Smith	Robert N.	94
★ Smith	Rodney A. M.	76
★ Smith	Roger	96
Smith	Susan	80
Smith	T. F.	72
Smith	Valerie	84
Smithers	Stephen	95 (SF)
Smyth	Ian M. M.	75
★ Snailham	Richard G.	73 (SF)
Snowden	George	84
Southon	Margaret	78
Sparrow	Dr Gerald	79
Speedie	Dr Julie W.	89
★ Spencer	Neil	78
★ Spiller	Margaret J.	87 (Finalist)
★ Spinks	Judi M. A.	92
★ Spitz	Heinz	87 (SF)
Spruytenburg	Nicholas J.	76 (Finalist)
Stafford	Ross	96 (SF)
Stainthorpe	Wayne	89 (SF)
Stark	Rev. John	74 (SF)
Starling	Boris	96 (SF)
★ Stedman	Maurice B.	92
★ Steele	David K.	90 (SF)
Steele-Smith [Beshir]	Lynne	85
★ Stein	Roger	85 (Finalist)
★ Stephen	Alec	75
★ Stevens	Ian G.	80
Stevenson	David	81
★ Stevenson	Dr Iain	92
★ Stevenson	Leo	97
★ Stewart	Margot	84, 96
Stewart	Seamus	78
Stewart	Timothy S.	86 (SF)
Stirk	Tim D.	81
Story	Belinda	92
St Quintin	Simon	76
★ Strange	Rev. Canon Peter	73 (SF)
Strathearn	John	78 (SF)
★ Stratton	Bill	95 (SF)
Stringer	Karen	83
★ Stringer	Pamela M.	90
★ Strivens	Dr Thomas E. A.	83
Strudwick	Christopher J.	84
★ Stuart	R. A. Gordon	93

Stubbs	Herbert	85
★ Sturch	Rev. Dr Richard	Champion 96
Suckling	Norman C.	74 (SF)
★ Sutherland	John M.	87 (SF)
★ Sutherland	Robert J.	89 (SF)
★ Sutton	Ian	89
Swanson	Ian	73
Sweeney	Tom	93
Sykes	*Dr John B.*	*76 (SF) (d. 1993)*
Syms	Beatrice	79 (SF)
Tabb	Peter	77
★ Taggart	Andrew J.	91
★ Taggart	Bill	88
Tatton-Brown	Tim	84
Taylor	Briony	86
★ Taylor	Joan M.	72 (Finalist)
Taylor	John	76
Taylor	John B.	93
★ Taylor	John S.	87
★ Taylor	Kate	90
★ Taylor	Katherine	97
Taylor	Marcus	86
★ Taylor	Michael	88, 95 (SF)
Taylor	Paul	95
Taylor	W.	72
★ Tedds	Julie M.	89, 96
Tenby	*David (Viscount)*	*75 (d. 1983)*
Thackrah	J. Richard	84
★ Thomas	Geoffrey	94 (SF)
Thomas	Jeremy	93
★ Thomas	Margaret	90, 96 (SF)
Thomas	Perry L.	90
Thomas	Siân R. E.	83 (SF)
★ Thompson	Barbara	95
★ Thompson	Chantal	90 (Finalist)
★ Thompson	Ella	84 (SF)
Thompson	Major Peter	94
Thompson	Richard	77
Thompson	Stewart	76
Thornton	George	84
Thwaytes	Joy	87 (SF)
Tickell	Fergus	90
Tight	William	86
Todd	Charles	89
Todd	Dr Maxwell	79

★ Todd	Peter M.	92 (Finalist)
Todd	*Stanley C.*	*87 (d. 1993)*
★ Tombs	David	93 (Finalist)
Tomlinson	Jack W.	75
Tonge	Jacquelyn	80 (SF)
Tooher	Anthony	78 (SF)
★ Torr	Thelma	94
Towne	Edward	83
Tozer	Dawn	89 (SF)
Traynor	John	95
Trevor	Jane	91
★ Troughton	Gordon B.	94
★ Tudor	James	91
★ Turek	Andrew	86 (SF)
Turnbull	Stephen R.	74 (SF)
★ Turner	Mark	88 (SF)
Turner	Mary	86
Turner	Russell	96 (SF)
Turpin	Robert	80
Turton	*Peter*	*89 (d. 1990)*
Twyman	Leo	76
Tyson	Kathryn M.	83 (Finalist)
★ Van-Cauter	Doreen	96
Vandervelde	V. Denis	76
★ Vaughan	Andrew J.	91
Veitch	Tony	80
Venitt	P.	72
★ Verber	Dr Ian	89 (SF)
★ Vernon	Peter	95
★ Vernon-Parry	Dr Kate	84 (Finalist)
Verso	Lorna	77
Vickers	Raymond	77
Vickers	Susan	85
Viney	Nigel	80
★ Vlaar	Maureen M.	93
Wadey	Clifford J.	72
★ Walden	Robert	76
★ Walford	Rex A.	85 (SF)
★ Walker	Dorothy	96
★ Walker	Francis M. G.	85 (SF)
★ Walker	Rev. Ian	96
Walker	Michael E.	78
Walker	Susan S.	75
★ Walker-Kinnear	Dr Malcolm H.	96 (SF)
Wall	Robert W.	79 (SF)

Wallace	Derek M.	88
Wallace-Murphy	Timothy	76
Walling	Catherine	85 (SF)
★ Ward	Ray	78 (SF)
★ Warman	Christine	97
Warner	Clifford J.	75
Warner	John	84
Wate	David	72
Waters	Rev. Donald	78
Watson	Bruce	90 (SF)
★ Watson	Michael	94 (SF)
Watson	Trudy	73
Watt	John	81 (SF)
Watt	Katherine I.	75
Watts	David	91
Waugh	Rosemary	87
Weaver	Heather	80
★ Webbewood	Paul	90 (Finalist)
Webley	John	80
Webster	Dr Reginald	73 (Finalist)
★ Weir	Michael G.	89 (SF)
★ Weir	Yvonne E.	87
Welch	Dr Patrick J.	90 (SF)
Weller	John	79
Wells	Bob	89
★ Wells	Jeffrey D.	87
West	Alan	73
West	Rev. Derek	85
West	Capt Joe K.	79 (Finalist), 96 (SF)
West	Dr John F.	77
★ Westcott	Tim	94
★ Weston	Andrea	97 (Finalist)
★ Wharmby	Philip J.	89
Wharton	Patricia M.	86
★ Wheatley	Rev. James	96
Wheeler	Dr John	83
★ Whipp	David G.	92
★ Whitaker	Alan R.	96 (SF)
White	Cyril V.	80
White	Elizabeth	78
Whitehead	Alan	72
Whitton	John B.	74
Widdowson	*John B.*	77 *(d. 1993)*
Wilcockson	Peter	81
Wilcox	Ingram	80 (Finalist)

Wildman	R.	72
Wildman	Stephen	73
Wilkins	Gwyn	97
Wilkinson	Det. Constable Anthony	90
★ Wilkinson	Nancy	Champion 72
Willbourn	Simon	83
★ Williams	Dave	90
Williams	David	74
Williams	Elizabeth	73
★ Williams	Janet C.	86, 95 (SF)
Williams	John G.	96
Williams	Kate	81
Williams	Morris	77
★ Williams	Steve	Champion 92
★ Willmot	Mary	94
Wilson	David	76 (Finalist)
Wilson	Hilary	74
★ Wilson	Ian	92
Wilson	Dr Jean	79
★ Wilson	John M.	94 (Finalist)
★ Wilson	Philip	88
Winpenny	David	86
Withers	Margaret	90
Withrington	John	81
Wood	Andrew C.	77 (SF)
★ Wood	Angela	94
Wood	Paul	79
★ Wood	Primrose	84 (SF)
Wood	Rev. Ron	89 (SF)
Wood	Stephen	94 (Finalist)
Woodcock	Bob	83 (SF)
★ Woods	Jim	94
★ Woods	Roger D.	89 (SF)
Woodward	Nicholas J.	81 (Finalist)
Worger	Robert G.	75
Wright	Brian L. D.	74 (Finalist)
Wright	Chris	92 (SF)
Wright	Gordon N.	78 (Finalist)
★ Wyatt	Martin	88
★ Wynne	Alan	94
Yates	Alex	83 (Finalist)
York	Michael	73 (SF)
Young	Don	80 (SF)
Yule	Donald	91 (SF)

Index

Page numbers in *italic* refer to the illustrations in the main text.

I.L